12/19

.60

WALL
STREET
JOURNAL
BOOKS

Herd on the Street

Animal Stories from
The Wall Street Journal

EDITED BY

KEN WELLS

Foreword by Bruce McCall

A WALL STREET JOURNAL BOOK

Published by Free Press

New York   London   Toronto   Sydney

A WALL STREET JOURNAL BOOK
Published by Free Press
Rockefeller Center
1230 Avenue of the Americas
New York, NY 10020

For information about special discounts for bulk purchases,
please contact Simon & Schuster Special Sales:
1-800-456-6798 or business@simonandschuster.com

Manufactured in the United States of America

1   3   5   7   9   10   8   6   4   2

Library of Congress Cataloging-in-Publication Data

Herd on the Street : animal stories from the Wall Street journal / edited by Ken Wells ;
foreword by Bruce McCall.
p. cm. — (A Wall Street journal book)
1. Animals—Anecdotes. I. Wells, Ken. II. Wall Street journal. III. Series.
QL791.H52 2003
590—dc22
2003057649

ISBN 0-7432-5420-1

Contents

CHAPTER THREE
ODD DUCKS

CHAPTER FOUR
PASTORAL PURSUITS

CHAPTER FIVE
FISH STORIES

CHAPTER SIX

WILD THINGS

CHAPTER 7

BUZZ

Foreword

by Bruce McCall

In the following pages, that famously warm and fuzzy chronicler of nature and its wondrous ways known as *The Wall Street Journal* ladles out the cream of its coverage of man's relationship with the animal world from over the past four decades.

Do not snicker. Our finned, feathered and four-footed friends pump billions of dollars every year into the American economy, via everything from gourmet pet food to racetrack betting to aquarium supplies to my veterinarians' bills; the *Journal* would be remiss if it didn't regularly check in. But it's about much more than just the money. The man-animal interface is so spiced with scientific and psychic and emotional oddities that it's catnip to the curious mind—and the paper's readers know that no mind is more curious than that of the typical *Wall Street Journal* reporter, who is an adept at finding newsworthy pay dirt in odd places. This guarantees a virtual grand tour of the offbeat, the weird and the bizarre, and animal stories that elevate information to a level somewhere between entertainment and astonishment.

Perhaps best of all, the stories in this book are mercifully free of both Disneyesque anthropomorphic treacle on the one hand and killjoy dismissiveness on the other, because also absent are personal bias and its evil twin, personal advocacy. The same deadpan, objective eye more familiarly trained on big business and Alan Greenspan's latest prognostication, here trained on dog dancing and astrochimps and the medical challenge of emergency surgery on pet goldfish, yields similarly satisfying rewards. And oh, by the way, the writing is really good.

All of which combine to make this an absolutely unique book about animals. Of course, you still have to like animals. Reportorial objectivity notwithstanding, it's implicit that you're thinking of plunging into this collection because you'd agree that a love of animals is what separates us from, well, animals. You don't see chimps feeding gourmet Simian Snax to monkeys, after all, and grizzly bears almost never adopt badgers and tie red bandanas around their necks. And what other than a deep bond with the animal world could induce you to even pick up a book—without pictures—about such things as the International Ox Pulling Contest, Polish buffalo stalkers and freeze-dried permapets?

So the working assumption here is that you're part of the pro-animal team. And the odds are good that if mixing with the animals brings you daily pleasure and spiritual reward, you've joined the 73 million other Americans who keep a pet. Happily for us pet lovers, a good many of the stories herein chronicle aspects of the human-pet relationship—mainly the wackier aspects. If you're occasionally embarrassed by the extent of your emotional involvement with Fido or Cleopatra or Pete the parrot, and what pet lover isn't, you'll find something in here—the very polite Marin County way of settling dog-custody disputes, for example, or birds on Prozac—to make you feel almost boringly normal.

If you don't keep a pet, this book might well convince you to do so. It plunges you knee-deep into the animal world, and to spend any time at all with animals (certain irritable crocodiles and this or that charging hippopotamus excepted, of course) is to become *ipso facto* an animal lover.

But beware. Once declared, the animal lover finds himself bound by moral contract to cherish every living four-footed creature regardless of circumstances and national origin and what the prosaic world calls common sense. This can combine with a morbid turn of imagination to inject the most torpid life with an urgent sense of purpose while visibly thinning the wallet, turning a vacation into work and earning you fame on two continents as a sentimental idiot.

At least, that's my experience. One recent summer in Umbria, an obviously lost or abandoned housecat showed up on our farm-house doorstep, starved for food and human warmth—evidently one of an estimated thirty thousand pets discarded in Italy at the end of every summer. He was immediately fed a three-course breakfast and we immediately gained a lodger. This was impolitic given our landlady, who just as immediately scorned our guest as another mooching four-footed hobo to be shooed off the property, pronto. Any animal lover, or hapless sucker, naturally saw not just another stray cat but an Oliver Twist in feline form: abject, unloved, imperiled. We took our feeding underground. We dared not bring him out of the damp chill of that particularly wet and cold Umbrian August but we did provide him a nest, crafted from my old underwear. For Umbro, as we called him, was no stringy, feral little killer but a big, soft, amiable lunk. The stormy night when a door flew open and in raced Umbro to snuggle in our bed—only to be bounced out like a drunk by wifely command—was decisive. We must adopt him. My wife's protests that he wasn't our responsibility, that saving one cat out of the thousands just like him was a pointless gesture and that anyway we didn't need another cat, melted under my hoarse pleas.

Adopt him we did, racing all over Umbria in a bureaucratic and logistical roundelay involving vets and tests and shots and Polaroid portraits, multistamped certificates from the Italian Bureau of Feline Affairs, fees paid to the Umbrian Department of Animal Export, a plane reservation and the search for a cage built to British Airways' strict specifications.

Floyd, as he came to be called once safely landed stateside, lies sound asleep on the couch nearby as I write this, on his back with feet in the air like an overturned coffee table. To create this cozy scene cost us several vacation days and well over $1,000 (in cash), not to mention the chortling disbelief—"it's just another cat, for God's sake!"—of most of our friends.

So dive in, Dear Reader, and immerse yourself in tales of

Introduction

In the summer of 1998, I found myself paddling down the Zambezi River in a canoe, hoping to run into a hippopotamus or two. Well, run into is an exaggeration. I actually was hoping to get a look at a hippo from a relatively safe distance—say, 50 yards away.

My river guide had informed me that hippos, if so inclined, can swim as fast as a trotting horse, and that they usually swim that fast for two reasons. One: when they're running from you. Two: when they're coming *after* you.

I didn't want to be too close should the latter occasion arise— enraged hippos have been known to bite canoes in two. I was *working*, after all, and there was no use getting mauled on the job.

Ah, the things we at the great, gray *Wall Street Journal* do to properly report critter stories. My account of paddling among the hippos appears in these pages, along with more than 50 other features that cover a remarkably wide swath of the animal kingdom.

When I joined the *Journal* 21 years ago in the San Francisco bureau, I expected to write about many things—stocks, bonds, oil, the environment. But I hadn't anticipated this most serious newspaper's infatuation with animals and animal stories. Yet when Ken Slocum, my bureau chief at the time, dispatched me on my second Page One feature assignment for the paper's legendary "Middle Column," he sent me out to Idaho to write a piece about modern-day falconry. "I myself cut my teeth on critter stories," I recall Mr. Slocum telling me. He had, by that time, been at the paper about 20 years.

I can't say for certain when this infatuation started. But based upon archival research, I do know that animals, and people's relationships with them, had become a staple Page One *Journal* feature by the early 1960s. (A number of the features in this book are taken from other sections of the paper as well.) One explanation is that the modern *Journal* was edited in its formative years mostly by solid Midwesterners who came from places where animals, given the Midwestern interest in hunting, fishing and livestock, were core to the fabric of life. Beyond that, the *Journal*'s peculiar, stylized Page One format—the Middle Column in particular— makes it a perfect vehicle for telling an engaging critter tale now and then.

Add to that the seemingly innate knowledge of writers that almost everybody loves a good shaggy dog story. Glynn Mapes, who served as Page One editor in the 1980s, ran a lot of critter features during his watch, and later wrote a number of memorable ones (his pieces on a British hedgehog hospital and why toads cross the road are included herein). Mr. Mapes, now retired, explains the allure: "I guess it's because animals are always fascinating, sometimes cuddly and, most importantly, they don't ever give you any back talk. One can't say the same for humans."

As important, however, is that animals are often at the center of the news. While most of the stories in this book tend to the humorous (pets on Prozac, we think you will agree, *is* a laughing matter), the animal-rights movement that emerged in the late 1960s gets some attention here. Geraldine Brooks's story about the plight of chimpanzees retired from the Air Force space program is one example, as is Jim Sterba's piece about whether feral cats ought to be awarded "native status" the same as the songbirds they are killing.

Animals also make great stories because they often become metaphors for the great issues and controversies that roll through society. Mr. Sterba, who is perhaps the most prolific critter writer in the paper's history, explains why his several features on frogs over the years amounted to core *Journal* coverage:

"The first story I wrote for the *WSJ* was a Middle Column piece about the national frog shortage. After Sputnik, the Eisenhower Administration raised the alarm that we were behind the Russians in science. Eisenhower created the National Science

Foundation, which started showering schools with money for science education. What did the schools buy? Frogs. Soon, every kid in freshman biology was taking a frog apart. To supply them, the biological-supply houses were paying frog catchers more than restaurants would pay. Frog legs disappeared from menus."

This would later lead to Sterba features on the conundrum of imported frog legs (a congressman got sick eating salmonella-tainted Asian frog legs at Richard Nixon's second inaugural, setting off a federal investigation) and to get-rich-quick frog-farming schemes pitting American entrepreneurs against international competitors.

Says Mr. Sterba: "No newspaper has more thoroughly and tenaciously covered the ups and downs of America's long national frog-shortage nightmare than the *Journal*. Ronald Reagan is the hero of frog lovers: His cuts in federal aid to education greatly depressed the dissection frog market, allowing wild stocks to rebuild. A ribbeting saga!"

One of Mr. Sterba's frog pieces appears herein, along with numerous other riveting Sterba sagas, including a tale about an eight-foot-long earthworm.

Lest you think the *Journal* has paid too little attention to the insect kingdom, this book also takes you deep into facets of bug life that you perhaps had not previously contemplated. I recommend Carrie Dolan's story on the on-the-job travails of a bug wrangler—the person in charge of supplying and directing things like ants, flies and spiders in movie scenes. And surely you will be as amazed as we were by Bob Ortega's piece about the exploits of Cockroach Dundee, a man who had acquired great (if not particularly marketable) skills at training roaches.

Enjoy!

—KEN WELLS

Herd
on the
Street

CHAPTER I

PET THEORIES

———

1. Listening to Prozac: "Bow-Wow! I Love the Mailman!"

Prozac has greatly improved life for Emily Elliot. She had tried massage therapy, hormone treatments, everything; but she couldn't relieve the anxiety, the fear, the painful shyness.

Or the chronic barking. So, after three years Ms. Elliot recently put Sparky, her dog, on Prozac.

Sparky (not her real name) suffered from "profound anxiety" of strangers as well as "inter-dog aggression," says Ms. Elliot, a veterinary student at the University of Pennsylvania. The pooch "has a problem thinking through solutions to what is bothering her," she adds. So, in March, along with other therapies, doctors at the animal-behavior clinic where Ms. Elliot works prescribed Prozac.

Sparky, a show dog, quickly lost that hang-dog attitude. "It's been a big relief," says Ms. Elliot, who asked that Sparky's real name not be used because her Prozac use might influence dog judges.

Among American humans, of course, Prozac has become fashionable as a treatment for depression and obsessive/compulsive disorders. "It's the designer drug of the '90s," says Bonnie Beaver, chief of medicine at Texas A&M University's department of small-animal medicine. "People think, 'Gee, if I can have Prozac, why can't my dog?'"

The field is still new, but the growing potential for using Prozac and other human psychiatric drugs to treat destructive or antisocial animal disorders will be discussed at next month's meeting of the 52,000-member American Veterinary Medical Association. Prozac proponents say the drug, particularly for dogs, may represent the last chance to keep a maladjusted canine off of death row. Unruly behavior, which leads owners to abandon pets to shelters, is "the leading cause of canine and feline deaths" in the U.S., says Karen Overall, a University of Pennsylvania veterinarian.

"These vets are dedicated to finding ways to help pets stay with their owners," says an AVMA spokeswoman. "It's important to use all the avenues they can."

The University of Pennsylvania animal-behavior clinic has put depressed puppies on Prozac, feather-picking parakeets on antidepressants and floor-wetting cats on Valium (Prozac, for reasons not completely understood, has proved toxic and ineffective for cats, some veterinarians say). The clinic has also treated emotionally troubled ferrets, skunks and rabbits.

Some dogs on Prozac will be weaned off the medication,

while others may be listening to Prozac for the rest of their lives, says Dr. Overall, who heads the clinic. "It's a great drug for some animals," she adds—though she stresses that owners and pets should never take each other's medication.

The number of animals, including some birds, on Prozac is currently small, but anecdotal evidence as to its effectiveness is encouraging. In a letter to be published in the upcoming issue of *DVM Newsmagazine,* a veterinary journal, Steven Melman of Potomac, Md., describes a five-year-old dog suffering from "tail-chasing mutilation disorder." Conventional treatment failed and one vet suggested amputating the tail.

After five days on Prozac, though, the pooch was a "much more mellow, less restless patient," he writes. After five weeks on the drug, the dog's disorder was cured. Dr. Melman writes: "I had literally saved my patient's tail."

Using human drugs to treat certain animal conditions is "not at all controversial in mainstream medicine," says Dr. Melman. But Prozac has long been dogged by controversy. Thus, when Dr. Melman published a paper in the April edition of *DVM* describing Prozac use for dogs' skin problems caused by obsessive/compulsive urges, the fur began to fly. "I mentioned Prozac and people went nuts," he says.

The Church of Scientology, for example, responded with warnings that pets on Prozac could "go psycho." Since Prozac's launch six years ago, the Scientologists, who oppose the use of mind-altering drugs, have called it a "killer drug" linked to murder and suicide—a charge roundly derided by the medical community.

If owners put pets on Prozac, "You may be forced to defang your dachshund or put Tabby in a straitjacket," warns a recent press release from the Citizens Commission on Human Rights, a group founded by the Church of Scientology. Yet, when reached for comment, the commission conceded it hadn't received any reports of injuries from Prozac-deranged pets.

Other groups are concerned as well. "There's a lot of room for fear and worries," says Bob Hillman, vice president of the Animal Protection Institute, a Sacramento, Calif., animal-rights organization. "Giving a Rottweiler or a Doberman Prozac could be dangerous for the neighbors" should the drug have an unintended effect.

The Food and Drug Administration and Eli Lilly & Co., Prozac's maker, have denied any link between Prozac and acts of violence or suicide. But "our clinical data support use of Prozac in treating only humans," says a spokeswoman for Eli Lilly. "We're not actively pursuing the study of Prozac for veterinary use."

Some animal advocates argue that, instead of turning to wonder drugs, people need to look for "gentle, noninvasive ways" of getting along with their pets, says Ken White, vice president for companion animals at the Humane Society of the U.S. in Washington. Ellen Corrigan, director of education for In Defense of Animals, another animal-rights group, suggests "a more holistic approach" that might include alternative treatments like acupressure and herbal remedies.

Indeed, doctors to humans often counsel patients to first try conventional therapy or behavior modification before they turn to Prozac. Pro-Prozac vets agree. With the appropriate diagnosis and dosage, drugs like Prozac can help pets, says Texas A&M's Dr. Beaver, but owners and doctors must find the real root of a pet's distress. "If you don't remove the stress, you don't fix the problem," she says.

Pennsylvania's Dr. Overall, who has plumbed the minds of pooches, notes: "If you pet them while they're moping, it just reinforces sad behavior." Instead, she recommends trying to get them to "take an interest in something they enjoy: Play with a ball, go for a car ride, sit on the sofa and watch TV. When they look happy, relaxed or outgoing, then give them a treat."

But determining a pet's neurosis takes time, and even Sigmund Freud wouldn't have gotten far with Fido on his couch. "We can't go up and say, 'Tell me about your traumatic puppyhood,'" says Dr. Overall. Still, she points out that depressed dogs exhibit many of the same signs that down-in-the-dumps people do: They don't eat, they don't sleep and they don't make eye contact. Many problems occur when the animal reaches social maturity, notes Dr. Overall. "The teen years are when we see a lot of social disorders in humans; gang involvements, schizophrenia. It's the same thing with cats and dogs."

Dr. Overall knows there are some people opposed to pet drug use of any sort. But she has put one of her three dogs on human antianxiety medication (though not Prozac) and is high on the idea. "I go home to normal dogs," she says.

—CARRIE DOLAN, June 1994

2. Surgery on an Odd Scale

RALEIGH, N.C.—Three veterinarians stood over a $4.95 goldfish named Hot Lips, prepping her for surgery. The senior vet, Craig Harms, slipped a syringe into the nine-inch-long fish's swollen belly. He drew out clear fluid—a bad sign.

Dr. Harms retreated to the hallway, pulled out his cellphone and called the owners in New York's Catskill Mountains. It was Wednesday morning, August 14.

"Hot Lips is doing OK," he said, before delivering the bad

news about the liquid. "It puts the possibility of liver disease or kidney disease back in the picture. . . . We'll keep you posted as we move along."

Dr. Harms and his colleagues are among about 20 vets in the nation who perform surgery on pet fish. Not one of them makes it his sole practice. But the need for such services is growing. Americans are building more backyard fishponds, stocking up on pets that they swear have personalities of their own.

Large "pond-kept fish" rank as the fastest-growing fish-pets in the nation, while the broader category of fish ownership grows faster than dogs, cats, lizards or any other pet type, according to the American Pet Products Manufacturers Association in Greenwich, Conn., and pet fish tend to grow bigger when they have more room to swim. Koi, the goldfish's fancy and often-expensive cousin, are particularly popular. They can live well past 30. So when these much-loved pets grow lumps or quit swimming, some owners give surgery a shot.

More are reaching out to Dr. Harms and his colleagues at North Carolina State University's College of Veterinary Medicine. One reason: Surgeons there have developed an advanced way to keep their patients alive on the operating table—a portable device that pumps fluids, including anesthesia, into their mouths and out their gills.

The North Carolina surgeons will take cases that other vets consider hopeless. In March, they fused two crushed vertebrae along the spine of a 21-inch, $900 koi named Ladyfish. The three-hour procedure followed X-rays and a CAT scan. Ladyfish's owner, a North Carolina Roto-Rooter manager named David Smothers, recently brought in a smaller koi named Wendy for similar work. "To see this little girl swimming again, it's just incredible," Mr. Smothers says.

That expertise caught the attention of Deb and Greg Ireland, who live in Liberty, N.Y., about 90 miles northwest of New York City. The couple, in their mid-50s, bought Hot Lips three years ago when she was a three-inch baby. They picked her out of a pet-store tank because of the fish's striking snow-white body, reddish-orange back and small spot of color above her mouth.

The Irelands acclimatized Hot Lips to their pond, in a back-yard oasis of gentle waterfalls, a barbecue grill and lounge chairs. Hot Lips grew into a svelte beauty, making friends with the couple's 25 other fish, among them Pinto, a large koi, and Alice, a naturally round oranda, a type of goldfish.

Last fall, the Irelands noticed some lumps on Hot Lips. "Maybe she's got some oranda genes in her," Mr. Ireland told his wife, hoping to ease her concerns. By spring, Hot Lips's stomach had swollen like a baseball. Mrs. Ireland gave her regular injections of antibiotics. That cleared up the sores but didn't reduce the swelling.

Mrs. Ireland began looking for a surgeon. By early August, she was telling surgeons at North Carolina State about a pink, bumpy growth protruding from Hot Lips's vent.

"How soon can you get her here?" veterinarian Greg Lewbart asked.

Three days later, the Irelands took Hot Lips to an aquatics shop in Warwick, N.Y., where she was specially packaged for overnight shipping. "Hang in there, Champ," Mr. Ireland said.

That night, Mrs. Ireland couldn't sleep and spent her time tracking Hot Lips's travel itinerary on the UPS Web site. By 10:00 A.M. the next day, Hot Lips had arrived safely in North Carolina. The operation was to take place the following morning.

The Irelands had reason to feel good about their surgeon. A native of Iowa, Dr. Harms earned his bachelor's degree in biology at Harvard, where he became taken with the idea of working with aquatic animals. He then went to vet school at Iowa State University. He has since had advanced training in microsurgery.

During the past eight years, Dr. Harms, now 41, has operated on about 125 fish, for pet owners and while teaching seminars for other vets. All but one fish survived. The pet owners generally pay between $350 and $1,000. Dr. Harms's research-journal articles have chronicled, among other cases, the removal of a hematoma the size of a pencil eraser from a three-inch gourami.

Operating on Hot Lips, Dr. Harms wedged the Irelands' goldfish into a V-shaped bed of foam rubber. The sedated fish was still, save for the motion of her gills as water and chemicals flowed through. A water pump provided the only constant sound in the room.

Dr. Harms, wearing aqua surgical scrubs and a light-blue mask, cut and retracted enough of Hot Lips's sides to reveal the first of two growths. With his fingertips, he gingerly probed beneath the yellow, slimy mass. "Looks like we got a big ol', fluid-filled, nasty ovary," Dr. Harms told his team.

The growth had been pushing into Hot Lips's central organ cavity, wending its way around her tiny colon. At Dr. Harms's request, one of the other vets inserted a catheter into Hot Lips's vent, hoping that it would support the colon as he cut near it.

No good. By the time Dr. Harms's instruments reached the colon, it had torn. He would have to repair it with surgical thread the thickness of a human hair.

At 11:04, Hot Lips stopped gilling.

Pam Govett, a vet assisting in the surgery, switched the anesthesiology flow device to pure, dechlorinated water. This supplied Hot Lips with oxygen in the same way a ventilator keeps human patients alive in a hospital. Next, the fish's heart became the big concern. Jenny Kishimori, a former U.S. Army intelligence officer now in veterinary school, put a tiny audio probe just below Hot Lips's throat. They couldn't hear a pulse, just water sloshing through the gills.

The team adjusted the probe. Finally, the sound of a steady, though slow, beat filled the room. "Thump-thump . . . thump-thump . . ." A low-normal 28 beats per minute.

Dr. Harms eventually removed two growths, which together accounted for about 40% of Hot Lips's weight, which had been 13 oz. But it was then clear exactly how sick she'd been. Damaged kidneys, scant body fat and pale gills suggested anemia.

Dr. Harms turned back to the frayed colon. He pinched its underside with forceps, rotating it enough to sew together a lateral tear. An assistant retracted the catheter slightly as saline solution ran back into Hot Lips's colon to test the fix. It held.

In New York, Hot Lips's owners waited by the phone. Nervous, Mrs. Ireland finally called the vet school, but could reach only an intake room. "Hot Lips hasn't made it back yet," she was told.

Forty minutes later, her phone rang. "It's not looking real good," Dr. Harms told her. He explained all his team had done. "The biggest concern for me right now is: She's been on pure water for over two hours and she hasn't started gilling," he said.

"Keep trying," Mrs. Ireland said.

Back in the operating room, Hot Lips's pulse had faded to 14 beats per minute. Dr. Harms injected her with adrenaline, which spiked her heartbeat to 32, but he didn't really expect that to last.

"Come on, Hot Lips," the soldier-turned-vet-student Ms. Kishimori pleaded, "wake up!"

Dr. Govett smoothed out Hot Lips's tail. "Such a beautiful fish," she said.

Nearly five hours after the procedure began, Hot Lips's pulse faded to nothing. Dr. Govett extended her thumb and forefinger into Hot Lips's chest, applying several minutes of CPR to try to start her heart.

"I think not," Dr. Harms said finally, walking out of the room to call New York.

—Dan Morse, September 2002

3. A Horse Is a Horse,
Unless of Course . . .

LEXINGTON, Va.—The world will little note nor long remember what was said here, but many will never forget the weirdness of what they did here this week. Six score and 14 years after his last ride in battle, Thomas "Stonewall" Jackson's war-horse was finally laid to rest in a walnut casket with prayer, pomp and a parting carrot.

At least part of him was.

"I wish they'd bury the whole horse," says Martha Boltz, gazing at Little Sorrel's hide, mounted on a lifelike frame on display at the Virginia Military Institute's museum here. Studying the horse's oft-repaired flank, she adds, "He looks like he's been re-upholstered one too many times."

Mike Whitaker, another visitor, disagrees. "I've got deer mounts on my wall that look a whole lot worse," says the cookie distributor from North Carolina. "I say let the ol' boy keep riding as long as he's able."

How Little Sorrel came riding here at all is a long, strange story winding back to 1861, when Jackson, a brilliant Confederate commander, procured the reddish-brown horse from a captured Union train. Jackson, an awkward rider, liked the gelding's gentle gait—"as easy as the rocking of a cradle," he wrote—and often slept in the saddle. Mount suited master in another way; both were unimpressive physical specimens whose attributes weren't obvious. "Little Sorrel was as little like a Pegasus as he [Stonewall] was like an Apollo," wrote one Jackson aide. Others recalled "a dun cob of very sorry appearance" and an ugly "old rawbone sorrel."

But the small, dumpy mount proved tireless on the march and

calm under fire, surviving a bullet wound and bolting just once, when Jackson was accidentally shot in the arm by his own troops as he rode in the dark during the battle of Chancellorsville in northern Virginia. His arm was amputated but the wound proved fatal to Jackson, who had earned his nickname for his "stone wall" defense of rebel lines at the first battle of Bull Run.

After the war, Little Sorrel toured county fairs and rebel reunions; souvenir seekers tugged so many hairs from his mane and tail that the horse required guards. In death, at the age of 36—just three years short of Stonewall—the horse's fate again mimicked its master's. Jackson was buried in pieces, his amputated arm at Chancellorsville, the rest of him in Lexington, where he had taught at VMI before the war. His horse, meanwhile, was mounted on a plaster of Paris frame by a taxidermist who took the bones home to Pittsburgh as partial payment.

Both bones and hide eventually found their way to VMI, where the skeleton was used in biology class and the mounted hide displayed in the school museum. Then, when the science department relocated in 1989, the bones languished in moving boxes in the museum storeroom.

"It seemed weird and sad to me that Little Sorrel was never buried," says Juanita Allen, head of the Virginia division of the United Daughters of the Confederacy. Not long ago, she visited the horse's boxed remains. "I picked up his teeth and rubbed his nose bone. I was petting it and talking to him, telling him how sorry I was and how we'd take care of him."

Ms. Allen, an executive assistant at McKinsey & Co., a consulting firm, decided the Daughters should bury the horse with military-style honors. To her, this seemed the Christian thing to do, as well as a natural extension of the never-ending interest in the Civil War. "You can only talk so many times about what your great-grandfather did at this or that battle," she says. "But no one ever talks about the animals, who had no choice in the matter. They were just faithful beasts of burden who suffered terribly." An estimated 3.5 million horses and draft animals died in the war. Ms. Allen got VMI to agree to bury Little Sorrel's bones on the parade ground where the horse had once grazed, but this raised a ticklish question. What about the hide? Standing stiffly in a diorama-like display scattered with stones and leaves, Little Sorrel's hide has cracks on its face and lines on its flank where the leather has separated over the years.

"He's done with the Yankees—humidity's his worst enemy now," says the museum's director, Keith Gibson, who calls in a taxidermist from the Smithsonian Institution every few years to glue the hide's tears and seal the cracks with beeswax. Despite its flaws, the horse remains the main draw at VMI's small museum, which attracts 50,000 visitors a year. The gift shop sells Little Sorrel postcards, refrigerator magnets and cuddle toys. Visitors even leave apples at the mounted hide's feet.

"This place is a reliquary, it's a piece-of-the-true-cross kind of thing to be close to Sorrel's remains," says University of Pennsylvania Civil War historian Drew Gilpin Faust, visiting Lexington to witness the horse's burial. Even so, Ms. Faust finds the mount's fate and enduring appeal a tad strange. "You have to wonder," she says, "if Southerners wanted to stuff Stonewall Jackson but stuffed his horse instead."

Nor is Little Sorrel's hide the only shrine in Lexington, a Shenandoah Valley town of about 7,500. Robert E. Lee, the South's most prominent general, also worked here. For Civil War pilgrims, the town's other holy sites include the two generals' graves, Stonewall's house, an exact life-size statue of Lee and the nearby grave of his war-horse, Traveller. Visitors often leave carrots and coins on Traveller's grave, and flock to the stable—now a garage—where he was kept.

"If it wasn't for our dead generals and their dead horses this town would be, well, dead," says Doug Harwood, publisher of the *Rockbridge Advocate,* a Lexington newspaper. He is often bemused by the town's idol-worship. "You turn a corner in the VMI museum and come face to face with the mighty Stonewall's mighty war-horse—and it looks like it couldn't pull Donald Duck in a wagon." But even Mr. Harwood turned out this week for the burial of Little Sorrel's cremated bones. Originally, VMI hoped to keep the interment quiet, even planning a night burial for fear of turning the event into a circus. But as word leaked out, and interest grew, it became clear that Little Sorrel would not ride quietly into the night. In the end, it took a minister, bagpipe player, fife-and-drum band, color guard—even a Stonewall impersonator astride a horse meant to resemble Little Sorrel—to lay the horse's remains to rest.

Nikki Moor, who bought the horse for her Stonewall-playing husband, concedes that the handsome Arabian isn't a perfect match of Jackson's mount, but it is the closest she could find. "Most people don't advertise that they have a short, fat ugly horse for sale," she says.

The interment, held beneath a statue of Stonewall, drew about 500 people, including women in period mourning garb. After prayers and speeches and the playing of "Dixie," pallbearers clad as rebel soldiers lowered the coffin as Confederate riflemen fired musket volleys. Then the crowd filed past the grave and scooped in clods of dirt gathered from 14 battlefields where Little Sorrel served. Some mourners also tossed in carrots, oats and horseshoes.

"Once again, Little Sorrel is beneath Stonewall Jackson," intoned James Robertson, a Jackson biographer. "May you continue to have good grazing in the boundless pastures of heaven."

After the burial, the crowd proceeded to the nearby museum to pay their respects to Little Sorrel's hide, still on its frame. Even the cynical publisher, Mr. Harwood, was struck by the dignity of the event. "You didn't see anyone trying to cash in with T-shirts or tacky mugs," he said. "There wasn't even a politician here."

But Mr. Harwood did wonder if the remains might have been put to better use. "We could have traded these bones for Stoney's arm up in Chancellorsville and brought the limb back here," he said. "Now, we've got no more relics to swap."

—TONY HORWITZ, July 1997

4. Much Chow, No Hounds

CARNATION, Wash.—Edward Kane is up to his whiskers in cats. Cat posters adorn his office walls. Cat food crowds his shelves. Cat magazines clutter his desk. Cat eyes stare from a pin on his starched white lab coat.

The 37-year-old Mr. Kane talks cats, cats, cats. Cat business litters his mind: cats to mate, cats to groom, sick cats, cats that won't eat.

Especially cats that won't eat. Cats that won't eat are a real problem.

Mr. Kane sneezes, then excuses himself. "Allergic to cats," he says sheepishly.

The bespectacled, affable Mr. Kane runs Carnation Co.'s "cattery." Here in the pastoral Snoqualmie Valley about 20 miles east of Seattle, more than 500 cats reside in a sort of feline commune—and eat for, not into, the corporate profits.

They are the cat version of gourmet food tasters, nibbling a pungent pâté of this, sampling a crunchy nugget of that. Their food preferences are computerized and scientifically translated by Mr. Kane and others for Carnation's pet-foods division, based in Los Angeles. There, product managers and marketers gamble that what tickles these feline palates will please cats all across the nation.

The cats, which taste-tested about 250,000 cans of moist cat food and 70,000 pounds of dry varieties last year, seem to be doing a good job. Carnation, the nation's No. 2 pet-food maker (behind Ralston Purina Co.), had pet-food sales of $486 million in fiscal 1983. About 60% of the total came from sales of the company's Friskies, Fancy Feast and other cat-food brands.

"The cats," says Ronald Stapley, Carnation's farm-research director, who formerly ran the cattery, "aren't just necessary: They're critical."

Dwight Stuart, Jr., a great-grandson of Carnation's founder, E. A. Stuart, says, "It's kind of neat knowing that our success is largely in the hands of those little beasties." The 38-year-old Mr. Stuart is, so to speak, the Top Cat of Carnation's pet-foods division. At least once a year, he visits the cattery to look in on his furry helpers.

The cattery, as it happens, is just down the hill from the barns where Carnation's famous Contented Cows still lead an idyllic bovine life. It's also one of only two large-scale cat taste-testing and nutrition-research facilities in America. Ralston Purina runs the other, near St. Louis.

Carnation began its cattery with only 44 cats in 1953, about the time commercial cat food was beginning to jump onto supermarket shelves in quantity. The cattery grew slowly to about 300 cats by 1970. Until then, Carnation and other pet-food companies concentrated on the lucrative multibillion-dollar dog-food market, which had its beginnings in the 1930s. (Carnation has operated a taste-testing kennel for dogs since 1932.)

But in the 1970s, pet cats, to the surprise of pet-food producers, climbed sharply in popularity. Mr. Stuart attributes the boom partly to the "mystique of the cat"—cats not long ago even made the cover of *Time* magazine. But the main factor, he thinks, was a shift toward urban living, which favors pets that fit into compact living space and need less attention. The cat, small, cheap to feed, independent and fastidious, answers the job description, he adds.

Today, cats have begun to challenge dogs as America's favorite pets. Though dogs still hold the lead—there are perhaps 55 million to 60 million pet dogs in America—cats have almost doubled in just the past 15 years to 43 million currently.

And cat-food sales, a modest $500 million nationwide in 1973, grew to about $1.6 billion last year and are expected to hit $2.7 billion by 1992. Americans also spent another $1 billion or so last year on feline vaccinations, vitamins and veterinary services.

"The cat-food side of the industry is where the growth is," Mr. Stuart says.

To capitalize on that growth, Carnation decided to get even cozier with cats. So, since 1970, it has almost doubled the cattery's capacity to 550 cats and has stepped up its research to answer lingering questions about cat nutrition and food preferences.

The nutritional requirements are fairly well known, Mr. Kane says. The mysterious things are the finicky feline appetite and the cat's penchant to seem bored one day with the very food that it downed voraciously the day before. This "food fatigue," as Mr. Stapley calls it, helps explain why pet-food companies make so many flavors and textures of cat food—and why they are as nervous as cats at a dog show.

"We know we've basically got one chance with the consumer," Mr. Stuart says. "If the cat walks up to the bowl, sniffs at it and walks away, the owner is probably off to the supermarket for someone else's brand."

So, Mr. Kane spends long hours trying to demystify cat idiosyncrasies about food. He oversees perhaps 200 to 250 tests a month, mostly dealing with "food acceptance." The tests are straightforward: White-coated clinicians scoop out measured portions of cat food into stainless-steel bowls. The food is weighed, the weight punched into a computer.

The cats, each with his own computer number, eat. The bowls are taken away, and the food is weighed again to determine the amount consumed. That information is also punched into the computer, which calculates how much the cat liked the vittles. The tests not only involve new products, which can take up to two years to develop, but often cat food on the market for years.

"Quality control," Mr. Kane explains. The cat palate is so sensitive to even minute changes in flavor that Carnation uses taste testing results to make sure that its longtime products don't drift from the tastes that made them popular.

Sometimes, too, the company has to change an existing recipe slightly because it can't get a customary ingredient from a supplier. In those cases, the cats—under considerable deadline pressure—help make multimillion-dollar business decisions.

"If we have to change an ingredient, we don't want to make a large batch of food using the new ingredient without knowing how the cats will react," Mr. Stuart says, so, a factory often airfreights a test batch to Mr. Kane, who feeds it to his cats overnight, quickly runs the results on his computer and phones headquarters the next day with the results. Whole factories sometimes are held up until the cat data are digested. Sometimes, so much is at stake that the cat stats go all the way up to

Carnation's chairman, H. E. Olson, before the company decides what to do.

"The results are only a tool. We might say, 'Well, it looks pretty good to our cats.' But they [pet-foods division officials] make the final decision," Mr. Kane adds.

The cats also help Carnation check up on the competition. They often eat rival brands, served in identical bowls alongside Carnation products. The company concedes that now and then, its cats devour competing food with disconcerting relish.

"If that happens, I don't get depressed, at least not right away. But I get very inquisitive and want to find out what's going on," Mr. Stuart says. Mr. Stapley adds cryptically, "We probably know as much about our competitors' products as they do."

Though the testing is done with scientific efficiency in a hospital-clean environment, all sense of clinical decorum is lost at feeding time.

"Hold on, it's coming," says a cattery worker as she pushes a large cart full of pungent cat food into a room where about 25 cats live in airy, stainless-steel "apartments." She is greeted with a cacophony of meows. Cats in the next room join in, and suddenly the whole place is vibrating with hungry-cat noises.

Down the hall, a few cats are singing different tunes: wails, purrs, shrieks.

"Oh, that," Mr. Kane says. "Mating season, you know." Mr. Kane, in fact, is the principal matchmaker, importing one or two male cats a year to add vigor to the cattery's bloodlines. But almost all the cats here are descendants from the original 44. Most are just plain tabby cats; Carnation discovered long ago that what common cats eat, fancy cats eat, too.

Common or not, the cats here seem to be treated royally. They all have names—such as Faustus, Pong, Sly, Secret Agent and, yes, Garfield—and Mr. Kane knows practically all of them.

Each cat is groomed and weighed weekly, gets regular physical checkups and is fussed over by a full-time veterinarian on call 24 hours a day. There aren't any fat cats here; tubby tabbies are put on a diet. Every day, juveniles and young adults romp for several hours in a kind of cat gym. And mating cats are paired off in little private suites where cat love can flower without disruption.

Indeed, the cattery's only drawback is that the cats spend most of their time in cages—a necessity, considering the logistics involved in feeding, caring for and keeping track of research on more than 500 of them. There are some exceptions: Some taste-testing is carried out by cats living in large, open communal rooms, though the exact object of those tests, like much of what goes on here, is kept secret.

What isn't secret, however, is Mr. Kane's fondness for cats—despite his allergy, he has seven of his own at home—and his unabashed conviction that his cats are the best-fed felines in America. Mr. Kane, in fact, speaks from personal experience.

"I eat the cat food routinely," he says. "I like it." So does Mr. Stuart, who says key employees of the pet-foods division get together regularly to talk, and nibble, cat food.

"We get very close to the product," Mr. Stuart says.

—KEN WELLS, April 1984

5. *Polly Wants a Scholarship to Harvard*

EVANSTON, Ill.—It is always awkward for a reporter when a source stops answering his questions, moves closer and gently chews his ear. But allowances must be made for eccentric geniuses.

The biting intellect here is an African Grey parrot named Alex, a research animal at Northwestern University. For 13 years he has fraternized only with people and now regards them as members of his flock—sometimes even preening the scruffier ones about the ears. But identifying with humans isn't what makes him special.

Nor is his ability to whistle some Mozart and say things like "Tickle me." Parrots, after all, are uncanny mimics. But Alex isn't just a copycat. Asked the color of a bluish pen held before him, he cocks his head, ponders and expounds: "Baaloo!"

The Prof. Henry Higgins behind this former squawker is animal-intelligence researcher Irene Pepperberg. For 13 years she and her assistants have tirelessly acted out a kind of *Sesame Street* for Alex. Like Big Bird and friends, they perform simple word skits, day after day, while he watches in a small room stocked with toys, snacks and perches. They have slowly drawn him into the act.

Now he can name 80 of his favorite things, such as wool, walnut and shower. (Studiously copying Ms. Pepperberg's Boston accent, he says "I want showah" to get spritzed.) He knows something about abstract ideas, including soft, hard, same and different. He can tell how many objects there are in groups of up to six. When he says, "Wanna cracker," he means it: Handed a nut instead, he drops it and exclaims in his peevish old man's voice, "I WANT CRACKER." So much for the idea that our feathered friends are all just bird brains.

Some other animals, such as chimpanzees, have learned non-verbal communication. But Alex is the first animal to actually speak with a semblance of understanding. Ms. Pepperberg believes his conversational gambits prove that he can handle some simple abstractions as well as chimps and porpoises can.

When shown a group of varied objects Alex has learned to answer certain questions such as, "How many corners does the piece of red paper have?" with about 80% accuracy. That is, if he is in the mood. When bored, he tells his teachers to "go away" and hurls test objects to the floor. "Emotionally, parrots never go beyond the level of a three-year-old" child, sighs Ms. Pepperberg, a young 41-year-old, patiently picking up toys Alex has strewn about his room in an orgy of play.

Skeptics argue that Alex isn't as smart as he seems. He has "learned to produce a repertoire of sounds to get rewards," says Columbia University animal cognition expert Herbert Terrace. "The only thing distinguishing him from pigeons [taught to peck buttons for food] is that his responses sound like English."

But regardless of whether Alex grasps meanings as we do, he shows an "incredible, totally unexpected" power to make mental connections, notes Ohio State University psychologist Sarah Boysen, who works with chimps. Before Alex, scientists generally dismissed talking birds as mindless mimics.

For her part, Ms. Pepperberg sidesteps the fray, merely noting that Alex shows "languagelike" behaviors. But she adds that parrots in the wild routinely perform mental feats—such as learning to sing complex duets with their mates—that prove they have a lot on the ball. Biologists sometimes call them "flying primates"—they have even shown evidence of using tools. Once when Alex couldn't lift a cup covering a tasty nut, he turned to the nearest human assistant and demanded crowbar style, "Go pick up cup."

Parrots tend to go loco and pluck out their feathers when

caged alone, says Ms. Pepperberg, so they generally don't make good pets. Yet the talking-bird trade is booming, endangering many parrot species. Alex, whom Ms. Pepperberg bought for $600 in a Chicago pet store in 1977, may himself have been nabbed in the jungle. And he probably isn't an avian Einstein—he is just highly schooled. "It's possible I got a dingbat," his coach says.

If so, he proves how much inspired teaching can do for the dingy. Ms. Pepperberg, who took up bird research while getting her chemistry doctorate at Harvard University, has helped pioneer a new training strategy for animals that stresses humanlike learning by social interaction. "There's been a lot of resistance to my work," she says, "because I don't use standard techniques." But not from Alex.

Standing on a chair, he is all eyes and ears as she and an assistant hand back and forth a date nearby—they're trying to add it to his lexicon. "I like date," says Ms. Pepperberg. "Give me date. Yum." Suddenly Alex ventures, "Wanna grain." "No," says Ms. Pepperberg, "date. Do you want date?" Alex preens, seemingly mulling it over. Then he says, "I want grape." That's good enough for now. She hands it to him and he takes a bite.

Another of her tricks resembles the way parents help tug their toddlers into verbal being—by acting as if babbling is meaningful. When Alex says something new, Ms. Pepperberg tries to "map" it to something he is likely to remember. After he learned "rock" and "corn," and spontaneously said, "rock corn," she got dried corn and began using that term for it. Similarly, "peg wood" was mapped to clothespin and "carrot nut" to the candy Boston Baked Beans. Alex no longer gets candy, though, for it makes him hyperactively "bounce off the walls, saying 'I want this, I want that,' " says Ms. Pepperberg.

Alex often seems to play with words like kids learning to talk.

Overnight tape recordings revealed he privately babbles to himself, perhaps practicing new words. Once he saw himself in a mirror and asked, "What color?"—that's how "gray" was mapped. When a student blocked him from climbing on her chair, he uttered the only curse he's heard: "You turkey!"

These untrained signs of wit may be just "babble luck," says Ms. Pepperberg. Still, Alex sometimes seems to be groping for linguistic connections. Soon after first seeing apples, he called one a "banerry"—a word he hadn't heard. "No," Ms. Pepperberg gently reminded him, "apple." Alex persisted: "Banerry," he said, "ban-err-eeee"—speaking as his teachers do with new words. He still uses banerry, says Ms. Pepperberg, which after all makes sense: An apple tastes a little like a banana and looks like a big cherry, fruits he already knew.

Today, the gray eminence is again doing it his way. When Ms. Pepperberg holds up two keys and repeatedly asks, "How many?" he plays dumb. Finally, she calls a "time out," leaving the room. Moments later, Alex looks at me, eyes the keys, and spits out, "Two."

—DAVID STIPP, May 1990

6. *Two-Stepping with Four Legs*

HERSHEY, Pa.—As Julie Norman two-stepped across the dance floor, her partner, resplendent in a matching red bandanna, stayed flush by her side, sidestepping as she sashayed, two-stepping backward with her to "The Devil Went Down to Georgia." As the final guitar chords twanged, Ms. Norman knelt down to the Astroturf floor, tossing her cowboy hat into the air. Her partner, Sprint, a seven-year-old border collie, caught the hat, then leaped into Ms. Norman's arms. As the audience cheered, a three-judge panel sat poker-faced on the far side of the ring, judging the pair on technical merit and artistic impression.

Welcome to the Northeast Offlead Regional for the World Canine Freestyle Organization: Think Fred Astaire meets *Best in Show*. No longer is it enough for Fido to simply march around a ring. In this new sport, handlers perform (many aficionados eschew the word "dance") with their pups, to musical accompaniment. Worldwide, there are now dozens of freestyle competitions and exhibitions each year in which dogs and their owners disco, line dance and fox trot to tunes ranging from Rodgers and Hammerstein to the Rolling Stones.

At the moment, there are 2,500 or so freestyle competitors around the globe, and their ranks have been growing quickly, quadrupling in the last few years. In fact, there are already two competing freestyle groups, which differ on the extent of costuming and human involvement they allow. The World Freestyle organization (www.worldcaninefreestyle.org), founded by Patie Ventre, a onetime competitive ballroom dancer who sports rhinestone dog-bone earrings, is considered to be the more prohuman and procostume. Ms. Ventre has high hopes for the contests, aiming to get them included as a demonstration sport in the Olympics.

For now, though, freestyle has some distance to go in terms of garnering serious respect. Ms. Ventre has had a tough time winning significant sponsors—the major dog-food companies are devoting their resources to show dogs. ("The [show] dogs are generally better looking," says a spokesman for Heinz North America.) Meanwhile, the 50 or so competitors at the two-day Northeast Regional were relegated to the second tier of the parking garage at the convention center here in Hershey.

The venue may have been somewhat informal, but the competitions are anything but. Canine freestyle has two categories of events, heelwork-to-music (think ice dancing) and musical freestyle (more like pairs skating). Scores are then divvied up into a series of categories including content (three points), precise execution (two points), flow (two points), stepping in time to the music (one point) as well as use of ring space (75% is required for big dogs, 50% for those 20 pounds or under). Costuming counts: A maximum of 1 ½ points is awarded depending on how well costumes are coordinated with the routines. Points are deducted for excessive barking and canine inattention—scratching and floor-sniffing are definite no-nos, as is piddling in the ring, a misstep that got one Labrador disqualified at the North Central Regional in Michigan this May.

Maintaining canine concentration can be a challenge. As Peg Shambaugh and her border collie Belle did their routine to Lawrence Welk's "Beer Barrel Polka," Belle paused briefly to tend to a possible flea. Ms. Shambaugh tried to camouflage the slip by quickly mimicking the move. "Cute," said judge Mary Jo Sminkey, "but it won't win her any extra points." (Ms. Sminkey is a former competitor who got out of the ring because her own six-year-old Shelty, Taz, who nestled under the table as she watched the competition, "likes other sports better.")

Judges are trained to account for dogs' breeds—terriers are cut extra slack, while the bar is set a little higher for Shelties and border collies since they're considered easier to work with. "A Briard is difficult to train let alone dance with," explains the announcer. Meanwhile, in the ring, Mrs. Beasley, a buff Briard—a large French herding dog known for its lush coat and obdurate personality, defies her breed by doing figure-eights through the legs of her owner, grooving to Paul Simon's "You Can Call Me Al."

Linda Blanchard's German Wirehaired Pointer, Robbie, is

somewhat more reluctant, balking as Ms. Blanchard tries to coax him to prance with her to "I'm Looking Over a Four-Leafed Clover." Ms. Blanchard concedes she is as much a novice in some of the finer stylistic moves as Robbie. "I've done classical music and dog training—but I don't have much dance background," she says. "I just started classes this summer." What master and dog may lack in function, though, they make up for in form: Ms. Blanchard wears a custom-made green sequined number straight out of Busby Berkley, while Robbie wears a matching collar. The sequins paid off; though Ms. Blanchard and Robbie came in near the bottom of their division, they took the show's award for best costume.

As for rest of the performances, Ms. Norman and Sprint walked off with one of the top trophies; Mrs. Beasley the Briard and her owner took second, and a Schipperke who trotted to Elmer Bernstein's "Magnificent Seven" took the bronze. "I usually win," says Ms. Norman, "but this is the first time I've had any competition."

—LISA GUBERNICK , September 2001

7. *Big Bird Is an Emmy Shoe-In*

BEAUFORT, S.C.—In tidal marshes just a short distance from where scenes were filmed for *Forrest Gump,* R. J. Sorensen is making his own audience-pleaser. He lacks a big-movie budget. But luckily, his actors will work for chicken feed.

After pouring a bag of seed into a plastic feeder, he retreats behind his camera, waiting for his cast of grackles and cowbirds to arrive. "Take One!" he says, as the camera begins to roll.

Mr. Sorensen, 48 years old, is out to make the ultimate video for the bored house cat. His first movie, *Kitty Show,* took four years and half a million dollars to make. It featured a cast of bugs and fiddler crabs. It sold 100,000 copies, at $19.80 each, mainly through Mr. Sorensen's Web site. It got a "Two Paws Up" rave from *Catnip,* a publication of the Tufts University School of Veterinary Medicine.

Mr. Sorensen believes his new film will move its audience even more. "If I was a cat," he says as he looks through his viewfinder, "I'd tear the hell out of the TV."

People who live with cats know that some love watching television. Baseball and tennis are big with sports fans, who will perch atop the set and swat at the screen. And just about any old movie will satisfy a cat who's in the mood to sit and watch. It provides company if not companionship.

Between the cat owner's guilt about leaving Tabby home alone and Tabby's obvious affinity for television, there is opportunity for auteurs like Mr. Sorensen.

Ruth First, who lives in a New York studio apartment, says she no longer worries about leaving her cats alone at night. Before going out, she says she puts a little cat chair in front of the TV along with some catnip and treats. Then she pops a cat video into the videocassette recorder. Hannah, her domestic shorthair, "is mesmerized by it," says Ms. First, a spokeswoman for the American Society for the Prevention of Cruelty to Animals.

Cats, finicky in all things, have their niche favorites, be it *Kitty Safari, Feathers for Felines* or *The Adventures of Larry the Lizard.*

The genre was born in 1989 with *Video Catnip: Entertainment for Cats,* a 25-minute tape of chipmunks, birds and squirrels. Total sales: about 350,000 copies, says Steve Malarkey, the film's producer. Mr. Malarkey says he hadn't expected a perennial best-seller. "We figured we'd get a couple of years out of it and a few yucks," he says.

Video Catnip's success brought copycats and cat fighting. Steve Cantin (*Cat Adventure Video*) calls himself the Steven Spielberg of cat videos. "I know how to take creative energy and turn a profit," he says.

Before he made cat films, Mr. Cantin made "TV art," videos aimed at creating moods for humans. One was *The Ultimate Fireplace Video,* described on the box as "the next best thing to having your own fireplace. . . . No chopping wood . . . no cinders and soot to clean." Another was *The Ultimate Aquarium Video,* a fish tank that doesn't have to be cleaned.

Mr. Cantin economized by reusing Aquarium Video footage in his *Cat Adventure Video.* But this time a Tufts Veterinary reviewer wasn't amused. She panned the fish-swimming scenes, which, oddly, have a voice-over of birds chirping. She wrote that the scenes "bored all cats silly." She gave the video "Two Paws Down."

Mr. Cantin isn't fazed. *Cat Adventure Video* was picked up by Publishers Choice, a mass marketer owned by National Syndications, Inc., and advertised in *Parade*. Mr. Cantin is now working on a *Cat Sitter* DVD that can be played all day long. His goal for the year: $1 million in cat-video sales. "I'm out to sell volume," Mr. Cantin says.

As to his rivals, Mr. Cantin is less generous. He pans *Video Catnip* as gimmickry larded with "funky, goopy music." As for Mr. Sorensen's *Kitty Show* and its four-year gestation, he says, "I don't think they spent that much time on the atom bomb."

Says Mr. Sorensen: "It's a cutthroat business. . . . My goal is not volume, it's happy cats."

A onetime paramedic, Mr. Sorensen cut his cinematic teeth producing medical videos. But he says he would get home from two-day trips to find three depressed cats, "so I decided to invent a product that would keep their attention." Mr. Sorensen tested some of the other cat videos on his pets. His cat Milo, he says, hid under the bed after seeing *Video Catnip*—terrified by a close-up of a squirrel that made the creature look bigger than life. He says he took the tape out in the yard and "shot it to death" with his shotgun.

Out to make something more congenial, he lavished attention on *Kitty Show*. He filmed the tail twitches, raised fur and eye movements of several test cats as they watched a variety of critters pass across high-resolution monitors. He shaved cats' chests and hooked them up to electrocardiographs. He learned that cats are particularly excited by purple, green and yellow, but see reds and browns as grays. Rapid movements, he says, would increase a cat's heart rate by 40 beats. Cats, he decided, are crazy about insects and bugs.

Filming *Kitty Show* was rough. At night, Mr. Sorensen says, he illuminated his yard with floodlights. Two helpers ran around swooping up bugs with butterfly nets while Mr. Sorensen filmed in "the bug room," his studio. The biggest problem, Mr. Sorensen says, was keeping the insects moving. Also, his moths at first tended to immolate themselves on the lights.

To film the bugs, Mr. Sorensen says he invented a special lens filter that enhanced cat appeal by adding "low wave" purple colors to the white images. The result: two hours of fluttering moths, crawling beetles and creeping spiders set against backgrounds that alternate every 20 minutes.

This sort of action probably wouldn't interest anybody who isn't on drugs, Mr. Sorensen says. But then, "I'm not interested in what people think. I'm interested in what cats think."

To find out exactly what cats think of *Kitty Show,* Mr. Sorensen scheduled a screening at an animal shelter in nearby Hilton Head. As the shelter's director looked on, Mr. Sorensen turned on a TV set and slid a tape into the VCR. Not much happened at first, but soon enough, as the Fellini of feline film beamed, a pair of cats hissed and growled, as they competed for space in front of the set.

—JAMES BANDLER, July 2001

8. Barking Mad for Joyce

GRESHAM, Ore.—When you read to a dog and he seems to be sleeping through the best parts, he is actually "listening with eyes closed." That's the word from Natalie Shilling, youth librarian at the Gresham branch of the Multnomah County Library.

Ms. Shilling introduced a "Read to the Dogs" program here last year after learning about the Salt Lake City Public Library's literary, listening dogs. They are certified therapy dogs guaranteed to act interested (or at least not run away) while a child reads aloud, even if they've already heard *George and Diggety* a zillion times.

Children tend to choose pack-pleasing, canine-themed books for their 30-minute sessions with the dogs and their unobtrusive handlers. When I visited the Gresham library, I found 11-year-old Shawn Helgeson about to launch into a spirited reading of *Watchdog and the Coyotes* to a yellow Lab named Patrick.

Shawn noted that the book had already scored a paws-up from Howard, another library dog. "It's hilarious," Shawn said. Sure enough, as he read about the watchdog that only watched, Patrick appeared to be laughing. Minutes later, however, the dog closed his mouth, along with his eyes, and commenced listening with eyes closed.

Patrick's owner, Rachel Timmon, said that before Shawn

came along, two little boys had been showing Patrick picture books. One book was about taking a bath. "Patrick hates baths," Ms. Timmon revealed. But Patrick had tactfully concealed his distaste for the topic, possibly even laughing in the face of it.

Ms. Shilling, the librarian, has five dogs of her own, all pint-sized Cavalier King Charles spaniels, and every one a therapy dog certified through Portland's Dove Lewis Emergency Animal Hospital. The hospital has trained an entire menagerie of pets (including dogs, cats, birds and llamas) that visits patients in hospitals and nursing homes.

When Ms. Shilling read in *School Library Journal* about the Salt Lake City library's partnership with Intermountain Therapy Animals, she realized that the key to a similar, local program lay snoozing in her lap.

Results from the Salt Lake City library's "Dog Day Afternoons" and related school programs showed that reading aloud to a nonjudgmental, unconditionally loving canine audience was having a positive effect on erstwhile problem readers. There was a marked increase in technical skill and personal confidence. Furthermore, petting while reading provided a natural tranquilizer for high-strung children.

In 1999, critical-care nurse and animal lover Sandi Martin literally dreamed up the Utah program, springing up in bed at 2:00 A.M. and jotting down her thoughts. After refining her idea with Intermountain Therapy Animals, for which she is a board member, she called Dana Tumpowsky, the library's community relations manager, and asked her to try it. "I thought, `This woman's crazy,' " confessed Ms. Tumpowsky.

Crazy like a fox, perhaps, or even a Portuguese water dog, like Olivia, Ms. Martin's own reading therapy dog, which before dying of cancer helped build READ (Reading Education Assistance Dogs) into a nationally known, copyrighted program. In this year alone, READ has fielded more than 400 inquiries from libraries and schools.

The READ program had its debut in November 1999, when six dogs and their handlers settled down on the library floor with six young readers. Ms. Martin and Olivia composed one dog team that day.

"You'd see kids with their finger in a book and a hand on a dog," recalled Ms. Martin. "It was just kind of magical."

By January 2000, children's librarians at all six branches had requested the literary dogs, which are washed with antidander shampoo before their visits. They are identified by their red bandannas and their handlers' red T-shirts.

"It's not like anybody can walk in with their dog," explained the library's Ms. Tumpowsky, who not once has had to say "Shhhhh!" to a READ dog.

Ms. Martin said the handlers take their jobs as seriously as the dogs do. The owner of an Akita is busy trying to teach her dog how to turn pages of the kids' books. The trick is placing a small morsel of kibble between pages.

"The kids think he's mesmerized by the story, but he's really waiting to turn the page so he can get the treat," she said.

When I visited Portland's Hollywood branch library, one of five local branches that has adopted the "Read to the Dogs" program, the dog on duty didn't appear to possess similar talents. In fact, Alyx, 10, an interesting mix of golden retriever, Labrador retriever, Newfoundland and border collie, was most adept at listening with eyes closed.

Her handler, Liz Johnston, was the one with all the tricks: a Polaroid camera, so the young reader's session with Alyx would be immortalized, and a reading certificate featuring Alyx's portrait.

I arrived just as Emma Crabtree, age seven, was gathering up her books and preparing to pose with her reading audience. Ms. Johnston set to work rousing the deeply listening dog, while Emma's mother, Linda Crabtree, kept her distance.

"I'm allergic to dogs," she explained. "If they lick me, I break out in hives."

The next scheduled reader was a no-show, so Ms. Johnston invited me to read to Alyx. Just as the children usually do, I scurried through the stacks, desperately looking for anything with dog in the title. But by force of habit, I had gone to the adult fiction section. No dog tales leaped out at me. So I took a copy of James Joyce's *Finnegans Wake* from the shelf. Alyx, as usual, was non-judgmental, while Ms. Johnson clearly would have preferred hearing yet another "Henry and Mudge" story. But that didn't stop her from snapping my photo and awarding me a certificate.

Back home, I tried reading aloud to my dog, Daphne. But, lacking the appropriate training, Daphne ran away, tossing me a look that seemed to say, "Reading? That's for the birds!"

—SUSAN G. HAUSER, August 2001

9. *Little Beauties*

SOWERBY BRIDGE, England—Jack Wormald, the founder of the Calder Valley Mouse Club, says his "fancy" for these furry little animals began more than 50 years ago when he attended the local agriculture show.

The owner of the best-mouse-in-show that day was a man who would become a legend in the world of exhibition mice, the late W. Mackintosh Kerr from Glasgow. "I was just so excited and thrilled by Mr. Kerr's mouse—it was an all-black with a lovely sheen—that I couldn't get over it," says Mr. Wormald.

Mr. Wormald wrote Mr. Kerr, expressing his admiration for these show mice, and Mr. Kerr mailed him "a trio"—a starter set of two does and a buck. The rest, as they say, is history. Mr. Wormald estimates he has bred 200,000 mice in the last half-century, twice winning the coveted Woodiwiss Bowl, named in honor of Sam Woodiwiss, who founded the National Mouse Club and became its first president in 1895. The solid-silver punch bowl goes to the best in show at the highlight event on the mouse-show calendar, held annually at Bradford. "There is," says Mr. Wormald, "no greater honor."

The 74-year-old Mr. Wormald was here in industrial west Yorkshire the other day for the Calder Valley show, which attracted about 50 exhibitors and 230 animals. It was a lively scene on the top floor of the St. John's Ambulance Corps rooms, with three judges, all dressed in long white coats (two of them with Mouse Club patches), inspecting the contestants, one by one.

The mice are packed in little green "Maxey cages," invented by the most famous mouse man of all, the late Walter Maxey, almost always referred to as the "father of the mouse fancy." Mr. Wormald is proud to say he owns the original Maxey cage, which was recently repaired by his friend and fellow mouse fancier, Frank Hawley.

"We took off layer after layer of paint," says Mr. Hawley. "When we got down to the original wood, we could dimly make out the letters EVILLE ORAN. Sure enough, he'd made the cage out of a box that had contained Seville oranges."

The judge reaches—carefully—into the cage and pulls the squirming mouse out by its tail. He examines its ears, checks its coat, measures the length of its tail. Sometimes he blows on the animal, to ruffle its fur, so he can look at its undercoat. He lets the mouse run up and down his arm, to see how lively it is.

"This is serious business," says Edward Longbottom, the longtime secretary of the Calder Valley club. "We are as careful in the way we breed mice as horse owners are in the way they breed Thoroughbreds."

Standards are rigid. "The mouse," according to the rules of the National Mouse Club, "must be long in body with long, clean head, not too fine or pointed at the nose. The eyes should be large, bold and prominent, the ears large and tulip shaped, free from creases. . . . The tail must be free from kinks and should come well out of the back and be thick at the root, gradually tapering like a whiplash to a fine end, the length being about equal to that of the mouse's body."

Graham Davidson, one of the judges here, says the most famous mouse of all—Mickey—"would never get out of the cage at one of our shows." Mickey Mouse, he says, is "too fat, his ears are too round and his tail looks like somebody pasted it on."

Mouse judging usually begins with the "selfs"—animals that come all in a single color. Recognized colors are black, blue, champagne, chocolate, cream, dove, fawn, red, silver and white. A perfect self would win 100 points—50 for color, 15 for general condition, 15 for overall shape and carriage, and five apiece for shape of ears, eyes, muzzle and tail.

There are other varieties with special markings and combinations of colors—Himalayans, chinchillas, silver foxes, argente cremes, marten sables, silver agoutis, rump whites, seal point Siamese.

It costs about 10 cents to enter a mouse in any of the recognized Mouse Club shows, the same price exhibitors paid 50 years ago. And the cash prizes haven't changed, either—50 cents for first place, 30 cents for second and 15 cents for third.

"We do it out of love—and for the social companionship involved," says Mr. Hawley, who won the Woodiwiss Bowl several years ago with his all-black Jetset Prince, still a legend among the mouse-fancy set. Jetset Prince, unlike most exhibition mice, which are killed when they pass their prime, was allowed to retire, living out a full three-year life, rich with honors.

Mr. Hawley estimates he travels 6,000 miles a year to compete in mouse shows. He is usually accompanied by three fellow mouse fanciers, who share the cost of the gasoline. "You've got to be out there almost every weekend between March and October if you expect to come up with grand champions," Mr. Hawley notes.

Most mouse fanciers are amateur geneticists, constantly attempting to come up with a mouse with new and unusual colors or markings. Your name, then, goes into the book (G. Atlee, for example, is credited with the Himalayan mouse, in 1897; Miss Mary Douglas discovered the champagne mouse in 1911). Mouse breeders understand that you begin to create cinnamons by crossing an agouti with a chocolate, yielding a litter of all agoutis. Breed these agoutis together and you come up with three cinnamons per litter of 16 babies. Each generation, the breeder culls out—kills—the babies that won't serve the purpose.

The mouse fanciers' bible, Tony Cooke's *Exhibition and Pet Mice,* spells out with charts and diagrams how it is accomplished.

It's a far cry from the ordinary wild mouse, Musmusculus, which has a shorter tail and smaller ears and which is normally a dull gray-brown in color. These exhibition mice, the experts say, carry a little Japanese strain in them, introduced by the legendary Mr. Maxey, who bought Oriental mice from sailors who brought them home as pets at the turn of the century.

Pink-eyed mice, in fact, can be traced back to Japanese mice called "Waltzers." They got that name, according to Mr. Davidson, the judge, "because they had a brain disorder that caused them to run around in circles." Waltzers were crossed with ordinary wild mice—and the babies appeared with pink eyes. Better still, the babies didn't waltz.

The mouse fancy, with nine clubs active in London and the industrial Midlands, is largely an English phenomenon (there are no clubs in Wales, Scotland or Northern Ireland). The only other countries that show much mouse interest are Holland and Germany. Efforts to interest Americans haven't been too successful. "They tend to be namby-pamby; they don't take it seriously," says Frank Hawley. He thinks there may still be an active mouse group in Fontana, Calif.

Most of the mouse fanciers come from quite ordinary working-class and middle-class backgrounds (Mr. Maxey, the fancy's father, was a mailman). They are warm, cheerful people, hoping outsiders will try to understand their innocent fun.

"These shows are social events as much as anything else," says Mr. Longbottom, the secretary of the local club. His wife, May, has been coming to shows for 50 years, even though she doesn't care for mice at all. "I despise them," she says. But, all the same, she has been voted a life member of the National Mouse Club.

The mouse fanciers look down on the rat fancy.

The National Fancy Rat Society holds regular shows, too, though, nationally, it is much smaller than the mouse group. "I don't care for rats," says Jack Wormald, twice the winner of the Woodiwiss Bowl. "They are very coarse."

— JAMES M. PERRY, March 1986

10. Fido Forever

Jackie Hibbard's voice softens when she recalls how her dog, a terrier-mutt named Itchy, was hit and killed by a car two years ago.

But even in death, Itchy is there every morning when the 40-year-old Gilliam, Mo., resident wakes up. Itchy lies on the bedroom floor, her head on her paws and her eyes wide open.

Ms. Hibbard had her freeze-dried.

More of the nation's estimated 73 million pet owners are having their departed companions freeze-dried, instead of buried or cremated. The bereaved say turning their furry friends into perma-pets helps them deal with their loss and maintain a connection to their former companions—at a fraction of the cost of preserving them through traditional taxidermy.

Freeze-drying, generally used for preserving food or purifying chemicals, also retains some individual characteristics like facial expressions that don't survive standard taxidermy, proponents say. "It's comforting," says the 40-year-old Ms. Hibbard. "If you can see her all the time, you really have those wonderful memories."

Freeze-drying has also given the sleepy taxidermy industry a new lease on life, letting many studios expand beyond their traditional hunting-and-fishing clientele. Mike McCullough, owner of Mac's Taxidermy in Fort Loudon, Pa., started freeze-drying animals about five years ago. About all he needed to get started were two freeze-dryers, which cost him $22,000. In addition to dogs and cats, he says he also gets the odd request to do a family bird or lizard. Pet preservation now accounts for 5% of his shop's annual revenue of about $80,000.

"It's getting to be a really big deal," says Mr. McCullough. "The profit margin is phenomenal."

Freeze-drying pets is still rare. Elden Harrison, president of the Joppa, Md.–based Pet Lovers Association, estimates that less than 1% of the dogs that die each year end up freeze-dried. And it upsets many animal lovers. In a recent survey by MeowMail.com, a Massachusetts-based electronic community for cat lovers, the 2,600 subscribers who responded overwhelmingly rejected freeze-drying. "It's kind of disgusting and demented," says subscriber Heather Marshall, a 23-year-old in Phoenix. "The question is, would you freeze-dry your child or mother or sister or father? Probably not."

Some taxidermists also turn up their noses at transforming family pets into permanent fixtures. "I don't do it here. I don't want to skin a dog," says Cally Morris of Hazel Creek Inc. Taxidermy of Green Castle, Mo.

Still, the practice is gaining acceptance. "We endorse it," says Mr. Harrison of the Pet Lovers Association, which advises owners on "disposition options" for dead pets.

Gail Timberlake, who owns a catering business in Winchester, Va., doesn't care what others think. Her Chartreux cat, Father Ron, is in the freeze-dryer right now. He will return home in March to resume his spot on the white bedroom chair he once used for afternoon naps.

"I just loved that little guy," says Ms. Timberlake, who found the alternatives to freeze-drying distasteful when she had to put the cat to sleep at age 21. "Ashes? I don't think so. Buried in the ground with the worms? I don't think so," she says. "This way, I can always look at him and kiss him goodnight."

Alan Anger, president of Freezedry Specialties Inc., which sells freeze-drying equipment, says he began promoting pet freeze-drying to taxidermists about five years ago after working with museums to preserve animal specimens. "We saw that the process was the same for doing trophy animals and domestic animals," he says.

He now promotes the practice through what the company calls "Friends Forever," a marketing scheme under which taxidermists purchasing the equipment pay a licensing fee in return for training and referrals from the company.

Taxidermists who favor freeze-drying say it's far easier than traditional wildlife mounting. Preserving a deceased animal the traditional way involves skinning it, removing internal organs, cleaning away muscle and other tissue through cooking, rebuilding the bone structure and tanning the hide. Then the skeleton must be padded with foam and other materials, and the preserved skin refitted and sewn on. Mr. McCullough, the Fort Loudon taxidermist, charges as much as $2,000 for a traditional job on a small dog.

Freeze-drying avoids nearly all of that labor, preserving the animal with much less expense. Mr. McCullough, for example, charges between $550 and $600 for a poodle, depending on the size.

The virtue of the process, which was commercialized after World War II to preserve blood plasma, lies in its ability to evaporate water directly from ice to vapor without it ever turning into water.

Al Holmes, who runs a taxidermy studio and wildlife museum in Wetumpka, Ala., starts by manipulating the animal's body into an appropriately meaningful pose. He works from snapshots and consultations with the owners. Then he puts the animal in a regular freezer until solid. From there it goes into a special freeze-dryer. In Mr. Holmes's studio, this is an imposing steel cylinder with a four-inch-thick Plexiglas window. As refrigerators cool the interior to 12 degrees Fahrenheit, a powerful pump sucks out the air, creating a near-perfect vacuum. Little by little, the ice in the corpse escapes as water vapor, which is pulled out of the chamber.

Small animals take about two months to dry completely, while large dogs need as long as six months. "We go by feel," says Mr. Holmes. "We open the machine every other week. When all the water is gone, there's nothing to freeze and they actually feel warm. Then you know he's ready."

Once dried, the animal's bodies don't decay.

Early efforts to freeze-dry family pets produced specimens that later became infested with insects. Taxidermists say they've solved that problem by injecting the pets with solutions of formaldehyde and other preservatives before putting them in the freeze-dryer.

Family pets can also be difficult because so many are over-weight. Sometimes, all the fat doesn't completely dry, leading to problems in the afterlife. "You start getting some oozing," says Anthony Eddy, owner of Anthony Eddy Wildlife Studios, Slater, Mo.

But this is nothing a little cotton batting and some household repair equipment can't solve. After surgically removing fat deposits, "I go in there with a caulking gun," he says.

The technical subtleties don't matter to Tauna Hadley of Kansas City, Kan. Her Weimaraner, Weimar Lee, died of cancer in 1999. Now she sits proudly atop a living room wardrobe. "It's like she's asleep," says Ms. Hadley. "She's still a pet. She's just not a live pet."

—JEFFREY KRASNER, January 2001

CHAPTER 2

POLITICAL ANIMALS

━━━━━

11. Kill Kitty?

OLD BRIDGE, N.J.—Skunk work is a breeze for Frank Spiecker. Removing chimney raccoons, no sweat. When he turns up in his Garden State Pest Management pickup to trap a wild animal, he often receives a hero's welcome. Many residents of this leafy suburb are newcomers from cities, and they are terrified of the wild animals that live among them.

But when property managers, fearing health complaints or lawsuits, hire Mr. Spiecker to trap and remove stray cats, it's a different story. Cat jobs have gotten him screamed at, threatened and jostled. His truck has been jumped on and pounded, his traps run over, and his trapped cats freed.

"The screamers I can handle," he says. "It's the quiet ones you have to watch."

Mr. Spiecker is a mercenary on the front lines of the cat wars. To cat lovers, he abets feline mass murder, since most of the cats he traps end up dead. To many others, cats are the murderers, wreaking environmental havoc by killing billions of animals, birds and other wildlife every year. Fights between cat people (who often feed birds) and bird people (who often have cats) have sputtered for decades. But as the cat population has exploded—to well more than 100 million by most estimates—the conflict is re-arranging the landscape of environmental politics.

How serious the problem is and what should be done about it are questions that have split veterinarians and wildlife biologists, divided animal-protection groups into rival camps, and united such strange bedfellows as bird-watchers and bird-shooters.

In one revealing battle, the Humane Society of the United States and the American Society for the Prevention of Cruelty to Animals in 1998 funded a signature drive in California for a state ballot initiative to ban leg-hold and other traps as cruel, promoting it with gruesome TV ads.

As soon as it passed, the National Audubon Society sued in federal court in San Francisco to block enforcement of the ban, claiming that the law didn't apply to federal lands and that trapping feral cats, foxes and other predators is an important tool in saving endangered and migratory birds. The National Trappers Association joined the suit.

In his ruling in favor of Audubon, Federal District Judge Charles Legge wrote: "Most such litigation pits environmentalists against industry or government. Here we have an unusual alignment of birds versus mammals. That is, two competing groups of environmentalists are in court to protect their respective wildlife constituents against one another."

The Humane Society, a national animal-welfare and -rights group unaffiliated with state and local Humane Societies, appealed. Late last month, the Ninth U.S. Circuit Court of Appeals in San Francisco upheld the lower court, saying that saving endangered species trumps the trapping ban. Wayne Pacelle, a senior vice president of the losing Humane Society, said: "We're disappointed that the Audubon Society essentially aligned themselves with commercial fur trappers and duck hunters."

Behind the shifting alliances are big changes in where people and animals live in America. A century ago, most cats lived in towns and cities separated from wildlife habitat by huge belts of cleared farmland. Farmers kept cats as mousers. The cats also preyed on other animals and birds around the farm. But their overall rural numbers were small.

Today, many farms are gone. The eastern third of the U.S. is home to the largest natural reforestation success story on the planet. Between splotches of big cities, trees, bushes and meadows have reclaimed abandoned farmland across hundreds of millions of acres, recreating a lush habitat for wildlife. At the same time, suburban sprawl has pushed relentlessly deeper into that habitat. That's where the majority of Americans—and their cats— now live.

To let cats roam freely in this prey-rich environment is criminal, bird people say. They say cats aren't native; they're an introduced species, like kudzu vine.

"Like West Nile virus," says Linda Winter, who runs the five-year-old "Cats Indoors!" campaign for the American Bird Conservancy, a bird-protection group in Washington. Keeping cats from roaming freely outdoors saves cats from passing cars, disease and predators, and saves wildlife from cats, she says.

While the Humane Society supports the initiative, Washington-based Alley Cat Allies, a vociferous defender of stray cats, denounces "Cats Indoors" as "a new environmental witch hunt."

For millennia, the cat wasn't a warm fuzzy pet. As an elegantly efficient predator, it was pressed into service to patrol granaries and ships for rodents. Cats evolved only slowly as house pets until the 1960s, when odor-absorbent clay Kitty Litter became widely available, eliminating the cat's biggest drawback as a pet: its concentrated, foul-smelling urine.

Today, the number of pet cats in the U.S. is somewhere around 73 million, according to the American Pet Products Manufacturers Association. That number doesn't include feral cats—strays that live on handouts, garbage and hunting. "Feral cat numbers are pure guesses," says Martha Armstrong, vice president for companion animals at the Humane Society. "There could be 30 million ferals, or 150 million."

If the high figure is anywhere close to the actual number, the total U.S. cat population exceeds the combined populations of cattle (99 million), pigs (61 million) and sheep (eight million). By contrast, the estimated U.S. population of white-tail deer, another controversial species, is 33 million.

The numbers are one reason many environmentalists are returning to a concept associated with the earliest days of the wildlife conservation movement: triage, or controlling one animal to protect another.

The conservation movement arose in the late 19th century in response to the ravages of commercial hunting for food and fashion. Conservationists lobbied successfully to outlaw hunting of threatened species and then nurtured them back by restocking deer, wild turkeys and other creatures. They then managed the species by setting bounties on their predators and, eventually, establishing seasons and catch-limits for hunters and trappers.

In the 1960s, many modern environmentalists began to view any human interference in nature as negative. Some sided with animal-rights groups to condemn any killing of animals for sport or economic gain or to manage wildlife populations. In recent years, they got trapping banned in several states, thwarted efforts by some local governments to kill white-tail deer and Canada geese, and stopped medical and other research using animals for experiments. They also attacked animal shelters as death rows for pets. Privately run shelters began advertising themselves as "no-kill," promising to find a new home for every animal taken in. (They often turn away unadoptable animals, which are then abandoned or taken to municipal shelters and killed.)

Now, in wildlife refuges and in the urban and suburban settings where man and animal directly confront each other with increasing frequency, killing is making a comeback. "We've shifted more and more to supporting hunting and trapping as tools of wildlife management," says Frank Gill, an Audubon senior vice president.

That thinking has figured largely in a series of setbacks for cat defenders. This year, municipal and county governments across the nation, responding to cat complaints, have adopted cat control or anti-cat-feeding laws, stiffened the ones they had and promised to begin enforcing long-ignored regulations.

In June, for example, the Akron, Ohio, City Council passed a law requiring that all cats be licensed, vaccinated against rabies and not allowed to run loose. By late August, 575 stray cats had been picked up and more than 400 of them euthanized. A local cat-defense group then filed a lawsuit in Summit County, Ohio, alleging that the law is inhumane. The case is pending.

The same month that Akron passed its law, scientists at the University of California at Davis said runoff tainted with cat feces may be killing the state's endangered sea otters. Nearly half of 223 live and dead otters tested were found to be infected with a parasite called Toxoplasma gondii. Cats are the only known source of the parasite.

In January, the U.S. Navy outlawed feral-cat colonies from all of its installations. Military bases become dumping grounds for pets when personnel are transferred. Feral cats also thrive on college campuses, where departing students abandon their pets, and around factories, restaurants, hospitals and other institutions where people feed them.

In its announcement, the Navy said two programs it used to manage the colonies don't work and harm wildlife. For more than a decade, so-called trap-neuter-release, or TNR, programs and trap-test-vaccinate-alter-release programs were embraced as an alternative to killing strays. The idea is that once the cats are castrated and released, they gradually die out because they can't reproduce. Volunteers feed and monitor the colonies, keeping out new strays. TNR advocates say cats in the colonies also defend their territory themselves against intruding newcomers.

Wildlife biologists call TNR a pipe dream that allows feral cats, neutered or not, to kill more wildlife. Bird people cite a new 13-month study of two Miami colonies by Dan Castillo, a graduate student, who found that the colonies encourage people to illegally dump their unwanted cats, which have kittens before they can be trapped and castrated.

Trapping pros such as Mr. Spiecker say another obvious flaw in TNR is that you can trap feral cats once and give them a rabies shot, but that it's nearly impossible to trap them a year later to give them a necessary booster. They learn quickly to avoid traps.

Alley Cat Allies, a TNR promoter, called the Navy decision a "death sentence" for feral cats. The group also announced that it would switch the focus of its energy from promoting TNR among cat lovers to fighting the backlash against them.

The Humane Society says that one fertile female and her offspring can produce 420,000 cats in seven years. As strays, they lead short, brutal lives. Sterilization rates for pet cats jumped dramatically, to 80% in 1990 from 10% in 1970, says Peter

Marsh, a Concord, N.H., lawyer who founded Solutions to Over-population of Pets to promote neutering and reduce euthanasia in shelters. But feral reproduction more than makes up for non-breeding pets.

To underscore the damage these cats do, bird lovers often cite Stanley Temple, a wildlife ecologist at the University of Wisconsin. His study team reported in the late 1980s that densities of free-range cats in some parts of rural Wisconsin outnumbered all midsize native predators—foxes, raccoons, skunks and the like—combined. The report said a "good guess" was that these cats killed from eight million to 217 million birds annually. It added that "most reasonable estimates indicate" that 39 million birds are killed by cats in the state. Citing other studies, the report went on:

"Nationwide, rural cats probably kill over a billion small mammals and hundreds of millions of birds each year. Urban and suburban cats add to this toll. Some of these kills are house mice, rats and other species considered pests, but many are native songbirds and mammals whose populations are already stressed by other factors, such as habitat destruction and pesticide pollution." It added: "World-wide, cats may have been involved in the extinction of more bird species than any other cause, except habitat destruction."

Dr. Temple says he was bombarded with hate mail.

Since then, bird people have seen cause to hope that nature is starting to deal with cat overpopulation in its own way. Coyotes and fishers, two predators of cats, are making dramatic comebacks. "Coyotes here have adapted to feeding on cats in urban areas," says Ron Jurek, a California Fish and Game Department wildlife biologist.

Fishers, which look like large weasels, have the advantage of being able to follow cats up trees. Just having these predators around keeps cats closer to home, says Roland Kays, curator for mammals at the New York State Museum in Albany, who studies cats in the Albany Pine Bush preserve.

But they aren't likely to put people such as Mr. Spiecker out of business anytime soon. When he was growing up in Old Bridge and learning to trap, this part of New Jersey was still farms and small towns. Now 35, he drives his truck down roads lined with fast-food joints, auto-parts outlets, malls, gas stations and the other fixtures of suburban sprawl.

To point out change, he pulls into a large apartment complex on a hill and drives to the back-fence Dumpsters. Beyond them, where farmers used to till fields, forest stretches as far as the eye can see—a habitat full of the animals and cats that fuel his business. About 40% is cat trapping.

When a woman said her small dog was attacked by a stray cat at the 1,200-unit Glenwood Apartments two years ago, Mr. Spiecker was hired to trap strays for $50 apiece. In the year ending September last year, he trapped 370 cats and nearly 600 raccoons, opossums and skunks. He relocated the wild animals to a state refuge and delivered the cats to the Old Bridge Township Animal Shelter.

Nearly half the 65,880 cats brought to New Jersey animal shelters last year were euthanized, according to the state health department. About 100 of the cats Mr. Spiecker brought to the Old Bridge shelter found homes, thanks to Barbara Lee Brucker, who has worked there for 21 years. The additional 270 were judged too wild or sick to keep and given lethal injections. Their carcasses were frozen.

"This is considered to be a no-kill shelter," Ms. Brucker says with a raised eyebrow. "Trap, neuter, release? We did it by the book for four years and it just didn't work." Dumped cats and new strays kept turning up.

When Ms. Brucker's freezer is full of dead animals, she calls the Abbey Glen Pet Cemetery in Morris County. They send a truck and incinerate the carcasses for 35 cents a pound.

—JAMES P. STERBA, October 2002

12. *Anglers Away!*

ENNIS, Mont.—Jasper Thomas was fly fishing for rainbow trout on the Madison River near here one recent morning when it suddenly began raining rocks.

Two young men were bombarding his fishing spot with baseball-size stones. "I said, 'Hey, you'll scare the fish!' " recalls Mr. Thomas, a retired Texas contractor. "They said, 'That's the point.' " Mr. Thomas reacted as many a fisherman might. He zinged casts at the trout protectors until they fled—but not before plastering his truck with anti-fishing leaflets.

The animal-rights movement has a new angle: It wants to ban fishing. Not just big commercial operations that vacuum up tons of fish and sometimes maim dolphins and seals. All fishing— from the pursuit of the wily trout here in Montana to cane-pole catfishing down at the local pond.

And while they're at it, they want compassion for crustaceans too.

The goal, say animal-rights leaders, is to spare the creatures from agonizing deaths. "Just because fish and lobsters aren't cute and cuddly doesn't mean they don't suffer excruciating pain," says Tracy Reiman, an organizer with People for the Ethical Treatment of Animals, or PETA, a group based in Washington, D.C., that is spearheading the fish-rights campaign. "You wouldn't sink a hook into your cat and leave it flopping on the deck gasping for air, would you?" she asks. "You wouldn't boil it alive."

Activists dressed in lobster suits have berated diners entering Gladstone's, a restaurant in Pacific Palisades, Calif., that serves as many as 10,000 lobsters a month. The shadowy Crustacean Liberation Front has tagged San Francisco cafés with pro-lobster graffiti. In England, underwater saboteurs in scuba gear have prowled the deep at fishing tournaments, herding away trophy carp and snipping off lures.

The campaign is bound to hit snags, given fishing's widespread popularity: An estimated 54 million people fish in America, including many members of Congress. Even some mainstream animal-welfare groups are skeptical. Wayne Pacelle, a lobbyist with the Humane Society of the U.S., says tackling fishing "is somewhat silly and possibly counterproductive when the movement has so many other priorities."

The reaction of fishermen is more biting. "Those anti-fishing folks are cuckoo," says Virgil Ward, a member of three fishing Halls of Fame and former producer of weekly television fishing shows. The 84-year-old Mr. Ward, who recently retired so he could devote more time to fishing, says anti-fishing groups periodically send him letters asking him to join their cause. "They make me so damn mad I just throw 'em in the trash can," Mr. Ward grumbles. "Then I go fishing to calm down."

Pro-fish forces are undeterred, though. Last month, PETA declared a National Fish Amnesty Day, and plans to call for more fishing-free days in the future. Not everybody got the message: On National Fish Amnesty Day at Fisherman's Wharf in San Francisco, the usual cast of fishermen were baited up and ready to go before dawn. "Anybody tells me I can't fish, I consider making them the bait," says Antonio Caldera, a Fisherman's Wharf regular.

Last spring, PETA led a band of about 30 protesters to Anglin's

Pier in Fort Lauderdale, Fla. Amid scattered boos and shouts of "Get a life!" the protesters waved banners reading "Fishing: Cold-blooded Sport" and "Get Hooked on Compassion, Not Fishing."

Activists considered the outing a success, but Will Harty, manager of Anglin's, says the action there is hotter than ever. "What these protesters don't understand is that people here love fishing more than anything—with the possible exception of their mamas."

Still, when it comes to protests, American fish-rights campaigners are pikers compared to the English. Pro-fish groups across the pond deploy saboteurs who shut down fishing tournaments by, among other things, flailing the water with 20-foot bamboo poles to scatter fish. More daring are the subsurface "sabbers"—scuba divers who slip beneath the water to spook fish and cut lines.

Earlier this year, a local borough council in South London tried banning fishing at Clapham Commons. Signs proclaiming "All Fishing Strictly Prohibited" went up around the park's largest pond—and were promptly ignored. "The anti-fishies are off their rockers," carps Steven Jones, an out-of-work South Londoner, as he flings a handful of wriggling pink and yellow maggots into the water to attract fish. The ban has since been repealed.

Anti-fishing forces' main beef is that fishing is cruel and immoral. And contrary to what many beginning fishermen are told by Grandpa, fish do feel pain, according to many scientists. Ditto for lobsters. "They are sentient organisms, so of course they feel pain," says Dr. Austin Williams, a National Marine Fisheries Service zoologist. But Dr. Richard Rosenblatt, an ichthyologist at the Scripps Institution of Oceanography, notes that life at sea is naturally rough, and that getting caught and eaten by a fisherman is probably no worse than getting caught and eaten by, say, a shark.

"No sardine ever died a happy death," Dr. Rosenblatt says.

Fishermen put it in more striking terms. "To say fishing is

cruel is just ridiculous," says Ann Lewis, spokeswoman for the Bass Anglers Sportsman Society in Montgomery, Ala., which is currently seeking a site for a bass theme park (one possible name: Bassanation Center). Adds famed fisherman Mr. Ward: "Fishing, cruel? That's the biggest fish story I've heard yet."

Still, anti-fishing forces have won a few fights. Last year, actress and vegetarian Mary Tyler Moore hooked up with activists defending Spike, a 70-year-old, 12-pound lobster, who was to be raffled and eaten at Gladstone's restaurant. Ms. Moore offered $1,000 to free Spike, prompting Rush Limbaugh to offer $2,000 to eat him. In the end, Gladstone's kept Spike in his tank as a tourist attraction. "Kids come by all the time to get their pictures taken with Spike," says Alan Redhead, president of the company that owns Gladstone's.

Mr. Redhead says his suppliers now have a new name for big lobsters: Mary Tyler Moores. "They say, 'how many MTMs do you need?' I say: 'As many as you can ship me.' "

Ms. Moore's reaction? "Good," she says. "At least people are thinking about our message."

— CHARLES F. McCOY, October 1995

13. Bite the Lawyers

NOVATO, Calif.—In the cool confines of a Marin County seniors' center, Diane Greer lays out the rules: No dog-eat-dog behavior here.

"This room is a bubble, a space where we can talk," the veteran dispute mediator says. Her "clients"—neighbors at each other's throats over a domestic issue—eye each other warily.

"No character defamation, please," Ms. Greer instructs. "Use 'I' messages, not, 'You did this,' but 'I feel.' "

Respect, it seems, is a vital element in nonbinding pet arbitration. Ms. Greer is Marin County's official pet mediator. In these well-to-do suburbs north of San Francisco, she straightens out pet peeves ranging from noisy hounds to snakes worn at public pools to puppy custody battles. Today's case: the barking of Rocky, a German shepherd whose serenades have infuriated his owner's neighbor and have become a police matter. Ms. Greer's goal is to stop "the kind of anger that has the opportunity for spontaneous eruption."

Ms. Greer has handled several hundred cases in the four years that she has had the post, a half-time job for which Marin County pays her about $15,000 a year. Most come to her from the police, after they get sick of showing up to referee chronic pet disputes. Rocky's barking, for example, generated more than 20 complaints during the past few months alone. Though mediation is voluntary, most disputants agree to it after learning how expensive it is to get a lawyer and fight it out in court.

Ms. Greer's job is complicated by the storied wealth and unorthodox enthusiasms of Marin, a place inordinately supplied with retired rock stars, rich cyber gurus and New Age retreats. Excess, even in choice of pets, is normal: Consider the county's problems with exotic beasts, like the recent brief escape of a pet Komodo dragon, a five-foot-long Indonesian lizard that commonly dines on live goats. Not long ago, too, a pet tiger at play on a lawn caused the city of Larkspur to ban large jungle cats in residential settings.

Her post may also reflect the modern notion that, in this age of overwork, anxiety and Oprah, all things are solvable with talk.

"These days, all kinds of disputes go into mediation, from multi-million-dollar lawsuits ... to crushes students have on each other," says Maria Volpe, president of the 3,500-member Society of Professionals in Dispute Resolution. She was surprised to hear about Ms. Greer's animal angle but says, "Pets can be very difficult—what is a lovely creature to one person is a monster to somebody else."

Steve Waldman knows all about that. He has twice submitted himself to Ms. Greer's mediations in a two-year dispute with a neighbor who chronically complained about the barking of his Labradors and Bichon Frises. "Before Diane helped," says Mr. Waldman, he had referred to his adversary as "the little toad" and was "ready to commit a felony."

Dealing with that much aggression takes its toll on Ms. Greer, who often starts cases with a phone call that requires her to take clients through stress-reducing breathing exercises. She encourages free expression during the mediations, however. Some clients even bark, in imitation of the dogs in the docket.

Things aren't yet that extreme between the two sides at the seniors' center, which loaned Ms. Greer a room for Rocky's mediation. But the talk is intense.

"That dog barks and barks and barks and barks and barks," says retired art teacher Joan Debruyn, who made all the police calls. "I want peaceful weekends, with no barking, or yapping, as some people call it."

For her part, Christina DeMartini, Rocky's owner, says Ms. Debruyn's constant cop-calling is harassment. "It's offensive to have the police come to your house," she says.

Ms. Greer smooths her mint-green business suit and firmly raises her hand. It is an anger-deflecting mediating gesture gained from training in aikido, a form of Japanese martial arts. "Do we get to agree that the dog barks?" she says.

Ms. DeMartini pauses. "I don't want to get trapped. The dog barks . . . appropriately. Barking is the function of a dog."

To Ms. Greer, the concession is progress. Ms. DeMartini and Ms. Debruyn talk things over some more, and then break for one-on-one sessions with their mediator.

"Maybe I can convince Christina to go for a 'flower power' collar," the 43-year-old Ms. Greer says privately. Dogs wearing these collars get a big whiff of pungent citronella oil when they bark; usually a whiff or two renders a pooch barkless.

Barking is of course just one of a dog's many functions, lots of which end up before mediators at some point. The messiest disputes, however, Ms. Greer acknowledges, involve human attachment. She was recently assigned a custody dispute that arose when two women claimed to own the same yellow Labrador. The dog's first owner claims she put Sarah in a foster home when she left town for four months. The new owner says she adopted Sarah after the animal ended up in Labrador Rescue, a local service for abandoned pets. "They couldn't agree at all," Ms. Greer says. The case is now in court.

While dogs get the lion's share of Ms. Greer's time, plenty of other pets come to her attention. She has been called into disputes involving house cats that were running wild and eating the neighbor's pet birds. She recently took up the case of a runaway "renegade rabbit"; the owner has been trying to catch the bunny for a year, while a neighbor complains that the rabbit has incessantly nibbled and destroyed $10,000 worth of landscaping.

She also intervened on behalf of a woman who, when high on drugs, gave her pet bird away. When she came down, she wanted her bird back. Ms. Greer convinced the new owner to relinquish it.

Some disputes resolve themselves. A woman who insisted on showing up at the pool of her apartment complex with a boa constrictor draped around her neck drew complaints from neighbors who thought it was creepy. She decided to move out.

At the seniors' center, the air seems to be clearing. Both women vent their feelings, which Ms. Greer attentively validates with nods and tiny waves, leaning forward in her black plastic chair. Maps of the neighborhood are unrolled and options, like taping Rocky's barks to gather evidence, are discussed. Day surrenders to twilight, and a square-dance class starts nearby. At last, Ms. Debruyn agrees to call Ms. Greer, instead of the police, with weekly reports on the dog's activity.

Ms. DeMartini, shaken by the police visits, agrees with the plan but is still hoping for new conditions. "Why don't we suggest she move?" she asks, before signing the agreement. She doesn't like the flower-power collar, though, worrying that citronella, often used as an insect repellent, could harm her children.

The paper signed, the disputants leave the room together. Ms. Greer quietly closes the door, and with a deep sigh gives the "thumbs up" sign. "That's the best sign—they left talking," she says. "After days like this, I remain amazed that people communicate at all."

—QUENTIN HARDY, June 1997

14. Bambi Uncensored

Deer season. It's that time again. But before you rush out and nail your trophy whitetail, do yourself a favor. Take another look at *Bambi*. Not Walt Disney's gooey 1942 animated cartoon *Bambi*. Rather, the original 1923 antifascist allegory, *Bambi: A Life in the*

Woods, by Felix Salten, a Viennese Jew (and former drama critic) who fled Austria for Switzerland as the Nazis rose to power. Translated into English by a 27-year-old American Communist named Whittaker Chambers, it was published by Simon & Schuster in 1928. You'll find it in the children's section at the library, a perfect place for this 293-page volume, packed as it is with blood-and-guts action, sexual conquest and betrayal. Real '90s stuff, as it turns out. Lots of what Steve Chapple, writing in *Sports Afield,* calls "dark adult undertones."

No kidding. Disney obviously made the wrong movie. Its version has only one bad guy: a powerful but careless hunter. This book has a forest full of cutthroats and miscreants. I count at least six murderers (including three child-killers) among Bambi's associates. With the right agent and a little script-doctoring, we're talking about a Hollywood bidding war here.

Oh sure, there's mushy stuff. But the action starts early. Only eight pages after Bambi is born, mayhem ensues: "A threadlike, little cry shrilled out piteously; then all was still." A ferret kills a mouse and prepares to eat it as Bambi watches. One page later, two jays plunder another bird's nest.

"Get away, you murderer," cries one jay. "Keep cool, you fool," says his partner in crime.

Bambi has fun, but growing up is no walk in a theme park. He isn't allowed to play, or even move, during daylight hours. Thunderstorms terrorize him. His mom leaves him home alone, time and again. He doesn't know who his father is. A hunter spots him in a meadow one day and almost blows him away. Bambi whines a lot for absent Mom. When an old stag catches him at it one day, he scolds the little deer, "Shame on you!" He does not say anything like, "That's OK, little fella. Let it all out. Get in touch with your feelings."

Bambi falls in with a local gang of young bucks called "the

Princes." They prance around arrogantly, brandishing their big racks like Uzis, trying to lure Bambi into trouble.

When the hunter shows up, he's a Luddite. No camo. No all-terrain vehicle. No global positioning satellite navigator. No scrape juice. No Buck Stop Mate-Triks Doe-In-Heat scent lure. No tree stand. Not a single truckload of carrots and apples. He simply aims and decks a young buck with a single shot through the shoulder. This guy's a Fair Chase poster boy!

Winter brings hard times, cold and hunger. Crusting snow cuts Bambi's legs. Forest animals badmouth the hunter, telling horrible stories "full of blood and suffering." Things really get depressing in Chapter 10, as winter drags on: "It was silent in the woods, but something horrible happened every day. Once the crows fell upon Friend Hare's small son who was lying sick, and killed him in a cruel way. He could be heard moaning pitifully for a long while."

Then the ferret bites the squirrel in the neck. The squirrel escapes but "clutched his head in terror and agony while the red blood oozed on his white chest. He ran about for an hour, then suddenly crumpled up, fell across a branch, and dropped dead in the snow. A couple of magpies flew down at once to begin their meal."

Halfway through the book, hunters stage a drive through the forest—today's "game harvest." Among the animals harvested are a pheasant and a rabbit. Bambi's friend Gobo is wounded. "It seemed to him as if he saw his mother hit but he did not know if it was really she or not," Mr. Salten writes, leaving open other possibilities. (This is Disney's big weepy scene.) In any case, Bambi's mom is out of the picture.

And what's in? Sex. In Chapter 12, a "restless desire" so rages inside Bambi that he no longer recognizes his childhood friend Faline. She's now a sex object. "I love you terribly," he tells her. He'll obviously tell her anything she wants to hear. Jealousy raging, he fights off old friends he sees as rivals for Faline's affection.

Then it happens. "He made merry with Faline all night," is the way Mr. Salten demurely puts it. (We can do a lot with this in the screenplay.) Bambi's so turned on he forgets to eat. He's so tired he drops into Z-land.

In Chapter 15, Gobo, whom Bambi had left for dead during the game drive, turns up alive and well and singing the praises of the hunter who rescued him, nursed him back to health indoors, fed him "whatever I wanted," and played with him. "You all think He's wicked. But He isn't wicked," Gobo says.

The old stag dumps on Gobo for collaborating with the enemy. "You poor thing," he says. Sure enough, Gobo is betrayed by his human friends. He gets shot and Bambi watches "his bloody entrails oozing from his torn flank," and listens as he lets out a "wailing death shriek."

Bambi's on a downer. He gets tired of Faline, who "no longer satisfied him completely." And as Chapter 20 opens, "Bambi was alone . . . his whole life seemed to have become darker." Life is depressing. A fox nabs a mother duck. "Please tell us," her baby ducklings appeal, "have you seen our mother?" Bambi needs space. He dumps Faline, and then only one page later, as if to serve him right, gets shot in the left shoulder.

The big old stag, who's been hanging around the edges of this story making sage comments, now reveals himself to be Bambi's father. And turns Bambi on to drugs. He shows him a dark green plant near the ground. It "tasted terribly bitter and smelt sickeningly." But it works. Bambi blisses out, obviously zonked. And after many days in an opium-like daze, he heals.

But things don't get much better. A screech-owl dives on a mouse, tearing it to pieces and gobbling it down. Somebody saws down the squirrel's old oak tree. Bambi grows a studly set of antlers, but constantly remembers what his dad has told him, "You must live alone"—not exactly a formula for happy family values.

Another winter comes. More snow. Dogs chase a fox. "We're brothers almost, you and I," the fox argues. "No, no, no," man's best friends respond. They side with the all-powerful hunter. "He's above all of you. Everything we have comes from Him. . . ."

"The most dreadful part of all," says the old stag, "is that the dogs believe what the hound just said. They believe it, they pass their lives in fear, they hate Him and themselves and yet they'd die for his sake." Could anyone ask for better dogs?

In the last big scene (which doesn't work, really), a poacher somehow gets shot. More mythic payback, as if the old stag or Bambi shot him. Anyway, they move in for a closer look. "His horrible head was split in two. The poacher's shirt, open at the neck, was pierced where a wound gaped like a small red mouth. Blood was oozing out slowly. Blood was drying on His hair and around His nose. A big pool of it lay on the snow which was melting from the warmth." Justice. And great visuals.

"He isn't above us. He's just the same as we are," the old stag tells Bambi, who responds inspirationally, "There is Another who is over us all, over us and over Him." (Perhaps these words made an impression on Chambers, who later found God.)

Bambi glides into the final chapter by telling a couple of fawns whining for their mom, "Your mother has no time for you now." He says it, the author says, "severely."

That's pretty much it. No Disney forest fire, no Bambi heroics, no King of the Forest. But, hey, we can fix it.

Meanwhile, happy deer season.

—JAMES P. STERBA, October 1997

15. Horns of a Dilemma

MANISTEE, Mich.—Five weeks ago, David Gutowski, a self-employed painter in this little town, killed a six-point buck with his bare hands and a brown leather belt.

After strangling the white-tailed deer, Mr. Gutowski gutted it and hung it in his garage to skin it. Then a state conservation officer came to confiscate the animal. She explained that Michigan has seasons for killing deer legally with guns or bows-and-arrows. There is no season for garroting deer.

Hearing that angered Mr. Gutowski, 41 years old, a stocky man in a crew cut and goatee. He had killed deer before, he told the officer, but never in self-defense. He wanted the head on his wall and the venison in his freezer. "Please don't take that deer," he told the officer. "You don't know what happened."

This was his story: Around noon on October 30, Mr. Gutowski took a break from a painting job and went looking for stray fishing lures along the shore of Manistee Lake. The lake hugs the eastern edge of this town of 6,586 people in Michigan's northern lower peninsula. Mr. Gutowski grew up here and has hunted and fished in the area most of his life.

As he crunched across clam shells on the beach in his paint-flecked tennis shoes, he heard stirring in the brush along the bank. He turned to see a buck staring at him. He tried to scare it away by roaring and stamping his feet, he said, but the deer lowered its head and charged.

Mr. Gutowski said he caught it by the antlers and it drove him back into the frigid lake. He hung on, desperate to avoid being gored, as the two spun down the beach and up the bank, past an overturned rowboat and into a clearing littered with driftwood. The buck fell and Mr. Gutowski scissored it between his legs. It squealed and snorted while Mr. Gutowski whacked it with chunks of driftwood and gouged its eye with a branch.

Then, with the antlers in one hand, Mr. Gutowski slipped off his belt, looped it around the deer's neck and pulled. Grunting with exertion, Mr. Gutowski told it, "You're mine."

When the deer seemed dead, Mr. Gutowski let go of his belt and walked toward his Dodge minivan, which was parked several hundred yards away. He said he hadn't gone far when he heard something at his back and wheeled to see the buck moving at him, the belt flapping at its throat. Mr. Gutowski snatched the belt and forced the deer down. He stepped on the belt and yanked so hard that the buckle broke.

Lying nearby was a pair of two-by-fours nailed together. Mr. Gutowski picked them up and swung them down on the buck's head like an ax. "I don't know how many times I hit him," he said. When the animal stopped quivering, he loaded it into his minivan.

There were no witnesses.

That evening, Mr. Gutowski reported the killing to the state Department of Natural Resources. His girlfriend, Lisa Hankins, went to Kmart for a $14 hunting tag. The buck was hanging in Mr. Gutowski's garage, minus its organs, when DNR field officer Carla Soper arrived. Mr. Gutowski showed her scrapes and bruises on his wrists and a knuckle. He said he had fought for his life.

She told him he had every right to defend himself, but no legal right to the deer. It was bow season, but he hadn't used a bow. Mr. Gutowski cut the hanging carcass down with a swipe of his filet knife. Ms. Soper hauled it away in a DNR pickup truck, the belt still cinched around the deer's neck.

The next day, Mr. Gutowski's story shared the front page of the *Manistee News Advocate* with articles on Halloween and terrorism. Ms. Soper relayed the tale to Lt. Dean Molnar at the DNR's district office in Cadillac. Both officers were skeptical.

Deer in the wild usually flee when humans come near, Lt. Molnar says. If a healthy buck did attack, a man could easily be hurt or killed by a hoof or an antler. "I wouldn't want to have to fight a deer," says the lieutenant, a trim 45-year-old in a gray-and-olive DNR uniform. "They are one powerful animal."

There were possible explanations. The buck was in rut, the weeks-long mating season, and rutting deer "get a little crazy," Lt. Molnar says. Also, an injured or sick animal might defend itself if it felt threatened.

Normally, the DNR would have given the meat to a needy family and forgotten about it. But Lt. Molnar sent Mr. Gutowski's kill for a DNR laboratory examination.

Killing an animal illegally is a misdemeanor in Michigan, punishable by fines and restitution up to $2,000, loss of hunting privileges, and at least five days in jail. Lt. Molnar didn't think Mr. Gutowski had done anything illegal, but he says "the story was so wild, we wanted to make sure we thoroughly investigated."

Lt. Molnar also was under fire for refusing to give Mr. Gutowski the deer. More than a dozen Manistee folks called the lieutenant to berate him, he says, and Mr. Gutowski told the *News Advocate,* "I'm going to call my congressman. I have every right to that deer." Big Al's Pizza put up a sign reading, "DNR, give back the deer."

At the Rose Lake Wildlife Disease Laboratory in East Lansing, Dan O'Brien donned coveralls, rubber gloves and knee-high rubber boots to perform the post-mortem. The veterinarian spends most of his time investigating infectious diseases in wild animals. Occasionally the DNR requests a necropsy when poaching is suspected.

Dr. O'Brien X-rayed Mr. Gutowski's deer, then skinned it and carved it into pieces. At 158 pounds, it weighed about 40 pounds less than Mr. Gutowski does. The veterinarian guessed its age at 18 months, based on its baby teeth.

The forensic evidence supported much of Mr. Gutowski's story. The deer's left eye was nearly obliterated. Bleeding in the animal's brain indicated repeated blows to the head. Bruising and bleeding around the neck suggested the animal had been choked. Dr. O'Brien determined the proximate cause of death to be strangulation.

But there was more. X-rays showed that the deer's left hind leg had been broken so badly that the bone had torn through muscle. The right side of the pelvis also was broken, with muscle sheared off the bone. It was the kind of damage typically inflicted by an automobile.

A check with the Manistee police revealed that a deer had been hit the day before Mr. Gutowski's encounter, not far from where he killed the buck. Steven Kott of Manistee had been driving to work when he heard something slam into his pickup. He stopped and saw a deer with antlers struggling off the road, dragging its hind legs. It disappeared into the brush along Manistee Lake. The truck sustained $1,859 in damage.

Dr. O'Brien's two-page report concluded that the deer probably would have died from the injuries to its hindquarters. It would have had minimal use of its hind legs and been in great pain, the veterinarian says.

Lt. Molnar concluded that Mr. Gutowski's story was essentially true, although he doubted that the deer could have charged. "Maybe it felt like it was cornered and maybe it felt like it was trying to defend itself," he says. "It may have stepped toward him." The lieutenant doesn't believe Mr. Gutowski knew the deer was injured.

Mr. Gutowski says he resents the implication that he took advantage of a wounded animal. "That deer kicked the crap out of me," he says. "He threw me around like I weigh five pounds."

Lt. Molnar issued a "highway kill" permit that lets Mr. Gutowski keep the animal. Only its antlers remain. Mr. Gutowski plans to have them mounted on a plaque with the belt he used to kill the young buck.

—BRYAN GRULEY, December 2001

16. The Military-Chimpanzee Complex

ALAMOGORDO, N.M.—Amid spiky yuccas and cholla cactus, a dry desert wind snaps the American flag above the tombstone of this U.S. Air Force veteran. "Ham," the inscription says, "world's first astrochimp."

It's an odd resting place for a chimpanzee born in the dense rain forests of the Cameroons. But there's little about this chimp's life that wasn't strange. Trained aboard a Mercury capsule, rocketed into space, featured on the cover of *Life* magazine, Ham— short for the Holloman Aeromedical Laboratory just a few miles from his grave site—made history before the age of four.

Stranger still, perhaps, is the sudden plight of Ham's fellow astrochimps 36 years after his flight proved space travel safe for humans. Most have spent their lives in cages on Holloman Air Force Base, wedged between a Stealth fighter runway and the White Sands missile range. This year, the Air Force declared the chimps "surplus to requirements" and called for bids on them and their housing to be submitted by June 1998.

"Chimps—right, wrong or otherwise—are basically personal property. They're like a piece of equipment," says Col. Jack Blackhurst, project manager for the divestment.

This isn't an attitude being saluted by the chimps' supporters, however, which is partly why the 144 chimpanzees are proving more difficult to dispose of than spare widgets or extra flight suits. Chimp champions, led by the newly formed Institute for Captive Chimpanzee Care and Well-Being, are desperately trying to raise $10.6 million—the cost of building and running a retirement home in a warm locale big enough for the Air Force chimps, plus surplus chimps from other research programs. They are pitted against Frederick Coulston, a controversial biomedical researcher who currently leases the Holloman chimps, using some in AIDS, hepatitis and Hanta-virus testing. He wants the Air Force to let him keep them.

But only last year, Mr. Coulston's foundation was fined $40,000 by the U.S. Department of Agriculture for breaches of the federal animal-welfare act for mistreatment of primates in his care. And chimp advocates say that after a lifetime of government service, the astrochimps deserve a break. "We've required them to contribute repeatedly to human welfare," says Roger Fouts, a psychology professor at Central Washington University who talks to chimps in American Sign Language. "Surely the survivors have earned a little peace and quiet."

The problem is finding the money. "Ideally, I'd like a billionaire to fall from the sky and land in my backyard," says Carole Noon, coordinator for the new chimp institute. "But none has so far."

The Coulston Foundation, on the other hand, has ample funds from government grants and pharmaceutical companies. It also has a fancy taxpayer-funded chimp house built for New Mexico State University. But the university pulled out of primate research just as the $10 million project was completed and gave Mr. Coulston a free five-year lease.

For the chimps, the stakes are high. Chimpanzees' DNA is 98% identical to that of humans, and they can live into their 50s.

The oldest Air Force veteran is 40-year-old Minnie, who trained with Ham. The youngest is Minnie's daughter, Lil Mini, age four. Although about 65 chimps went through at least part of an astronaut-style training program, only two traveled in space; Ham and a chimp named Enos, who orbited the Earth in advance of John Glenn's historic flight.

Others were used to assess "hazardous mission environments"—strapped into ejection seats, hurled down a rocket-powered sled and pumped with caffeine in studies of long-term sleep deprivation. Later, the Air Force leased the chimpanzees to nonmilitary scientists to test everything from the cancer-causing solvents in industrial cleaners to drugs for sexually transmitted diseases.

Meanwhile, two things happened. Behaviorists' studies of chimps uncovered the ability to make tools, use language and experience complex emotions. At the same time, biomedical demand for the animals plunged when they proved poor models for the study of AIDS because almost none of them, once injected with HIV, came down with the full-blown disease.

While many scientists say chimps are essential for some research, a National Research Council panel recently stated that far too many are languishing uselessly in lab cages. The panel supported a breeding moratorium and the building of sanctuaries.

Mr. Coulston doesn't agree. His Alamogordo-based foundation already houses 600 chimps—the largest captive colony in the world—and he wants to expand it. "I don't think there's an excess—I would like to have 5,000" to use, eventually, as organ donors and blood banks for humans.

The 83-year-old Mr. Coulston isn't afraid of courting controversy, and not just about chimps. He calls AIDS "a silly disease" whose sufferers should have been forced to display "a big sign on the door saying 'Quarantine.' " Chain-smoking through a recent interview, he proclaims that "nicotine is not addictive" and "you won't get cancer if you don't inhale." He says he had to turn to chimps when his work with human subjects—prisoners—was halted in the 1960s.

And that, says Mr. Fouts, who decries all invasive research on chimps, is the point. "Eventually we realized it was wrong to experiment on prisoners, and our closest relatives, the chimpanzees, are the next step," he says. "People say, 'You'd want to use a chimp's organs if it would save your child.' Well, I'd want to use my neighbor's organs if it would save my child, but that doesn't mean I should." .

If the chimps get their sanctuary, it will probably look much like the facility in which Mr. Fouts, 54, houses five chimps used in his language research. His students' study of the animals depends on whether the chimps want to take part. If they choose to interact with their human visitors, the chimps swing down from high outdoor perches, approach a glass partition and begin asking in emphatic sign language to "chase" or "tickle." One, remembering a Thanksgiving treat, asks if there's any "bird meat"—turkey—on the dinner menu.

The Air Force says the welfare of the chimpanzees will be the main consideration in assessing June's bid proposals (bids, until last week, had been due in February, but the Air Force pushed the deadline back). The Coulston Foundation's "state of flux" in veterinary care has "been a concern of the USDA and a number of other parties," says Lt. Col. Denver Marlow, chief of Air Force animal programs.

Mr. Coulston says he has bolstered his veterinary staff and plays down his regulatory run-ins. "Everyone has problems with the USDA from time to time," he says. "No matter how meticulous you are, they're going to find something when they go through. That's their job."

Whatever the outcome, it's too late for Ham, the original astrochimp. After his brief moment of "fame aboard the flame," he spent most of his life in a zoo where he was caged alone—a hardship for social animals like chimps. When he died prematurely of heart and liver failure, his skeleton was sent to the Smithsonian to be picked clean by demestid beetles before being shipped to the Armed Forces Institute of Pathology. The rest of him got a decent burial in front of Alamogordo's Space Museum, but only after a proposal to stuff and mount him brought howls of protest. "A chimpanzee is not a green pepper!" declared one outraged letter. Another asked: "Are you planning to stuff John Glenn as well?"

—GERALDINE BROOKS, December 1997

17. High on the Hedgehog

AYLESBURY, England—This hospital's intensive-care ward isn't for the spineless.

Medical charts attached to the beds of the 70-odd patients tell terrible tales: severed limbs, fractures, poisonings, internal injuries and brain damage. Some patients are blind, some are in shock. All endure their suffering silently, without complaint.

This is St. Tiggywinkles Hospital, and patients in the ward are hedgehogs. Animal lovers send the critters here from all over England and Wales, often by British Rail's overnight parcel service, which has a special rate for shipping injured hedgehogs here. The eight-year-old hospital opened a new $1.9 million building in November.

St. Tiggywinkles, named after a hedgehog washerwoman in the children's book *Tales From Beatrix Potter,* exemplifies the

growing affection Britons have for this cute but prickly beast. Informal networks of care-givers are springing up throughout
Britain. In their homes, they tend hedgehogs poisoned by pesticides, struck by cars or caught up in farm machinery. They feed
baby hedgehogs so they will survive the winter.

"Everybody loves the hedgehog. He's a good chap, with nothing at all against his character," declares retired British Army
Maj. Adrian Coles, head of the 10,500-member British Hedgehog
Protection Society. "All he does is eat beetles, wood lice and
slugs—and who likes beetles, wood lice and slugs?"

Indeed, in England hedgehogs are called "the gardener's
friend," quite a compliment in this nation of gardeners and a big
reason for hedgehogs' booming popularity. "They don't bark,
they don't bite and they do good works right outside your back-
door," says Tim Thomas, wildlife officer of the Royal Society for
the Prevention of Cruelty to Animals.

The hedgehog's appeal, however, isn't immediately apparent.
It sports 5,000 or so sharp quills. It is half the size of a loaf of
bread, very likely to be flea-infested and resembles a toilet brush.
With its tiny feet hidden by the spines, the animal trundles along
as if on wheels, looking like a windup toy. When in danger, it
tucks in its head and rolls itself up into a ball, bristling. That usually discourages large hungry animals but has little impact on its
biggest predator: the motor vehicle. Hedgehogs are the armadillos
of England, flattened by the thousand on roadways. (In Surrey,
drivers who hit a hedgehog can confess to a telephone hotline and
pay a small, voluntary fine.)

Unrelated to porcupines, hedgehogs don't exist in the wild in
North America. They first appeared in Europe 15 million years
ago—well before saber-toothed tigers and woolly mammoths—
and have always managed to survive their enemies. One was
Queen Elizabeth I, who declared them vermin and put a three-

pence bounty on their heads, falsely accusing them of sucking milk from cows' udders and stealing grain.

Nonsense, says Elaine Drewery, postmistress of tiny Authorpe, Lincolnshire (pop. 100). "These animals are our heritage—we should be nurturing them."

Considered the doyenne of England's hedgehog ladies, Ms. Drewery, a 52-year-old grandmother, runs Hedgehog Care, a network of about 150 volunteers in the English Midlands who nurse injured and orphaned hedgehogs in their homes. Her cottage, which is also Authorpe's post office and dog-clipping parlor, is teeming with the creatures.

"I regard hedgehogs as a priority—humans take potluck here," she says emphatically, leading a visitor through the kitchen (diagnosis and defleaing), the TV room (surgery and antibiotic treatment) and the bathroom (postoperative recovery). At the moment, 72 hedgehogs, in various stages of recovery, are in the house; more are in pens in the garden. Those that recover are set free; the less fortunate get a proper funeral, and Ms. Drewery sends a bereavement card to human benefactors.

Ms. Drewery has no regrets about the sacrifices she has made for hedgehogs. "It may seem like sentiment and sop," she says, "but I've gained from these animals. I haven't given up anything." After a moment's pause, she adds, "Well, I guess I've given up my bathroom."

When tough medical problems arise, however, Ms. Drewery and other hedgehog fanciers turn for advice to Les and Sue Stocker, who run St. Tiggywinkles Hospital. Mr. Stocker, 48, a former accountant, does most of the minor surgery and bonesetting himself in a well-equipped operating room, complete with mini anesthesia machine and heart monitor. A veterinarian, paid on an hourly basis, comes in for amputations and complicated operations. Hernia surgery is often needed for road accident victims.

Bad teeth plague all hedgehogs, so patients here get their teeth scaled before they are released.

A few patients even undergo brain surgery. Consider Hercules the hedgehog, who was kicked in the head by a rhinoceros in an English safari park. He survived the operation but is brain-damaged and walks in circles. Hercules is cared for in a volunteer's enclosed garden.

But why all this medical attention for such a common animal?

"A broken leg hurts an ordinary animal as much as it does an endangered species," says Mrs. Stocker, who handles fund raising for the hospital. This kindly approach goes down well with the animal-loving British public. St. Tiggywinkles, which has no government financing, operates in the black.

Schoolchildren are big contributors; so are some major companies: British Petroleum, for example, last year gave $98,000 to equip an operating-room suite. Mr. Stocker also contributes proceeds from wildlife books he writes, including *The Complete Hedgehog,* the U.K.'s No. 2 nonfiction best seller in 1987. Mr. Stocker last week was awarded the MBE (Member of the British Empire) by Queen Elizabeth II for his work with hedgehogs.

The hospital has expanded into the treatment of all forms of wildlife, from sparrows to deer. Some 10,000 animals were treated last year. In its new facility, the hospital aims to handle 50,000 a year, while offering courses for paramedics as Europe's first wildlife teaching hospital. Atop the new building is a hedgehog weather vane, "so we don't forget our roots," says Mrs. Stocker.

Brits definitely bristle when they think hedgehogs are being mistreated or merely treated with disrespect. Three months ago, bulldozers about to break ground for a nursery school in London's Chelsea district were turned back by irate hedgehog fans. This was the site of Beatrix Potter's childhood home, which was destroyed in the Blitz. The author's beloved pet hedgehog, Tiggy, is buried in the former garden. (Tiggy became Mrs. Tiggy-Winkle in the Potter book.) Because of the furor, the nursery school found another building site.

Hedgehog mania has accounted for at least one business success story: Hedgehog Foods Ltd., one of Europe's biggest makers of organic potato chips, or crisps as the British call them. In 1981, Philip Lewis, a pub owner in Wales and devotee of hedgehog jokes, decided as a lark to produce "hedgehog flavored" crisps. Sales boomed, but it didn't take long for angry hedgehog lovers to blow the whistle, fearing that the crisps actually were made from hedgehogs. In fact, they were flavored with pork fat.

But then, in 1982, Britain's Office of Fair Trading hauled Mr. Lewis into court for false advertising. A settlement ultimately was reached under which Mr. Lewis interviewed gypsies, who actually do eat baked hedgehog, ascertained what hedgehogs taste like and commissioned a flavorings firm to more or less duplicate the flavor. He changed the labels from "hedgehog flavored" to "hedgehog flavor," and all interests were satisfied.

Last year Hedgehog Foods had sales of $3.6 million and is now a major contributor to St. Tiggywinkles Hospital, plugging the hospital on every package. "Looking back, it was a bit gruesome, that flavor," Mr. Lewis concedes.

—GLYNN MAPES, January 1992

18. I've Got You, Babe

HERFORD, Germany—As his 1,500 pigs polish off their evening meal, Ulrich Krutemeier climbs into the stall for a snuggle with his schwein.

But it's clear the chemistry just isn't there. The pigs creep back nervously as soon as Mr. Krutemeier's mud-encrusted boots touch the floor. As a few of the more curious inch closer, he tickles a snout. The pig returns the affection with a bite.

"Ouch!" the sandy-haired Mr. Krutemeier yelps, jerking back his lanky arm. "Only someone who has no idea about pigs would think of this," he mutters as the pigs scurry away again.

That someone is the government of North Rhine-Westphalia, Germany's most densely populated state in terms of both people and pigs. Officials want to regain the confidence of meat-wary consumers in the wake of "mad-cow" disease and other food scares that rocked Germany this past year. Part of the answer, they say, is better testing and hygiene. Just as important is that farmers raise their animals with more of a human touch.

Lest any farmer wonder how, the state's agriculture ministry spelled out the new and improved rights of North Rhine-Westphalia's six million pigs in a recent decree. A pig should get one square meter of stall space and a straw or soft rubber mat for napping. When it's time to play, the pigs must have chains or chewy toys on hand. "Balls also can be made available to the pigs for activity material," the edict states. Each pig should get at least eight hours of daylight. During the darker, shorter days of winter, farmers must compensate with lamps.

But what really rankled farmers is a declaration that a farmer or farmhand must spend at least 20 seconds looking at each pig each day—and back up the loving care with paperwork showing he has enough pighands to provide quality time. Without it, a farmer can't get a license to expand or start a pig-rearing business. Many farmers have come to mock the edict as the *Kuschelregel*, or the cuddle rule.

So far, the rules haven't done much to bring farmers and their pigs closer. Egbert Storck, a 48-year-old farmer with 1,300 pigs in the rolling, wheat-covered hills on the outskirts of Herford, is be-fuddled. "What am I supposed to do exactly? Go like this?" Lean-ing over the fence of one of his pig stalls, he clinches his square jaw and fixes one of the pigs with an exaggerated bug-eyed stare, ticking off the seconds. Feeling the intensity of his gaze, the pig turns to hide its face behind the haunches of another. "See, they don't like it either," he says, throwing up his hands.

It's not that North Rhine-Westphalian farmers aren't fond of their swine. This is home to nearly a quarter of Germany's 26 mil-lion pigs. It's the source of Westphalian ham and more than 300 kinds of sausages. Most farms are small family operations, some dating to the 12th century. "I grew up with these guys," Mr. Krutemeier, 37, says of his pigs. As the youngest son, he inherited his father's farm, following local tradition here.

To protect their livelihood, Mr. Krutemeier and other local farmers already provide their pigs with agricultural innovations such as state-of-the-art central heating, homeopathic medicine and even toys. After years of experimenting with old tires, then miniature soccer balls, Mr. Krutemeier found his pigs preferred to gnaw on steel chains and wooden blocks for fun. "If my pigs aren't healthy, I'm not healthy," he says.

But farmers fret that the new rules could regulate them out of business. A farmer with 1,500 pigs, for example, would need eight hours, or one full-time farmhand, to spend 20 seconds a day with each animal. Farmers estimate the rules would cost them about 12 extra euros ($10) per pig, nearly as much as their current profit.

Many fear that will put them at a greater comparative disad-vantage to Southern and Eastern Europe, where pig rearing is held to lower standards and prices are cheaper. Just how real the threat is was unveiled in the Herford police blotter last year: A truck that had overturned on its way to a nearby sausage factory was found to be carrying pork from Spain, sparking a local scandal.

"If we were required to give every pig a reclining chair, we wouldn't have a problem with it, as long as everyone in the European Union did it, too," says Wilhelm Brueggemeier, a local farmer.

For farmers, two women personify the threat: local agricultural minister Baerbel Hoehn, who drafted the edict, and her fellow Green party member, Renate Kuenast, a spike-haired former lawyer who runs Germany's national ministry for consumer protection, food and agriculture. The Greens, who run the state and federal governments in coalition with the Social Democrats, devised the local rules and have attracted the farmers' ire. At a recent farmers' forum, bodyguards stood by with umbrellas to shield the two ministers in the event of flying produce.

Named to the post after the first signs of mad-cow disease were discovered in Germany a year ago, Ms. Kuenast already angered farmers by fingering industrial agriculture as a big part of the problem. She proposed increasing organic farming from 2.5% to 20% of German agriculture over the next decade. But even Ms. Kuenast's minor publicity stunts—such as "adopting" a Rhineland sow named Berta and her 16 piglets—cause farmers to gnash their teeth.

"She wants consumers to think of 'Babe' when they think of pigs," says farmer Anneliese Schulte-Steffens, referring to the 1995 movie about a talking pig that narrowly escapes the butcher. "We raise pigs to make a living, not to cuddle and let them sleep on our beds."

North Rhine-Westphalian agricultural-ministry officials point out the local edict is only temporary until a nationwide pig-rearing law is passed, most likely next year. But they hope it will serve as a model for the legislation. "People increasingly want to know where their meat comes from," says Leo Bosten, a ministry spokesman. "We need to make sure both animals and consumers are protected."

It's too soon to say whether consumers prefer pork from pigs reared with more affection. But at Haus Duesse, a nearby state-sponsored agricultural training and testing center, farming experts are checking the pigs' reaction—and getting mixed reviews.

Nocturnal animals by nature, the pigs don't mind low lighting. But as one of the center's agricultural engineers, Hans-Joachim Luecker, turns up the glare to simulate the different levels of state-prescribed light, some start to squint and nip nervously at the others. In one stall, the pigs have taken to their soft rubber napping mat, snoozing alongside each other in a neat row. In the next, though, the pigs prefer to stretch out on the perforated concrete floor instead, relegating the mat to their group litter box.

"We can make all the rules in the world," he says. "But the pigs sort out what they like for themselves."

—VANESSA FUHRMANS, March 2002

19. A Man Among the Predators

JORDAN, Mont.—John Graham grinds his dusty, mud-caked 4x4 Ford pickup up a steep rutted trail. A dead coyote and a smelly badger carcass bounce in the truck bed next to a jangling pile of Montgomery No. 3 dog-less, four-coil foothold traps and Amberg galvanized ⁵⁄₆₄-inch aircraft wire snares. His scope-mounted Ruger .22-250 bolt-action rifle strains at the Velcro straps in its mount above his head as the truck roars up, lurching left, then right.

Veering up a draw, he spots a coyote, its left front foot caught in the jaws of a trap he staked, chained and baited earlier. He brakes to a stop, hops out, walks over to the snarling animal, unholsters a .22-caliber Smith & Wesson revolver and delivers the coup de grace behind its right shoulder. He tosses the critter in the truck bed and resets his trap, sifting dirt over it through a wire-mesh screen.

John Graham always wanted to be a trapper. In Upper Michigan, where he grew up in the '60s and '70s, woodsmen's skills still mattered. He immersed himself in the lore, devouring trapping books and magazines. His grandfather had trapped in Ontario. His father's friend, Wilfred Eikey, let young John come along, walk his trap lines, learn about sets and scents. He did it weekends, after school, picking up know-how passed down through generations. In 1983, he turned 21 and set out for Montana like a rookie headed for the big leagues.

Today, at age 37, Mr. Graham is one of the few full-time, year-round trappers left in the U.S. He's predator-control trapper for Garfield County, an expanse of eastern Montana nearly the size of Connecticut. His job, essentially, is to kill coyotes before they kill sheep. He actually snares more than he traps. Sometimes he calls coyotes in by imitating their yelps, then shoots them. Last season, he bagged more than 500 coyotes, 350 red foxes, 43 bobcats, and assorted skunks, badgers and raccoons, some of them rabid. He is paid $39,000 a year, including medical insurance and retirement benefits, and gets to keep what he can make selling pelts.

"I've got the best trapping job in America," he says.

There's just one problem: As jobs go, trapping is one lots of Americans love to loathe. While plenty of local ranchers think he's doing the Lord's work keeping coyote populations at bay, people elsewhere pass more and more laws trying, essentially, to put trappers out of business. And when he goes to trappers' conventions, animal-rights activists sometimes arrive and call him a "murderer."

How times have changed. In the 18th and 19th centuries, fur

traders and trappers were indispensable to the nation's economic interests; indeed, the Lewis and Clark expedition was as much about exploiting the West's treasure trove of fur, especially beaver pelts, as it was finding a hospitable route to the Pacific Ocean. Through much of the 20th century, trappers like Kit Carson were romanticized in fiction and film with other frontier heroes. But by the end of the 20th century, in a profound twist in public perception, they have been reduced to cruel villains who torture and kill cute little animals.

And they aren't alone. The other men who practiced the manly arts, who did the tough, gritty but vital work of frontier America—hunters, lumberjacks, cowboys, soldiers, fishermen and others—were turned into mythic figures at the end of the 19th century. First, Eastern novelists Owen Wister in *The Virginian,* and Zane Grey, in *Riders of the Purple Sage,* transformed the cowboy into a romantic hero. Then came the movie makers, and finally, television. By 1959, there were 40 westerns a week on prime-time TV; Walt Disney's Davy Crockett wasn't just a character who kept trappers busy satisfying demand for the first baby boom mass-marketing phenomenon—the coon-skin cap. He was a rifle-toting, varmint-shooting, straight-talking role model for an entire generation of boys.

But consider how such archetypes are often portrayed these days:

The cowboy, unlike Roy Rogers, is an alcoholic with lung cancer who, when he isn't posing for cigarette ads, is riding around on his noisy ATV, scarring the landscape, while the cattle he tends overgraze the public lands.

The hunter-frontiersman who blazed trails and kept his family fed is now a beer-swilling weekend warrior blowing away hapless critters for sport; his professional counterpoint, having slaughtered frontier bison herds and practically wiped out once-vast populations of other indigenous animals for profit, has become an outfitter guiding rich men on junk hunts to bag trophy animals or, worse, rare or endangered species. The lumberjack, instead of the rugged woodsman with the outsize skills of a Paul Bunyan, is a tool of avaricious corporations chopping down America's last virgin stands of timber or committing arboreal holocausts on tropical rain forests.

The mountain man, unlike Jeremiah Johnson, is a deranged recluse sending letter bombs instead of pelts into the modern world. The commercial fisherman, having virtually wiped out the whales, is feverishly turning the oceans to deserts, and won't stop overfishing with his gill nets and long lines and factory processing ships until there's nothing left.

What explains this fundamental turnabout in perceptions? Most social observers see the early seeds of this in the turmoil of the '60s, when the underpinnings of American society came under sharp assault from a variety of forces: from minorities demanding not just civil rights but an overdue restructuring of a history from which they had been widely excluded; from feminists challenging male dominance and setting off an argument about the very nature of masculinity itself; from a rising environmental movement that demanded that Americans rethink their basic notions of nature as something whose only value is to be "tamed" and exploited for profit; from advocates who began attempting to apply and extend, often militantly, the concept of human rights to animals. Then came the "national guilt trip" over Vietnam that put America into what the Pulitzer Prize–winning historian William Goetzman calls the "post-heroic era." One indicator of that shift, says Mr. Goetzman: About that time, "cowboy" went from a noun to a verb meaning to behave wildly and recklessly—as in, "The arrest victim claimed he was cowboyed by the cops."

The sum of these forces set off a re-examination that, at its crudest, redraws Davy Crockett as a sort of neocolonialist who helped open the frontier to thugs who despoiled the forests and rivers while warring upon and stealing the land of Native Americans. Of course, it's also true that, even if these pejorative stereotypes are as overblown as the mythic heroes before them, they have some basis in fact. The market hunters who slaughtered the passenger pigeon in the last century come to mind. And, left to their own devices, commercial fishermen just half a decade ago seemed prepared to fish the gulf redfish to the brink of extinction to satisfy the craze for blackened redfish. Parallel to this came a shift in demographics and economics that has further marginalized frontier skills that once had been so valued. As rural populations drained into cities, America's agrarian industries like logging and trapping have shrunk in their importance to the American economy—in fact, some argue that the U.S. economy would still hum right along if every ranch in the nation was converted to parkland tomorrow. And practices that were part of the agrarian birthright—hunting and trapping, among them—simply no longer have the historical imperative that they once did.

Or, put another way, on the Lewis and Clark expedition, its members hunted or perished, and a gifted hunter was as valued then as a crack investment banker is today. Such people were seen as part of an altruistic vanguard that "give up the comforts of civilization to blaze new trails" for the common good, says Paul Fees, curator of the Buffalo Bill Museum in Cody, Wyo. The image of the hunter, he says, begins to turn for the worse with Teddy Roosevelt, though ironically it was Roosevelt and other sport hunters who ushered in the era of game conservation and the concept of wildlife refuges. "It became hunting for the sake of hunting, rather than for the sake of civilization."

No one is more aware of this somersault in popular perception than John Graham. He is working in what was, perhaps, North

America's first trade. So important was the fur trade to Manhattan Island's development that the beaver became part of the official seal of New York City. Ironically, Manhattan is now the center of the anti-fur movement. In Montana, John Graham can stand on a high ridge near his home and see the Missouri River, where Lewis and Clark paddled west in 1803. Congress, at the urging of Thomas Jefferson, had given them a slush fund of $2,500—a fortune then—with explicit instructions to use it to help steal the fur trade from the British.

Mr. Graham now wonders how to keep his profession alive in the face of a well-funded, politically connected anti-fur movement that he thinks doesn't care one whit for his historical or natural perspective. Mr. Graham isn't totally without intellectual allies; William Cronon, a Rhodes scholar and MacArthur fellow now at the University of Wisconsin, outraged fellow environmentalists four years ago by ripping into their notions of a natural balance, the supposed harmony in which native cultures existed within it and the notion of a wilderness that was pristine before modern man came along and corrupted it.

Mr. Graham doesn't know William Cronon, but they seem to think a lot alike. After years of intimate day-to-day contact with nature, he believes the wild is always out of balance, one way or another, with populations of prey animals rising and falling while predators take what's available—a volatile mixture into which man introduced himself along with sheep and cattle ranches.

While Mr. Cronon seeks "an ethical, sustainable, honorable human place in nature," Mr. Graham thinks he has found his: managing his portion of nature on behalf of prey—sheep and cattle, in particular, but also elk, antelope, deer, grouse, pheasants—and the people who benefit from them. Numbers of game birds and animals are way up in Garfield County, attracting hunters and their dollars for guides, outfitters and local businesses.

He thinks animal-rights zealots are plain loopy. "They're living in a dream world," he says, a sheltered urban or suburban environment full of balance-of-nature documentaries and cartoon depictions of humanlike animals and birds.

"I've killed thousands of animals," Mr. Graham says. "Remember, they're animals, not Disney characters." What is more cruel, he asks, choking a coyote to death with a snare or choking a lamb to death with the jaws of a coyote?

Today, people sometimes talk about man, with his suburban sprawl, encroaching on nature, out there in forests and fields, as if there was never anything between civilization and wilderness. Until well into the 19th century, the American frontier was east of the Mississippi River. There, across the Northeast, then Midwest and South, the great forests were hunted and trapped. Trees were both fuel and building material. They were also in the way of agriculture. So in giant swaths, the trees were removed, the land scalped in a gigantic deforestation that tamed the wilderness.

And into this bald landscape, to keep wild animal populations in check, marched millions of animal-control agents who settled in and did the job for more than a century. They were called farmers, and they had enormous self-interest in keeping predators at bay. To protect their livestock and fowl, farmers kept dogs and cats. They shot, trapped and used poison on everything from possums to hawks, coons to crows. A marked egg injected with strychnine, for example, was a good way to get rid of the fox raiding the hen house. These efforts helped turn America's vast Farm Belt into prime habitat for meadow birds, waterfowl and upland game birds, including grouse, quail and pheasant.

Then rural Americans began moving to town. In 1924, rural and urban populations balanced for the first and last time. Slowly but steadily, millions upon millions of acres painfully cleared and painstakingly settled and tended in the Northeast, the Midwest and the South went unfarmed. Bushes sprouted, then small trees. Today, forests are reclaiming hundreds of thousands of acres of former farmland.

Suburban sprawl, of course, has created its own set of disasters, often overrunning habitat critical to species—birds like the snowy plover or California gnat catcher, for example—that are not as adaptable as the fox or rabbit. But forests have reclaimed farmland at a pace that in some places outdistances suburban sprawl. At the same time, tens of thousands of artificial ponds, lakes and other water-impoundment areas were created. All these—new forests, suburbs and standing water—made wonderful habitat for certain kinds of wild animals.

Today, populations of many species are exploding. And not just deer. A coyote recently caught in Manhattan's Central Park and the beavers gnawing on Washington's beloved Reflecting Pool cherry trees are symbols of much bigger population distributions. Foxes, coyotes, bobcats, mountain lions, bears are all prospering, adjusting to life near people, and, increasingly, causing trouble—including, sometimes, eradicating the nests of songbirds and other beneficial or even threatened species.

But while this has been going on, many Americans have come to believe that wildlife management is wrong because it is being managed, in part, on behalf of the hunting industry, which caters to people who kill animals for sport. And trapping, as a management tool, is cruel. Through the efforts of such groups as the Humane Society of the U.S. and People for the Ethical Treatment of Animals, or PETA, trapping has been essentially outlawed in several states and increasingly restricted in others. In places where trapping is allowed, the collapse of the world's major fur market in Russia sent prices plummeting, turning old-fashioned trappers—those who make money selling pelts—into a dying breed.

Of the estimated 150,000 trappers in the U.S., the huge majority are weekenders and hobbyists.

But in a twist upon a twist, some of the very people who find trappers so loathsome and politically incorrect are now hiring them as helpful, come-to-the-rescue animal-control officers. Tim Julien, an Indianapolis resident, for example, never made more than $600 a year as a trapper. As head of an animal control company, A&T Wildlife Management Services, however, he made $36,000 last year saving suburbanites from troublesome raccoon, pesky opossums and, increasingly, cagey coyotes.

"Last year, if I'd gone out and trapped 150 raccoon, I could get no more than $2 apiece for their fur, or $300 total," he says. "But my minimum for a problem coon call is $90, so for the same 150 raccoons, I make $13,500. . . . Business is very, very good. I made $6,000 in May alone." He charges $165 to get rid of a problem beaver (instead of $12 he gets trapping one for its pelt).

Last year, Mr. Julien helped start the National Wildlife Control Operators Association, one of several such organizations, and became its president. One problem for the industry is upstarts advertising "nonlethal" nuisance-animal disposal, preying on people's gullibility, he says. "That's not reality," he says. Animals may be caught in cage traps, but most aren't released. There are too many of them now, and relocation doesn't usually work. More often than not, they're euthanized, a euphemism for killed. And thrown away.

"It's such a sad waste of an incredibly valuable resource," says Parker Dozhier, a former fur buyer who writes the fur-market column for *The Trapper and Predator Caller* magazine.

Mr. Dozhier calls trappers "benign loners" who, as a result, develop a knowledge of the natural world and skills to operate in it that few others can match.

"And if we lose these talents and skills, have we not lost something important?" he asks.

John Graham isn't losing them. He's devoted his life to their acquisition. For eight years after moving west from Michigan, he worked here and there, felling timber, building houses, guiding fishermen and hunters—all the while trapping on off days, honing skills, acquiring knowledge handed down through generations of mountain men. He often camped out or slept in his truck to save money.

When Mr. Graham arrived in Jordan in the spring of 1991, Garfield County was a predators' playground. Some ranchers were losing 200 lambs to coyotes each spring. Three ranchers chipped in $1,500 and gas money and invited him up for a month. He trapped 15 coyotes and 30 red foxes. The county offered him a full-time job. He took it. Four years later, he married Nicole Murnion, a local rancher's daughter. Today, they have two children—Collette, age three, and Tristan, two—and a blue-tick hound named Penny. And after years of living in a cramped house on Main Street, in Jordan, they are preparing to move into a bigger home on the edge of town.

In Garfield County, the concern is clearly on the well-being of struggling ranchers. Garfield is 4,455 square miles of mostly treeless undulating hills of scrub pasture laced with sagebrush and ground cactus that even residents call bleak. Movie stars don't buy ranches here. The wind can howl for weeks. Temperatures can drop to 47 below zero in January and reach 109 above in August. Ponderosa pines dot the high ridges, and a few cottonwoods flank the creek beds. Here and there, rectangles of wheat and barley grow.

Garfield County has 40,000 head of cattle and about 65,000 sheep—more than any other county in Montana. It is also home, thanks in part to Mr. Graham's predator-control efforts, to large herds of antelope, elk and deer, as well as grouse and pheasants that lure hunters and their money. About 1,500 people live here,

500 of them in Jordan, the county seat. The nearest doctor is in Miles City, 83 miles south. Billings, a three-hour drive away, is Paris. Sheep ranchers here are just holding on. The joke is that if the parents leave the ranch to the kids, the kids sue for child abuse. Wool prices dropped to one dollar a pound last year; they were 33 cents a pound this spring.

Mr. Graham has about 500 traps and 1,800 snares. He catches three out of four coyotes in snares, wire loops that choke the animal. He admires his prey as wily and adaptable. But he says it's a myth that coyotes kill only for food. "When coyotes come in contact with sheep, they're going to kill them," he says, "but nine out of 10 don't eat the meat." The majority of Garfield County's coyotes come in from outside, from surrounding counties where there's little or no predator control. Mr. Graham also knows the conventional wisdom that says low-level coyote populations aren't much of a threat to sheep. "I've worked low population densities and high ones. You gotta kill 'em," he says. Mr. Graham's $39,000 salary comes from a livestock head tax paid by ranchers. In addition, he makes nearly $10,000 selling the fur of the animals he traps—about $150 per bobcat, $20 to $25 per coyote, and $13 per red fox.

He probably knows Garfield County better than anybody— every ridge and creek, every draw and gully. He knows every prairie-dog town, every fence line. Three years ago, he showed the Federal Bureau of Investigation the back way into the farmhouse "compound" where the Freemen, an antigovernment group, were holed up, surrounded by Feds and vowing to fight. (They surrendered after an 81-day standoff.) In 1996, he paid $18,000 for the formulas and names of Gary Jepson's lure business and turned them into his own company: John Graham's Fur Country Lures. Through 11 dealers and his own catalog, he sells 22 lure concoctions and three baits. Typical recipe: bobcat meat, fish oil, skunk spray, dried beaver castor and a glycerin preservative. It's called Cat Creek and sells for eight dollars a pint.

"You're dealing with an animal that makes its living with its nose, so if it's a good lure, he'll find it," he says. "But I believe I can catch coyotes with grape jelly."

This spring, he bought out a snare maker who developed a special lock that won't let the wire slack up once an animal pulls it tight around its neck. "This is going to be the snare of the future," he says. "It kills so much faster, you know, more humanely. That's the way things are going."

—JAMES P. STERBA, June 1999

CHAPTER 3

ODD DUCKS

═══

20. Splat Man

GAINESVILLE, Fla.—It hasn't rained much in central Florida for three years, but a short while ago it rained for a week, giving Mark Hostetler a chance to check for bug splats at the bus station.

Bugs come alive when it rains. Mosquitoes hatch. Mole crickets try their wings. Flying ants take off to start new ant hills. Often, these bugs fly across roads and have fatal run-ins with vehicles. Dr. Hostetler, who is 37 years old and a wildlife biologist here at the University of Florida, identifies the remains.

"I can claim expertise in bug splats," Dr. Hostetler said, pulling his Honda into the Greyhound parking lot; he has determined that the front of a Greyhound bus is an ideal splat catcher.

"I've collected splats of various colors and sizes and matched them to carcasses," he said.

An afternoon storm had left Gainesville steamy at dusk. Midges flitted in the neon light under the bus station's overhang.

"Hello, Buggy!" Buford Turlington shouted from behind the ticket counter when Dr. Hostetler walked in. Just then, a bus arrived from Atlanta. In the bustle of passengers and luggage, Dr. Hostetler went out to the platform, stood at the front of the bus and leaned in close. "You see all these little guys?" he said. "Flying ants. They're out now. Here's a butterfly. No. Yeah—that's a butterfly. There's yellow in it. That's pollen. Moths tend to be creamier." He looked up at a splotch on the windshield. "That's a moth. They have scales. Comes off their wings like powder. Gets stuck in the gunk."

"What you all doing?" said a woman in a uniform who appeared at his side. "I'm the driver."

"I'm checking the bugs on your bus," Dr. Hostetler said.

"Bugs?" said Jeanne Maness.

"I'm not an inspector or anything," Dr. Hostetler said. "I study insects. Collect the splats off the buses."

"Gross," said Ms. Maness.

This is the kind of anti-bug attitude Dr. Hostetler gets all the time. "Most people's gut feeling is to get rid of all bugs," he says. But he thinks bugs are wonderful. "When they're not running into cars, insects lead amazingly unique and distinctive lives," he wrote a few years ago in a book meant for edifying entertainment on family drives. It was titled *That Gunk on Your Car.*

In his way, Dr. Hostetler is playing a part in a national movement to promote natural habitats—even in people's backyards, and in states where housing developers prefer to flatten anything in the path of their bulldozers. As a specialist in ecological education, he passes on that message in frequent contacts with the public. If humans follow his example in learning to recognize bugs by their splats, he reasons, they'll get to like bugs better. In Florida, however, the bug-vehicle encounter isn't popularly viewed as an occasion for enlightenment. When bugs whack bumpers here, drivers don't feel bug-friendly; they just want to get the gunk off.

Dr. Hostetler's splat book did win an "Ig Nobel" prize from the tongue-in-cheek periodical *Annals of Improbable Research*. It also prompted a physicist to speculate that aerodynamic car design may cause bugs to explode before impact. In Florida, though, public enthusiasm for participating in splatological studies barely outlasted the life span of a no-see-um.

At noon on a hot day, Dr. Hostetler stopped by Park Place Car Wash, where Jeremy Golz was toweling off an SUV that had bug fossils etched into its hood. "Bug juice," said Mr. Golz. "Sticks to the paint. I hate bugs."

Inside, Dr. Hostetler found the usual huge gunk-cleaner display. Florida is the epicenter of an anti-splat market for bug deflectors, dried-bug softeners and greasy spray-on stuff that supposedly renders fenders nonstick. Aquapel is a good seller here; it was invented by Northern scientists at PPG Industries Inc. to make water bead up so drivers can see better in rainstorms. By accident, it took off as a gunk-resister in Florida bug storms. The invisible car bra is flying off the shelves, too.

For those unschooled in gunk, a car bra normally comes in black vinyl and wraps around front ends to keep bugs at bay. The invisible car bra is a brainchild of Arthur Seligman, who lives near Orlando. He created it out of clear plastic and custom cut it for 3,000 models. He called it Invinca-Shield, sent out "splat reports" for his distributors and came up with a slogan: "The bug stops here."

Tony Dilello, the carwash manager, shook Dr. Hostetler's

hand and said, "I don't think there's any solution to bugs. Bugs give spiders something to eat, I guess, but I hate spiders, too." Then he asked Dr. Hostetler: "What are the contents of love bugs?"

For a splatologist, that is a hostile question. Love bugs come alive here in May and September. No other creature will eat them. They copulate in midair for 56 hours, on average, then look to lay eggs in anything rotten. But they mistake exhaust fumes for rot and swarm all over the roads, igniting a twice-yearly car-gunk crisis.

"Love bugs have no purpose, correct?" said Mr. Dilello.

"They put nutrients back in the soil," Dr. Hostetler began to explain, but he knew he was licked when Mr. Dilello shot back, "And they're not from the University of Florida?"

A myth flitting around the state has it that the love bug was brought to life by mad entomologists at the university where Dr. Hostetler works. "Everywhere I go, that's the story," he says later. "They invented them to eat mosquitoes." It isn't the best buttress for his grand design of splatological inquiry—which ultimately aims to send the American lawn back to its insect-infested origins.

Dr. Hostetler lives with his wife and son on a suburban street of tidy lawns. Their house, grown over with cabbage palm, native azalea and Spanish moss, looks like it's in a swamp. To get to the front door, you walk on raised boards over a sinkhole.

"My idea is to hook people into native yards," Dr. Hostetler said, standing in his. He slapped a mosquito on his cheek, leaving a blood streak. "People want more birds, but they don't connect birds and bugs. Birds eat bugs. The connection has been lost. This ties into the whole need to explain to people why bugs are good."

As a kid in Indiana, he fed flies to toads. While in the Peace

Corps in Senegal, he survived a locust plague. As a student in Florida, he wrote a thesis on cockroaches. Nothing puts Dr. Hostetler off bugs. Outside sympathetic ecological circles, he rarely meets bugaholics in Florida, but down at the bus station, he did meet John Pickett.

"You know all about bugs?" Mr. Pickett asked, approaching as Dr. Hostetler examined a sparsely splatted Greyhound. A man of 45 in a red uniform shirt, Mr. Pickett is a night luggage handler. "Bugs are cool," he said. "You know those slow ones? Armadillo shell?"

"That's a roly-poly," said Dr. Hostetler.

"Back where the faucet is, there's millions," Mr. Pickett said. "If I find one wandering around where it might get stepped on, I'll bring it back there. Them and ladybugs."

Mr. Pickett talks about banana spiders he has known, a dragonfly he mistook for an electric razor and a wingless bug Dr. Hostetler decides must have been a velvet ant. "Sometimes, there's none of 'em, other times, millions," said Mr. Pickett.

"Same like bug splats," Dr. Hostetler said, just as he looked around to see the 10:50 from Tampa roll in, splat-plastered from roof to bumper. "Now, look at that!" he yelled. "Hit the jackpot!"

Mr. Pickett's eyes lighted up like fireflies as the splatologist showed his stuff: "These here are grasshoppers. See those moths? Clear, kinda gray. That's a wasp. Mosquito. Ant. These green splats are lacewings. Those little guys are leaf hoppers. This is just a really gross flying cockroach. . . ."

Dr. Hostetler didn't stop until the driver climbed aboard, turned on the wipers to smear bug juice over the windshield and rolled out again into Florida's summer night.

—Barry Newman, July 2002

21. Next, They'll Want a Stadium

LONDON—It seemed like a bird-brained theory from the start. Now a British government study has ended the mystery: When aircraft fly over, spectating penguins do not lean further and further back until they finally tip over.

But the tuxedoed birds do perform the Wave, like the undulating rows of fans in a sports stadium, as planes pass by.

The question of whether plane-gazing penguins fall head over webs has burned in Britain since some Royal Air Force pilots reported the behavior on their return from the 1982 Falklands war. Ever since, millions of Britons, inspired by the lively imagination of local tabloid writers, have been mesmerized by the prospect. The U.K. hopes its $37,000 study has put the myth to rest.

"Not a single penguin fell over," says Richard Stone, an ecologist with the British Antarctic Survey, who spent a month studying the flightless birds on a remote Antarctic island. While Mr. Stone and an associate camped near the colony of king penguins, two RAF helicopters dispatched from the HMS *Endurance,* a survey ship, buzzed the place 17 times from varying directions and heights.

For all its remoteness, there is a growing amount of aircraft activity over the Antarctic, from cargo planes to scientific and survey craft. Some environmentalists worry about the effect on the local fauna, especially in breeding groups. The British Navy, for instance, has long banned pilots from flying over animal colonies. The latest study itself was meant to observe not toppling penguins but "the effect of aircraft noise on penguins' stress levels," according to a navy spokesman.

So, how bad is the stress?

"They go quiet when a helicopter approaches," says Mr.

Stone. "Then they walk away from the noise source." Aircraft at 1,000 feet or higher don't seem to bother them at all. Mr. Stone plans to study penguin video footage and write a formal report over the next few weeks.

The RAF says the birds remain curious about the approaching planes. "Are you familiar with a Mexican wave?" asks Elaine McCloud, a spokeswoman for the RAF. "You get that with the penguins. If you move your helicopter slightly, the birds will all turn" in the direction of the movement. "It's a penguin wave."

—GAUTAM NAIK, February 2001

22. *Pinky, Phone Home*

WALVIS BAY, South Africa*—Among the mysteries of Africa, confounding scientists and defying all search for the truth, is this vexing matter:

The flamingos have disappeared. Yes, again.

One night in 1976, it seems, 1,250,000 of southern Africa's 1.3 million flamingos flew off, and no one has reported seeing them since.

"They're not really missing," says naturalist Hugh Berry, with cheering, if somewhat confusing, logic. "They're around somewhere. We just don't know where." It happened like this.

---

*Walvis Bay is a Namibian seaport that was claimed by the former white-rule government of South Africa. It was turned back over to the government of Namibia in 1994.

The honeymoon hotel of flamingodom is Etosha national park, a 2,368-square-mile salt pan in South-West Africa, or Namibia as it is also called. In rainy years, which don't come often to this arid part of the world, the salt pan floods, becomes a vast salt lake and quickens the libido of flamingos everywhere.

Flamingos like privacy when they mate, and the flooded pan with its oozy soda floor keeps the curious away. (Even a four-wheel drive vehicle can't slurp through, so no one saw the flock breed until 1971, when Mr. Berry, who is the resident naturalist at Etosha, fought his way through the goo.)

The birds also like security, and their only serious predator, the fish eagle, won't fly over a large body of water like the flooded pan in search of a meal.

Flamingos want food, of course, to woo their lovers and feed the chicks, and the flooded pan turns into a pea soup of blue-green algae with crustacean croutons. And let's get another fact out of the way: It's carotene from the crustaceans that turns flamingos pink.

Finally, they want mud to build their nests—180-pound mounds they slap together in ghettos of up to 60,000.

When the ghettos and the salt pan begin to dry, and their food dries up too, Etosha's flamingos herd their chicks into huge nursery schools of gray fluff. A few adults are left to keep order and lead the chicks, on wobbling webbed feet, on a race with the receding water.

In 1969, the flood waters receded rather faster than usual, and bird lovers slogged through the mud to rescue some of the 100,070 stranded chicks that had been abandoned by their parents. But usually, after chasing the brackish puddles for about 50 miles, the chicks are strong enough to fly.

Then, in a whoosh of pink and gray, everyone heads west to cool-water lagoons along the Atlantic coast, and especially to

Walvis Bay, a deep-water port that is on South-West Africa's coastline but, because of the peculiarities of politics, is owned by South Africa.

Flamingos are the SSTs of the aviary, and they can make the 300-mile flight to Walvis Bay in one night. The birds are so much a way of life here that they don't turn heads as they go tramping by the thousands through the city's waste-water ponds, over its salt flats, and up and down its beaches.

There's a Flamingo cinema here, a Flamingo drive-in, a Flamingo flooring company, a furnisher, a packer, a transport company and a hotel. The Flamingo hotel, appropriately, has a seafood restaurant.

After the last mating, in 1976, about 50,000 flamingos took the regular flight path here to Walvis Bay. The rest didn't, and almost none of the birds have been back to Etosha since.

That's because South-West Africa is gasping through its worst drought in a century. There hasn't been any water in Etosha in five years. And when there's no water in Etosha, the flamingos of southern Africa have nowhere to mate.

Now, it's a safe bet that almost any other bird, flying over almost any other country in a flock of 1,250,000, would have been spotted in 1976 and tracked. But flamingos fly at night, apparently navigating by the stars. South-West Africa is thinly populated— about three people to the square mile. And the bushmen and tribesmen who live near Etosha haven't any telephones to phone in the news of a flamingo overflight, even if they saw the logic in it.

This isn't the first time a million flamingos have disappeared. It rains so infrequently in Etosha that flamingos have nested only six times in the past 25 years. Where they were between 1956 and 1963, or between 1963 and 1968, is anybody's guess.

Mr. Berry guesses that southern Africa's flock may have joined with the enormous flamingo flocks of East Africa: Four million flamingos live in Kenya's Rift Valley. Or, he says, they might be splashing around the remote, salty lakes of neighboring Botswana.

At any rate, flamingos are thought to have a communications system similar to that of honeybees. So whenever there's rain again in Etosha and the salt pan turns to sea, it's thought, flamingos will honk the message across the sky and return.

In the meantime, those long years of flamingos interruptus no doubt sadden flamingo hearts everywhere. But on the other hand, they have saved the rest of us from being swallowed in a poof of pink long ago. Flamingos live 70, maybe 80 years, breeding to the end.

Their only enemies, besides the fish eagle, are the indolent marabou stork, which is just as happy to chance upon a flamingo that has died of old age as to hunt down a young one, and the odd jackal, which never has much luck because it is loath to get its feet wet.

The ancient Romans considered flamingo tongues a delicacy. But now that that fad has passed, even man isn't a threat: No one wants those acres of salty goo that flamingos call home or the puddles of slime flamingos call dinner.

So that leaves drought as the only force preventing a flamingo baby boom, a carotene cataract. As long as there's no water in Etosha, southern Africa's honeymoon hotel is closed for the season.

—JUNE KRONHOLZ, January 1980

23. The Toad People

HENLEY-ON-THAMES, England—Why does the toad cross the road?

For love. And therein lies a tale of woe for the toad—and a story of the compassion of British animal lovers.

We're on toad patrol this miserable, rainy March evening, 30 miles west of London. All around us, thousands of lovelorn toads, awakened from hibernation by the suddenly warm weather, are making a beeline to their ancestral breeding pond, just across the two-lane road running between the towns of Marlow and Henley.

That road is the problem. When the toads are running, cars are running, too, often at speeds unsafe for amorous amphibians. The carnage is dreadful: toads squished by the hundreds, making a sickening mess of the highway. It's a scene repeated throughout Britain every March when, toad experts say, some 20 tons of toads are run over by cars.

But the British are a people concerned with all creatures great and small—especially small. So here on the Henley road, and at 400 other designated toad-crossings in the U.K., some 4,000 volunteers of the national Toads on Roads Campaign slop through the mud with their rain gear, rubber boots, flashlights and plastic pails to carry the toads to safety.

"I don't really like doing it," confides Michael Irwing, a 24-year-old gardener who often stops here on the way home from the local pub to carry toads across the road. "But otherwise, they'd get flattened, and that shouldn't be." Adds Roland Laycock, busy patrolling the side of the road with his two young sons: "It's just great when you hear the toads talking to each other in your bucket—well worth coming out on a night like this."

The toads of Henley are fortunate in more ways than one. In

1987, Toads on Roads volunteers constructed England's first toad tunnel here to help the creatures pass under the highway. Since then, five other toad tunnels have been built in the U.K., not counting one designed for newts. The 10-inch-high tunnels, made of plasticized concrete, are buried shallowly with air vents at road level to maintain a user-friendly degree of dankness.

(To answer the obvious question, toads don't bang their heads on the roof of the tunnel as they hop along. Toads waddle; it's frogs that hop. And toads don't croak like frogs: They peep like chicks.)

Germany, with fewer volunteer groups than Britain, instead applies Teutonic efficiency to its squashed-toad problem: It has built 150 toad tunnels in the past 12 years. The catalyst for the tunnel program was a car accident in Bavaria, where several people were killed or injured when a motorist skidded on rain-soaked toad bodies. New roads near toad breeding ponds are required to include tunnels; in Britain, there is no such law, and the few tunnels that exist have been built largely with donated materials and volunteer labor.

Toad tunneling has become a science. The world's first International Toad Tunnel Conference took place in Rendsburg, West Germany, two years ago. Amphibian specialists presented papers from 10 countries discussing such toad-tunnel arcana as "overshoot" (when the toad misses the tunnel entrance), "drift fencing" (tiny fences designed to overcome overshoot), "the rumble factor" (road noise that disorients the tunnel traveler) and, most mysterious of all, "tunnel hesitation" (why some toads sit for hours at the tunnel entrance, reluctant to enter).

All the concern about toads on roads has improved the critter's lousy public image. The word toad has long been a term of abuse; even Shakespeare dismissed the toad as an ingredient in a witches' stew. Its Latin name, *Bufo bufo,* and its Greek zoological classification, *herpes,* haven't helped matters. And many people firmly believe that touching a toad causes warts (not true).

Mr. Toad, the lovable rascal in Kenneth Grahame's *The Wind in the Willows,* published in 1908, helped give the toad a better name. (The author lived only a few miles from where the Henley folks carry toads today.) Toads also eat insects and grubs and play an important role in the food chain. But what's really helped their image is the Toads on Roads Campaign and its organizer, Tom Langton, Britain's unofficial toad czar.

"When you get close to toads, you just become very fond of them," says Mr. Langton, a young and very earnest conservation biologist. "We aim to give the toad as much popular appeal as the robin." To that end, boosters distribute such trendy toadiana as bumper stickers, posters and T-shirts emblazoned "Help a Toad Across the Road."

Mr. Langton certifies newly discovered toad crossings for the Department of Transport, which then authorizes erection of traffic-hazard signs bearing a toad silhouette in a red triangle. He also helps organize an annual toad census and maintains a computer database of the volunteer groups. Last year, he figures, Britons carted some 250,000 toads across the road.

Wyllan Horsfall of Thurgoland, England, has carried her share for some 24 years. She and her group of toad bearers, aged eight to 70, patrol Cote Lane, near her home. "People thought I was a nut when I first started. Now they all join in," Mrs. Horsfall says. The toads made their presence known right after she moved to Thurgoland. She had left her front and back doors ajar while working outside. Suddenly, hundreds of toads were ambling through her house, which apparently lies astride the quickest route to the breeding pond. "I hauled bucketfuls out of my dining room," she recalls grimly.

Frogs occasionally pop up in the buckets of toad carriers, much to the delight of any youngsters around. Daniel Laycock,

10, though an enthusiastic member of the Henley toad lift, confesses to being a frog fanatic. "Frogs are prettier," he explains, holding a toad in one hand and the lone frog of the evening in the other.

A visitor this night, however, finds it hard to tell the difference: Both creatures look an unpleasant warty brown; neither is anything like Kermit-green.

Janice Laycock, Daniel's mother and a schoolteacher in Marlow, provides some guidance. "Frogs are long and pointy. Think Fred Astaire," she advises. "Toads are squat. Think Jabba the Hutt."

—GLYNN MAPES, March 1991

24. Elvis Has Left the Forest

CROUCH, Idaho—There are signs all over the mountain: elk droppings and hoofprints, pines scored by antler rubs. But nothing of Elvis, the elk that Larry Jones loved and lost.

"I don't want to get my hopes too high," he says as he strides through the brush. The search is tough on his emotions and legs, but Mr. Jones moves quickly when his dog spooks something in the brush ahead—elk! But none of them is Elvis.

Mr. Jones is an Idaho native, and has hunted animals since he was 12 years old. In 1992, a wild bull elk and his herd wandered into the front yard of Mr. Jones's backwoods house, about 50 miles north of Boise. The other animals ran when Mr. Jones came out, but the big bull stayed. Man and animal communed from November to June. The next three winters, Elvis returned; when Mr. Jones beckoned, the two walked together with Mr. Jones's yapping dogs, man talking to elk, elk bugling back to man. It was inexplicable behavior for a wild bull elk, a beast known for its skittishness.

Mr. Jones, a former church pastor, came to see Elvis as a sign and gave up sport hunting. But in 1996, Elvis clattered away, never to return. Mr. Jones has been looking for Elvis ever since—and trying to save a few souls on the side.

When he isn't scouring the wilderness, the 56-year-old Mr. Jones travels the West, telling his story and showing a video of himself with Elvis. He also sells elk-centered records and books. The video is called *Rocky Mountain King: A Wild Bull Elk Adopts a Man & His Dogs,* and stars Elvis, as flappy-lipped as the crooner for whom he was named. The 800-pound ruminant has a rack of antlers five feet across. The soundtrack features Mr. Jones singing original songs, at times backed by guitars, synthesizer, and elk call.

He says he has sold 10,000 copies at prices of up to $19 a pop in 11 states. The money's nice, but mainly, Mr. Jones says, his elk-based productions are a great way to spread his Christian message to hunters and other outdoorsmen "who might never darken a church." "I tell them, 'A bull elk came down and became my friend, and folks, I think it was God that did it,' " he says. "Hunters have to conclude I am a nut case, or they have to buy into my faith."

He may be unorthodox, but he is not alone. There are people who minister through bass-fishing lessons, ventriloquism or rodeo singing. "People who would never go to a church will sit on a bale of hay or go in a barn," says Ann Corley, a Scottsdale, Ariz., resident who for 13 years has toured "rodeos, ranches and anything pertaining to the livestock industry," with her husband, Don, singing religious cowboy songs.

Mr. Jones acknowledges that some question whether he's sincere, or just out to exploit the Elvis story for money. He says he grossed about $60,000 last year, mostly on video sales. "There are a lot of charlatans, and some will paint me with that brush," he says. Even some close to Mr. Jones admit having to deal with the "nut case or faithful?" choice he asks that his listeners make. "By the fourth year he was filming, I just asked 'Why?' " says his wife, Debby.

But there was an upside for her: Before meeting Elvis, Mr. Jones had over the years killed 21 large animals as a bow hunter, often disappearing for weeks at a time to hunt. At least this elk kept him home. When Elvis's horns would catch in the trees below their bedroom at night, "I'd yell at him to go sleep someplace else," she says. "Larry would say, 'Let him stay, it's music to my ears!' " Soon, he hung up his bow, and though he still hunts occasionally for meat, he never hunts for sport.

Mr. Jones tailors his message to suit his audience. At prayer breakfasts or churches, he talks about the role elk have played in his spiritual life, beginning with the animal he shot at the moment of his conversion in 1969. "Inherently, there is nothing in an elk," he tells them, but elk are the way God signals to him. Secular venues, like seniors' centers or hunting clubs, get less about his background and more songs. "He gives tourists a real feel for Idaho," says Katrin Thompson, owner of a recreational-vehicle resort in nearby Cascade, who has booked Mr. Jones six times. "He doesn't push religion, but when he says how much Elvis changed him, it takes it to a deeper level than just an elk in your backyard."

Elk experts are mystified by Mr. Jones's experience. James Peek, a professor of wildlife management at the University of Idaho, says that "generally, elk are scared to death of human beings." He adds, "Not being tied into God, I have to look for another explanation." Elvis, Mr. Peek posits, "could be an escapee from an elk farm." Mr. Jones counters that a domesticated beast would have survived only briefly in the wild.

Either way, Mr. Jones's production is in demand, as the many calls on his answering machine from prospective buyers attest. Summers, he works the tourist camps in the Northwest, and in the fall, he hits the hunters' groups as their season opens. (He doesn't urge hunters to give up the sport.) Winter means trailer parks in the Southwest. Overhead in his living room, a massive stuffed elk head juts out four feet from the wall. This is the beast he killed 30 years ago, at a time when Mr. Jones was drinking heavily and his marriage to Debby was in trouble. After a particularly bad hunting trip, "I gave up on Larry Jones," he recalls. "Just then, that elk showed up and I shot it. Walking back to the truck, I felt that God had given me this critter," he says. "Of course, that raised the question of 'Why?' "

He sold his business and holed up for two years, wearing out Bibles and Bible commentaries. Soon after, he became a minister in nearby McCall but resigned in 1982 after burning out on the job. Elvis arrived in 1992, at another low point. Mr. Jones had lost an election to become pastor of the local church and couldn't finish his book combining hunting stories with religion. "I just couldn't get that last chapter written," he says. "Then Elvis showed up." The gentle elk became the coda of *The Challenge of His Call,* of which Mr. Jones says he has sold about 5,000 copies.

When he was around, Elvis was a minor sensation. There were write-ups in regional newspapers and a brief clip on CNN. There were plans for a big-budget nature film and calls from producers in New York. "I was all set to go national and make more money than you could say grace over," Mr. Jones says.

Just as he finished his short video, Elvis went back into the forest, a trip of about 15 yards from Mr. Jones's front step. There was a purpose to it, Mr. Jones now believes. It was only then that Mr. Jones determined that Elvis would be the instrument of his ministry. "Instead of Larry getting famous, Christ is reaching people" through the Elvis story, he says.

In his living room, he pops in the video and taps his foot as he hears himself sing "Rocky Mountain King," the Presley-redolent title song. "Look how relaxed he looks!" he says of Elvis. On-screen, man and elk nod to each other.

Elvis antlers rest below the television set in silent tribute. Nearby is a newer pair that Mr. Jones just found on one of his walks. They are virtually identical in shape to the others—a sign, biologists say, that they came from the same elk. Newly hopeful, Mr. Jones will comb the forest tomorrow.

"None of those have this pattern," he says, indicating the pile of non-Elvis antlers he has stacked outside his garage so far this season. "That son of a gun is still out there."

—QUENTIN HARDY, May 1999

25. *Bugged in Rhode Island*

PROVIDENCE, R.I.—Washington, D.C., has its monument. Texas reveres the Alamo. But only Rhode Island looks up to Nibbles Woodaway, the world's largest replica of the common termite.

Michelangelo it is not. Covered in screaming-blue paint, perched atop a roof overlooking Interstate 95, the two-ton bug is 58 feet long and hurricane-proof. It was sculpted, or shaped, in fiberglass 20 years ago for New England Pest Control Co., a local exterminator.

What started out as advertising evolved into iconography.

Nibbles—the moniker comes from a naming contest in 1990—
receives 2,500 requests a year for autographed pictures. Soccer
and baseball teams turn up to be photographed near the structure.
There are Nibbles T-shirts, a Nibbles song, a Nibbles hole at a
city-owned miniature golf course and a $7.99 Nibbles bean-
bag toy.

Victoria "Vicky" Vona, Mrs. Rhode Island International 2000,
says she plans to speak about the termite as part of next month's
competition for the title of Mrs. International. "Each contestant is
required to speak about her state," Mrs. Vona says, "and in my
opinion, nothing says 'Rhode Island' like the big blue bug."

Providence Mayor Vincent A. "Buddy" Cianci says, "It's kind
of our own little symbol of . . . uh . . . uh . . . I don't know what."

Grit, maybe. Or Rhode Island's quirky brand of self-effacing
humor. The Ocean State is in many ways a happening place—
from the glow of the hit TV show *Providence* to the new glitter
that developers have brought to the capital's downtown. But the
smallest state has a long tradition of anti-pretentionism.

For Halloween, Nibbles sports a witch's hat. For Christmas,
he wears lighted antlers. A video camera is anchored next to his
left foreleg, so Web savants can receive continuous live shots
every 30 seconds of a termite's-eye view of Providence, just south
of downtown, including vignettes of oil-storage tanks, the highway and goings-on at a neighboring asphalt manufacturer.

When Camille Ruggiero, 53 years old, of Providence, a former clerical worker, feels a little down, her favorite pick-me-up is
to hop in her car and drive by the termite. "I don't look at him as
an insect," she says. She has also collected a series of color
glossies showing Nibbles in his various outfits, including his Uncle Sam hat, which she plans to frame.

The bug has been featured on an instant state lottery scratch
ticket, infuriating other local exterminators like Paul Wyrostek,

owner of Arrest-A-Pest Inc., who argued in vain that the state should also promote his mascot: a German shepherd wearing a badge with a crossed-out insect.

No one intended this. New England Pest owner Stephan Goldman and his late father, Leonard, were talking about beefing up their advertising in 1980 when somebody suggested erecting a giant pest. "It was like a light bulb," Mr. Goldman recalls. "We said, 'Absolutely.' Then, it was a question of what bug to pick. A roach? An ant?"

They settled on a subterranean termite—*Reticulitermes flavipes*—since it was, in Mr. Goldman's view, the "No. 1 nemesis to the homeowner," in a state that is considered a moderate to heavy risk for infestation.

Pretty soon, the $30,000 bug took on a life of its own. Mr. Goldman periodically frets to his advertising agency that the termite has become so emblematic of Rhode Island that it is no longer associated sufficiently with pest elimination.

One of the preferred ways to advertise in Providence is to hang a banner from the termite's chin. So many groups now clamor to use Nibbles as their personal town crier that the chin is booked through 2001, with requests extending into 2002. Currently, the U.S. Navy has booked Nibbles to welcome one of its ships to the port.

When the U.S. Mint recently asked Rhode Islanders what they wanted on new ceremonial 25-cent coins honoring each state, a few skipped the usual suspects like founding colonist Roger Williams and suggested Nibbles instead.

Some citizens would prefer extermination. "Let's grow up, then blow up that eyesore," was the suggestion of one letter writer in the *Providence Journal* in 1997, after Nibbles was posed sipping from a giant cup of lemonade.

George Cardoza of Budget Termite & Pest Control Co., whose

slogan is "Free Alligator Removal," grimaces every time traffic reporters use the termite as a landmark—which is all the time.

Others grouse that Nibbles, who sits in the path of nor'easters blustering in off Narragansett Bay, doesn't always look so ship-shape. By the end of the Christmas holidays, his antlers usually hang down around his mandible.

"It's much-beloved, but it is not a work of art," says Edward Sanderson, executive director of Rhode Island's Historical Preservation and Heritage Commission, explaining why the bug is not included in a newly published book about the state's famous outdoor sculpture.

Of course, Nibbles isn't the only insect statuary around. For starters, there's the carving of St. Urho in Menahga, Minn., mythical patron of Finnish immigrants, with a grasshopper stuck to his pitchfork. Elsewhere, there are giant ants, a boll weevil, a beetle and more. But, nothing else is on the scale of Nibbles, says Doug Kirby, a coauthor of *Roadside America,* which chronicles the nation's bizarre highway attractions.

Nibbles has inspired its share of controversy. The insect was implicated in multivehicle pile-ups during one past rush hour, when a disk jockey broadcast from between its legs, accompanied by a bikini-clad model and a belly dancer in billowing veils. Six people were injured, but Mr. Goldman insists the stunt didn't trigger the accidents: "I'm here to tell you that happened a mile up the road."

Even the man who crafted the termite, George Cardono, says it has taken him years to overcome the embarrassment of creating the world's largest termite.

The lemonade promotion also went over badly with a city zoning inspector, who cited the exterminator, saying Nibbles couldn't advertise what wasn't sold on the premises. Mayor Cianci was moved to climb onto the roof to issue what he called a Stay of Extermination. "We're not pardoning Jack the Ripper here," the mayor added. "It's a bug, and it's been our friend for years."

It's certainly dear to Debbie Bettencourt, a 28-year-old administrative assistant. As a teenager, she says, she would ask friends for a moment of silence as they drove past Nibbles. Now, Ms. Bettencourt reports that her e-mail address is "bigblubug." On her left shin is a 3½-inch tattoo of Rhode Island's favorite termite.

—BARBARA CARTON, July 2000

26. *The Worm Economy*

KORUMBURRA, Australia—Mark Holmes thumps the flat side of his shovel down hard on a grassy creek bank and listens. Instantly, the ground erupts in gurgles and slurps that sound like water draining from a bathtub.

"There's one here, one there and one over there," says the 36-year-old local Subaru dealer as he begins to cut carefully through sod and peel back spadefuls of damp gray clay. Holes the size of garden hoses appear. Out of one, water oozes.

"Ah, one's in there," he says, chipping away more clay. "We've got lots of six- and eight-footers around here. We've found 12-footers, too."

Mr. Holmes is talking about worms—giant Gippsland earthworms in particular, worms so big they can be heard burrowing underfoot. They scatter cattle and cause dogs to bark, and they send shivers up the backs of visitors.

When some Malaysian farmers visited his mother's cattle ranch here last year, Mr. Holmes unearthed a five-footer that sent them scurrying up the creek bank. "After that, I told them about our saber-toothed possums, and I think they believed me," he says.

Then there is the story about the visiting Englishman out on the local golf course. He is said to have discovered an eight-foot worm on a putting green. He packed up his clubs and fled, muttering, "If your worms are that big, I'm not waiting around to see your snakes."

Residents of Gippsland, a region of Victoria state southeast of Melbourne, eagerly proclaim theirs to be the world's biggest earthworm. Scientists say species elsewhere in Australia, South Africa and South America are just as big or bigger. Locals denounce the scientists for putting down their worm.

For the 2,800 residents of the shire of Korumburra, worm hyperbole has become something of an economic necessity. Mr. Holmes says the worm helped save his village from becoming a ghost town. The local coal mine closed in 1956, costing hundreds of jobs. The butter plant went under in 1971. Korumburra, like lots of other rural towns, was shrinking as young people migrated to cities for jobs and as cattle raising became less and less profitable.

So in 1977, the town turned to its worm. Named *Megascolides australis* by a zoologist in 1878, the worm became known hereabouts as "karmai," after an aboriginal phrase for "land of the giant worm." They organized a weeklong "karmai festival," to be held each March with a carnival, street fair, games and a parade. Tourists began to drop in, partly because the place is on the way to a penguin preserve at Phillip Island on the South Coast.

The fuss, however, began to disturb Melbourne zoologists, who argue that by commercially exploiting the worm, local residents are calling too much attention to it and might thereby endanger a rare invertebrate.

Mr. Holmes, who helped organize the festival, says the worm is simply a symbol. This year's festival drew 25,000 visitors with money to spend, including tourists from Japan, Europe and America. No live worms were dug up or done in. Helen Anderson, an office receptionist, was crowned "Miss Karmai, 1985." And the grand parade, featuring a fanciful 180-foot cloth worm propelled down the main street by the 45 residents inside it, was the usual big hit.

Word of the worm has indeed spread. Television shows featuring strange or rare animals have introduced it to audiences throughout the world, especially in Japan. Japanese tourists are turning up in increasing numbers. And a few years ago, the king of Norway was given a worm for his personal animal collection.

Brian J. Smith, the curator of zoology at the Victoria Museum in Melbourne, says that the best way to study and to save species like this is to keep them out of the public eye.

"That's impossible in this case," he says. "It's now so widely known that we get letters from all over the world asking for specimens." The museum turns down such requests, he says, but collectors, including many from museums outside Australia, then write to local farmers offering to pay for specimens. The result: underground worm-trafficking.

Prof. Smith, who has written that next to nothing is known about the worm's abundance, habitat or life style, nominated it as "vulnerable" for inclusion in a list of some 600 threatened invertebrates. The list was compiled by the International Union for the Conservation of Nature, an environmental group in Geneva, Switzerland, affiliated with the World Wildlife Fund.

Last year, the Australian branch of the fund got the worm listed as one of the world's 10 most-endangered species, alongside the giant panda, the California condor and the black-footed ferret. "That had me spitting chips," says Mr. Holmes, who says his mother's 250-acre farm is so alive with worms that they endanger earthen dams.

Prof. Smith believes that if the cattle business doesn't pick up soon, area farmers will turn to truck gardening, plowing up their pastures and slicing through lots of worms just as railroad and highway builders did in years past. Mr. Holmes says severed worms grow new parts. Prof. Smith says that isn't clear. He wants to start a worm preserve to protect them. Mr. Holmes thinks that will only result in a lot of government meddling.

But even those who would exploit the worm aren't entirely happy with either the status quo or the possibilities the future holds. "Of all the things that are unique to Australia, we have to have a worm," says a Gippsland tourist official who notes that visitors want more than the candy worms, worm dolls and worm T-shirts that they encounter here. The trouble is, she says, the pickled worms on display at the local Coal Creek historic park are in corked-up plastic hoses and aren't very appealing. In live exhibits, on the other hand, the worms burrow deep into clay where tourists can't see them, or else they die and begin to smell.

—JAMES P. STERBA, December 1985

27. *Not Your Mother's Nutritionist*

BROOKFIELD, Ill.—The commissary at the Brookfield Zoo is no place for the squeamish, especially on Tuesdays, when some of the freshest food arrives.

The back door opens, to the piercing ring of an alarm bell. A deliveryman brings in two boxes of live munchies from Rainbow

Mealworms Inc. of Compton, Calif. These are earmarked for the lilac-breasted rollers and many other zoo birds. Soon the bell rings again. Another box arrives, this one resembling a giant pizza box, but with perforated walls. The soft chirping from the chicks within means the owls and other zoo carnivores will soon get a favorite treat. Older, bigger chickens loiter in a cage downstairs, presumably unaware that they too appear on someone's menu.

"They're for the alligators," says Susan Crissey, Brookfield's animal nutritionist.

Zoos are forever telling visitors not to feed the animals, and for good reason. Each animal has its own diet. Few people know this better than Ms. Crissey, one of only five Ph.D.-equipped nutritionists employed by the nation's zoos. As Brookfield's Julia Child, she devises menus for some 2,500 creatures great and small, from foregut fermenters like buffalo to hindgut fermenters like zebras, from tiny bats to a 10,500-pound elephant named Affie.

Keeping abreast of the variety inherent in the zoo's routine diets is taxing in itself—but there's always some creature who needs extra attention. Sam Orang, a diabetic orangutan, has to watch his sugar. He drinks artificially sweetened Tang. Oliver, an overweight aardvark, is now on a weight-loss diet. Claude, a Palestinian mole rat, needs to pork up.

Zoos confront some decidedly distinctive tastes. Vampire bats need their cow blood. Tasmanian devils—stout, voracious little flesh eaters—crave chicken heads. King cobras are notoriously picky, or, in zoo jargon, "stenophagic." In the wild they eat only snakes, but parasite-free "feeder" snakes are expensive. To get king cobras to eat mice instead, zoos resort to the lowest sort of trickery. A recent issue of Zoo Life magazine printed a recipe from the Oklahoma City Zoo for "Serpent Slumgullion," a thick soup of boiled rat snake used to impart the requisite snake flavor to mice and to "pinkies," hairless day-old mouse pups.

"Let cool," the recipe says. "Dip mice or pinkies in soup and serve immediately."

Fortunately, a supplier exists for just about every appetite. Jimeny Cricket Farm Inc., of Richmond, Va., sells crickets, a delicacy for primates. Brookfield's orangutans like to pop live crickets into their mouths and just hold them there as the insects bounce around inside. Arbico of Tucson, Ariz., sells maggots. "We prefer to call them fly larvae," says Sheri Herrera de Frey, vice president. Ever mindful of public sensibilities, the company named its standard live maggots "Tiny Wigglers." Dried dead wigglers are "Wiggler Tempura." "We want people to feel good about them," says Ms. Herrera de Frey. "Tiny Wigglers—they just sound so darling, don't they?"

Oddly, no U.S. zoo had a full-time nutritionist until the National Zoo in Washington hired one in 1978. Only Brookfield, the Baltimore Zoo, and the Bronx Zoo (recently renamed the International Wildlife Conservation Park/Bronx Zoo) have done likewise, though zoos elsewhere often seek their advice.

Zoos previously had used a so-called cafeteria approach to feeding animals, offering a broad array of foods known to be nutritious and letting animals choose what they wanted. But hidden deficiencies took their toll. Elephants that got too little vitamin E came down with debilitating white-muscle disease. Lions that ate only meat wound up with atrophied bones. Their diets lacked the calcium they would have gotten in the wild by crunching on the ribs of prey.

The new awareness of zoo nutrition evolved in tandem with other zoo trends, in particular the movement of the last two decades to make animal habitats—and diets—more realistic. Some zoos took this to extremes, as did the Detroit Zoo. Until 1991, it killed "surplus" animals and fed portions to its carnivores. The zoo's vultures, for example, dined on scimitar-horned

Oryx, a kind of antelope. But such realism works better in theory than in practice. "People like to see the cute polar bear," says Karen Fulton, the Baltimore Zoo's nutritionist. "They don't want to see him ripping the head off a harp seal pup."

Still, some animals won't eat anything but live food. The National Zoo, for example, finds it must feed live mice to its tawny frogmouths, small birds with gaping maws. Just before feeding time, the zoo makes an announcement suggesting that squeamish visitors move along.

Live prey poses some practical drawbacks. For one thing, it can escape. It can also fight back. Says Brookfield's Ms. Crissey, "If you've got a little snake and it's trying to go after a mouse, and the mouse bites it, then suddenly you've got a vet problem."

For some animals, frozen food offers a happy solution. Ms. Crissey walks into the commissary freezer, kept at 20 degrees below zero. Here are box upon box of frozen smelt, mackerel and herring. She opens a big yellow bin marked "mice and rats" and pulls out a plastic bag packed with dozens of frozen pinkies.

The commissary also stores less exotic fare—cases of peach nectar, five-pound tubs of peanut butter, Kretschmer wheat germ (for the bats), Gerber baby cereal, huge boxes of pasta and 50-pound bags of all sorts of commercial animal feed.

Ms. Crissey spends her days tinkering with diets, and regularly sallies forth for her favorite part of the job: watching the animals. The diversity she encounters each day is immediately evident as she strolls through Tropic World, a mammoth indoor exhibit complete with interior thunderstorms.

From high on a walkway overlooking a big fake canyon, she points first to Hose Nose, a giant anteater snuffling along the far wall. "He gets cat food," she says. The tapir wading through a shallow pool directly below gets hay and herbivore pellets. The sloth—"that bag of hair," Ms. Crissey laughs, pointing to a clump of fur protruding from a tree trunk—needs its fruit cut into long, thin strips. The vulture on a branch high overhead gets horsemeat and dead rats.

Freshly euthanized dead rats, not road kill. "He's getting what he needs," Ms. Crissey says, "but it's not gross. It hasn't been sitting out for two days."

Treats, she says, are a nutritionist's bane. When the orangutans began gaining weight too quickly, she slashed peanuts and raisins, eliminated the eggs. The orangutans were not pleased. They became agitated and started spitting at their keepers.

Ms. Crissey was unmoved.

"People call me the Grinch that stole produce," she says. "But I'm not the Grinch. I'm just trying to get better control over what the animals get."

She has her own weaknesses, however.

Over a lunch of sausage pizza, she confesses that her usual lunch is french fries drenched in melted cheese. Or, she adds, maybe a couple of chocolate-chip cookies.

—ERIK LARSON, February 1993

28. The Greening of Frog Dreams

ALAPAHA, Georgia—On December 7, 1982, we reported here that America's long national frog shortage was over. This was incorrect. It wasn't even close.

So we're being cautious this time. Could America's long national frog shortage now be on the verge of beginning to be almost over? Just read the headlines coming out of the swamps of south

Georgia: "Move Over Chickens, Here Come the Bud Boys!" "Fish-farming Pioneer Leaps Into Frog Business." "Frog farming: one man's effort to save the planet."

Behind these banners are 35 years of failure soon to end in a dream come true, says Hugh Kenneth Holyoak. He's the creator of such fish-farming innovations as Ken's Floating Raceway Fish Factory, the Scale-O-Matic Electric Fish Scaler, the E-Z Floating Fish Cage, the Bug-O-Matic Fish & Frog Feeder and his pièce de résistance: a monster hybrid bluegill, or bream, called the Georgia Giant that he says is selling like hotcakes to the fish-stocking trade.

Now, the 63-year-old owner of Ken's Hatchery and Fish Farms Inc., two pay-to-fish lakes and a wild-pig hunting operation, is unleashing on the free-enterprise system his exclusive "automated Bullfrog Chamber system," an indoor frog-raising breakthrough that could, he says, make a lot of prescient Americans rich and put the nation knee-deep in bullfrogs. In a world of mysteriously disappearing amphibians, this also amounts to an ecological service to mankind, he says.

The chamber's secret: a feeding system that Mr. Holyoak is absolutely not at liberty to discuss at this time. Indeed, anyone taking Mr. Holyoak's day-long $1,000 frog-raising seminar must first sign a "confidential disclosure and secrecy agreement." (Mr. Holyoak says he can't be too careful, since thieves of frog-tech know-how abound, and his patents are pending.)

But wait. For readers who may have spent the last 44 years unaware of America's frog deficit, a brief synopsis: The United States, once self-sufficient in free-range frogs for dining and dissections, sacrificed them by the millions in the Cold War. *Sputnik* started it. When the Soviet Union orbited the world's first satellite in 1957, Americans panicked. President Eisenhower signed the National Defense Education Act to close the science gap by pumping millions of dollars into schools to interest kids in science.

The schools bought frogs. Dissecting them was a hands-on experience thought to produce future Einsteins. By the mid-'60s, demand for biology-class frogs hit an estimated 1.8 million a year. Suppliers paid froggers more than restaurants paid. Coupled with pressure on frogs because of disappearing wetlands, frog legs disappeared from many menus.

What to do? The obvious answer: frog farms.

American frog-farming dreams go way back. James Harding, a Michigan State University museum herpetologist, remembers the ads of his boyhood: "Earn Extra Money Raising Frogs." It sounds easy. It isn't. Dump polliwogs into a pond and predators pounce. Fence off the predators and the frogs eat each other. Crowd them, and they get sick and won't copulate. Worse, frogs demand live protein. They want whatever is in their mouths to move before they swallow it.

America is dotted with failed frog farms. Probably the most famous was the Amphibian Facility at the University of Michigan. For 18 years, Dr. George W. Nace used tax dollars in a failed effort to farm frogs commercially indoors. The Feds cut off funding in 1982 and the project died.

"Frog farms are more myth than reality," says the Virginia Cooperative Extension Service's aquaculture Web site. "Those few individuals who claim to be successful frog farmers generally turn out to be distributors selling adult frogs, tadpoles or eggs, often harvested from the wild, to misinformed, would-be frog farmers. Beware of frog-farming schemes promising a new, quick way to make money."

Unable to farm them, America turned to imports. By 1971, the U.S. was importing 5.4 million pounds of frozen frog legs valued at $3.8 million annually, mainly from India. Salmonella bacteria came with them. President Nixon poisoned at least one unnamed congressman at his second inaugural dinner in 1973 by inadvertently serving imported, salmonella-laced frog legs. Food and Drug Administration inspectors cracked down, rejecting 90% of imported frog-leg shipments as contaminated.

Things got ugly. Insurance claims skyrocketed. Frog-leg fraud mushroomed. Unscrupulous dealers sometimes reboxed the legs, fumigated them, soaked them in chlorine, or dusted them with embalming-strength deodorants and reimported them as new shipments. Customs seized many of these shipments, preventing likely salmonella poisoning, and the FDA dispatched experts to India and Bangladesh to teach sanitary techniques.

Results were mixed. Salmonella gets in frog bones and joints where disinfectant rinses can't reach. (Irradiation now kills the bacteria in frog legs bound for Europe, but the U.S. doesn't allow it.) By the early '90s, the subcontinent's wild frog populations had plummeted from overharvesting. In 1993, Bangladesh banned frog exports, citing a rise in malaria and the overuse of expensive chemical insecticides that had replaced frogs in insect control. Importers turned to the wild frogs in Indonesia and Vietnam.

The U.S. frog shortage eased briefly in the early '80s as President Reagan held down federal education funds and students balked at dissections as cruel. But demand has again crept up to outstrip supply.

Today, virtually all frogs for food and science are imported. Last year, according to the U.S. Commerce Department, the U.S. imported 3,678,776 pounds of frog legs from Taiwan, China, Vietnam and Indonesia, including the 6,000 pounds served at the Fellsmere, Fla., Frog Leg Festival in January. Fellsmere, on Florida's central east coast, switched to imports three years ago when local froggers couldn't find enough in local swamps.

"They were beautiful," says Beth Perez, festival chairwoman.

They were, in fact, American bullfrogs, farm-raised in Taiwan. What U.S. ingenuity hasn't been able to do profitably, Taiwanese ingenuity (and cheap labor) has figured out. And Taiwan isn't alone. Brazil, Guatemala, Thailand, Malaysia and several other countries now farm American bullfrogs too. The key was to train them to eat pellets; one way was to use vibrating machinery to make the pellets move and mimic live food. Americans, too, are doing this now on a small scale, but labor costs here have so far damped high-volume frog-farming efforts.

So what's wrong with imports? Certainly not price. Sea King International Corp. offers small Chinese frozen frog legs by the ton from $1.43 to $2.03 a pound (16 to 20 legs), plus shipping.

Charles Trager, sales manager for Beaver Street Fisheries, in Jacksonville, Fla., the nation's biggest frozen frog-leg importer, says they probably get to restaurants at around $3.50 to $4.20 a pound.

But Mr. Holyoak, for one, won't eat them. Sanitation is still a problem, he contends, adding: "People don't want frogs shipped thousands of miles and frozen for months—the quality just isn't there." In his opinion, the untapped market is for live frogs and fresh legs. "This thing is on the verge of really taking off. It's going to be real big," he says.

"He's been saying that for years," says David Vohaska, of Specialty Game Inc. near Chicago.

China and Taiwan already compete in the fresh frog-leg market, air freighting live bullfrogs to Chinatown markets in California. David Dang, proprietor of Nguyen Loi Oriental Supermarket in Haltom City, Tex., buys live frogs at $4.35 a pound from Mexico. He sells 50 to 60 pounds weekly for $5.79 a pound.

Mr. Holyoak says he's so swamped selling Georgia Giant bluegills after a five-pound, 15-inch specimen was pulled out of a pond last year that he hasn't had time to build up his bullfrog breeder stock. (Besides shipping real fish, you can buy life-size plastic replicas for $395, plus shipping and handling.) But he says his five-year goal is to have 10 million frogs, which, along with his chamber system, will bring bullfrog farming to America big time. Each stackable three-feet by four-feet net-covered tray, he says, can hold 300 baby bullfrogs (or 150 adults), which are mechanically fed pellets and grow to edible size in 180 days (instead of the usual three years).

Soon, for only $50,000 or so, he says, he'll set you up with 50,000 giant jumbo bullfrog tadpoles (50 cents each) and a bullfrog chamber system big enough to grow them to edible adults. Just add water.

—JAMES P. STERBA, March 2001

CHAPTER 4

PASTORAL PURSUITS

———

29. *Shear Excitement*

REEDPOINT, Mont.—Before Montana, there was Spain. And in Spain, there is Pamplona. And in Pamplona each July, there is the running of the bulls, in which the mighty animals tear through city streets, from corral to bullring, while thrill-seeking humans try to dodge or outrun them.

Ernest Hemingway used Pamplona as a backdrop for *The Sun Also Rises*. As a symbol of adventure and romance, the running of the bulls there is world-famous.

Which brings us to Reedpoint.

Reedpoint isn't world-famous. It is hardly even Montana-famous. It has 96 citizens and seven businesses, and its high school this year should have a graduating class of one, assuming

Robert Ulmer doesn't stumble along the way. It is in the wide-open ranch country of the Yellowstone River valley, where the access ramps to interstates have grates to keep the livestock off the four-lane. Reedpoint has no water system, sewer system, mayor, police force, city government or city taxes. The signs on the highway south of town spell its name as one word; the signs on the railroad north of town spell it as two.

Nonetheless, little Reedpoint has at least one thing that puts it squarely, if gently, in the heroic tradition. As surely as July means Pamplona and the bulls, September means Reedpoint and the sheep.

Next Sunday, thousands of people are expected to flock to Reedpoint for what is being billed as the "101st Running of the Sheep." (It is actually only the second running of the sheep, but more about that later.) The festivities stretch from morning until midnight, but the main event comes around noon, when a thousand or so sheep will be herded the four blocks down Reedpoint's main street, from the abandoned grain elevators at the north to the Conoco service station at the south, threading their way through the humanity. People can race or pet or mingle with the sheep. The sheep, unlike the bulls at Pamplona, don't seem to mind.

"The sheep are so docile," says Russell Schlievert, an organizer of the event, which is a civic fund-raiser sponsored by a group called the Reedpoint Community Club. "It's a very hands-on thing."

Last year's thing started as a low-budget spoof of a high-priced cattle drive that was the biggest event of Montana's 1989 centennial celebration. Reedpoint ended up attracting an estimated 12,000 people, and it raised enough money to pay for doubling the size of the Reedpoint Memorial Library, to two rooms from one. This year's proceeds will go toward buying a used fire truck and emergency medical equipment for the town.

No one knows how big a crowd to expect this year—or what to expect from the crowd. Last year, many people arrived with their favorite sheep in tow and in costume. One sheep wore tennis shoes. Another was painted to resemble an American flag.

The winner of the Prettiest Ewe contest wore red-and-black satin garters on her legs and a lacy bonnet on her head; her owner, who led the sheep on a leash, wore a matching bonnet and turn-of-the-century satin dress. The Ugliest Sheep winner, by contrast, had a polka-dot look, its shaved coat punctuated with unshorn clumps of wool, which were dyed various colors.

Aside from the beauty pageant, events this year range from a parade to a street dance to a "sheep-to-shawl" contest, which is exactly what it sounds like and is expected to take six hours or so; the shawls will be auctioned. On the cultural front, there are sheepherder-poetry readings. (Sample from last year: The place I lived in wa'nt too clean / It smelled like somethin' died / When I talked to other people / They'd stay on the upwind side.)

And there's the Smelliest Sheepherder event. Last year, it began as a joke, with a few adequately groomed sheep men gamely getting up on stage to the hoots of the crowd. Suddenly, the real thing—a herder named Festus, straight from the hills—pushed his way through the crowd, climbed up on stage and literally overwhelmed the competition.

"Everybody else on stage just turned around and walked away and said, 'Hey, it's his,' " says Mr. Schlievert, who emceed the contest. "Then he got up and talked about living on the range with the sheep." (Festus couldn't be located for comment or for determining his last name. He's out with his herd.)

The idea for a sheep drive came when the Reedpoint Community Club began looking last year for a new gimmick to liven up its annual Labor Day weekend fund-raiser, Bachelor Daze. That event, which included the auctioning of bachelors, usually attracted a couple of thousand people to town, but the idea was getting old, as were the bachelors.

At the time, the Montana press was playing up something called the Great Montana Centennial Cattle Drive, a six-day extravaganza in which anyone could ride along with the herd and play cowboy at a price of not much more than, say, six days in Paris or Rome. Reedpoint decided that it might be fun to have something a little more down-to-earth. Sheep are about as down-to-earth as you can get; here in cattle country, they're treated as rather a joke. Soon, the Great Montana Centennial Sheep Drive was born.

The parallel with Pamplona's bulls was pointed out by a newspaper reporter in Billings, about 60 miles east of here; Reedpoint folks hadn't heard of Pamplona. But the small-town promoters proved adept at big-city media manipulation.

"We took our sheep to downtown Billings, unloaded them right in front of the TV stations and let them eat their flowers and stuff until they came out and interviewed us," says Chery Leicht, who was secretary-treasurer of the Community Club last year.

The word spread, and on Labor Day weekend, people descended on Reedpoint. Vendors ran out of food by midafternoon. Connie MacLean, the official silkscreener, ran out of T-shirts; after selling 560 of them that day, she later had to print up and mail another 400 to people who left orders. The event was thoroughly homespun: An elderly ranch woman set up a gas stove on a corner and made fried bread for passers-by.

"The Great Montana Centennial Sheep Drive must be the most successful spoof since Orson Welles's *War of the Worlds* was broadcast in 1938," an editorial in the *Billings Gazette* declared. "Certainly it was the most fun."

It also brought money into a town that doesn't have much of its own. The high-school girls' basketball team made enough from its hamburger stand to pay for new jerseys and a trip to Billings for the district tournament. And the Community Club netted enough—$9,131—for a 20-by-22-foot addition to the library, a former one-room schoolhouse roughly 12 by 14 feet.

"It was unbelievable," says Librarian Evelyn Burton, a retired schoolteacher, whose house is next door to the library. (People don't have library cards in Reedpoint, because Mrs. Burton knows everyone by name.) Mrs. Burton says that as a result of the expansion, she is considering increasing the library's hours—or, more precisely, hour: It's open from three to four every Wednesday afternoon.

Given the success of last year's event, there was no question but that it would be revived this year. Indeed, the only issue was what to call it. The organizers settled on the "101st Running of the Sheep"— even though it's only the second—because it's Montana's 101st birthday. "It didn't make much sense to me," says Ms. MacLean, the silkscreener. "But I think they just liked the sound of it."

It sounds like a tradition, an end-of-summer celebration that every year should give Reedpoint its moment in the sun. It might even become a continuing boon to the town's coffers. At least, say many residents, isn't it pretty to think so?

—ERIC MORGENTHALER, August 1990

30. Bucks, Sex and . . .

SPRINGPORT, Mich.—Dick Haley scratches the snout of Honey, a five-year-old whitetail doe. "She's a provider," he says, showing off a shed with slanted floors and drains where what she provides is collected for refrigeration.

Honey is one of 100 deer at Haley's Whitetail Farm. When he isn't tending them, Mr. Haley works second shift at a General Motors auto-assembly plant in Lansing, 20 miles up the road. It's a good job, but the 51-year-old millwright has a bad back and a retirement dream: making money from deer urine.

It's a dream beginning to come true. "Most mornings, I just turn on the TV to Kathie Lee and Regis, put on my gloves and start pouring," says Mr. Haley, who along with his wife, Nancy, and her son, James, bottle and hand-deliver fresh doe, buck and fawn urine to 35 hunting stores within 100 miles of their farm.

Sales are up, and a new musk-scented urine gel called The Hot-Doe-Formula is getting good word-of-mouth among Michigan hunters. The phone rang for days last month after the Haley farm was featured on satellite TV's Outdoor Channel; soon they were shipping orders to 22 states and Canada. "And we don't make any fantastic claims," says Mr. Haley.

There's a burgeoning market in deer urine; in fact, its bottlers and marketers are locked in a sometimes rancorous competition to win consumer loyalty. Once dismissed as a joke, deer-hunting scents, most of them urine-based, now rack up retail sales of about $15 million a year. For $3.50 to $12 an ounce, they cost as much as fine cognac and promise to lure bucks in for close-range shots.

Urine and glandular secretions help wild animals, including deer, find each other to mate, fight or, in the case of natural enemies, stay away. Whether they are effective when bottled is debatable.

"Conceptually, it will work," says Karl Miller, a whitetail researcher at the University of Georgia. "Whether it does when it comes out of a bottle, I can't say. And we haven't tested."

Still, anecdotal evidence and testimonials abound. Consider Gary Clancy, a bow hunter, writing recently in *Deer Hunter* magazine: "The biggest bucks are suckers for a properly used scent."

In fact, America's murky deer-hunting scents-and-lures industry has been built on such claims, along with sex and secrecy. The Haleys are small fry up against such heavily advertised big sellers as Buck Stop Lure Co.'s Mate-Triks Original Doe-In-Heat Buck Scent, Wellington Outdoors' Tink's #69 Doe-In-Rut Buck Lure, and Pete Rickard's Love Potion No. Nine; the last one, at $9.98 an ounce, is touted as "a fatal attraction of pheromones."

Mr. Rickard, a Cobleskill, N.Y., trapper, was among the first to market a deer scent when he began flogging Original Indian Buck Lure in the 1940s with quarter-page ads in outdoor magazines. It was made without urine and sold for two dollars a bottle.

Urine-based scents got a boost in the 1960s from George Robbins, a Connellsville, Pa., mink farmer who founded the Robbins Scent Co. He began supplying urine in bulk and bottle to scent sellers who touted "secret" formulas and blends. "I sold to everybody—thousands of gallons a year," says the retiree, now 83.

Two more recent developments are driving the current bull market in scents: a bow hunting boom and the use of sex as a marketing tool. Bow hunters needed to get close to their prey for good shots, and luring big bucks with the scent of randy does was a notion whose time had come.

Mr. Robbins says it was his idea to collect estrus urine from does in heat: "I tried it and it worked great. It gets bucks all excited."

This is where the matter gets a little cloudy. A Michigan mailman named Don Garbow says he gave Mr. Robbins the idea. He founded Buck Stop Lure and in 1972, using urine supplied by Robbins Scent, marketed Mate-Triks. In trade ads, Buck Stop introduced Bambi, a scantily clad (human) female model uttering such catch phrases as "Never too late to make a buck."

Then scandal rocked the industry. In 1989, Fred Trost, host of *Michigan Outdoors,* a popular public-television show, accused the scent industry of making fraudulent advertising claims for its sex scents. On his show, he poured plain ammonia and Aqua Velva after-shave on different patches of ground and showed that bucks came up to sniff them as readily as the high-priced bottled stuff. That might have been fine, except he accused Buck Stop of bottling cow urine.

Buck Stop sued for defamation, and in 1992, a civil-court jury awarded the firm $4 million in damages. Mr. Trost says he filed for bankruptcy; his program went off the air. A "truth-in-labeling of hunting scents act" died in the state legislature.

It was the Trost–Buck Stop hubbub that got Mr. Haley, a deer breeder, interested in the bottling business. To emphasize freshness, he has videotaped himself collecting urine in a pitcher held under a deer that performs on cue. He charges more for estrus urine than plain, but doesn't know if it's better. When hunters ask what's different about it, he says, "Three dollars."

"Right, but what's the difference?" they ask.

"Three dollars," he replies, smiling.

Most scent-product urine today is sold in bulk to bottlers by deer farmers such as Ray Hanson, who operates Indian Head Whitetails Inc., in Chetek, Wis. He sells 55-gallon drums of regular doe urine from $10 to $40 a gallon, and doe-in-heat urine from $30 to $70 a gallon, depending on the size of the sale. A single deer produces about a half-gallon a day.

It can be a rough business. Billy Vernon, of Wildwood, Fla., is of the opinion that most mass-marketed scents are "98% snake oil." He used to sell Scrape Juice, an old trapper's recipe of 14 secret ingredients, but sold out after eight years because he lacked the ad budget to go up against the big boys.

For example, to turn Tink's Doe-In-Rut into what is still the nation's best-selling brand, Aubrey "Tink" Nathan says he spent a third of his annual revenues—in 1989 he topped out at $4.5

million—on advertising. Mr. Nathan's company, however, filed for bankruptcy that same year and sold the trademark to Wellington Outdoors.

The Haleys don't have an ad budget. "We have to have a board meeting," says Mr. Haley, meaning he and Nancy and James need to sit down and plot strategy. Now, Mr. Haley thinks they may be ready for their first marketing campaign, perhaps with a Detroit Tiger baseball player he knows as a celebrity endorser. Nancy doesn't like the idea. Too much like the competition, she says. "It'll make us just like them."

—JAMES P. STERBA, December 1997

31. Yoking It Up in Maine

CUMBERLAND, Maine—A crowd of maybe 2,000 is packing the grandstand and piling three-deep against the rail on the open side of the Pulling Arena at the Cumberland County Fair, all waiting for the start of the International Ox Pulling Contest for the International Trophy. It is probably the biggest ox-pulling event in the whole country all season.

"It's sort of a similar deal to the Olympics," says George Hall, the fair's Superintendent of Oxen.

Sort of. Ox pulling isn't really a big sport any more; hasn't been since the tractor came in. But watching two big brutes that together weigh as much as a full-size car tug at a block of concrete three times as heavy as they are is still plenty exciting for the people who go to dusty little county fairs like this one, in places where being up-to-date might not be as important as it seems to be elsewhere.

A few people may be here from Portland for the contest. But this is mainly a farm crowd: round ladies in stretch pants munching French fries doused with vinegar; men with creased faces and bad teeth leaning out every so often to spit tobacco juice into the dirt. There are lots of kids, too, and some of these just climbed up on top of the chalk board in the corner. They'll have to get down from there before we can start.

There seems to be some movement at the far end of the arena. Here come the teamsters and their cattle, and the crowd is on its feet. Eight teams that qualified in last August's trials are competing. Four are from New England and the other four are from Nova Scotia. That's the way it is every year because other places never enter. Ox pulling just seems to have stuck mostly in the Northeast while about everybody else on the continent switched to horses and motors. First into the arena are the four Nova Scotians, smiling confidently, holding whips over their heads, leading broad-shouldered critters decorated with clanging cowbells and pompons resting on impassive snouts.

Nova Scotians are proud of their oxen; some farmers there still pull stumps and haul logs with them. "They're better than a tractor and as good as a pair of horses in the rough," says Gordon Lohnes, who came down for the contest. "When you get rid of an ox you can make beef; when you get rid of a horse you got to bury it. I guess that's why we hung onto 'em." (Oxen, by the way, are castrated bulls—it makes them less uppity.)

The Nova Scotia teams are bound by brass-studded head yokes that you hardly ever see in the States. The yokes are carefully carved and fitted to the horns so that the oxen can put the full strength of their massive necks into a pull.

Master of ceremonies George Edwards is talking into the microphone: "Just lookit the headgear on these cattle, folks. Let's give 'em a good hand for really polishing up these cattle. We're glad you're here, boys."

The cheering swells as the New Englanders move into the arena, marching with white-birch goad sticks resting like rifles on their shoulders. Their cattle, in plain hickory bow yokes that are fastened around their necks instead of to their horns, are stripped of finery and ready for a hard pull. These men, like most others in New England who keep oxen, do it more or less because their fathers kept oxen and because they think it's a good idea for their sons to keep oxen. They train them all year and in the summer they travel around to the fairs.

The New Englanders are convinced that their bow yokes are better for pulling than the Nova Scotian head yokes, and that's really why this contest was started in 1965, to settle that point once and for all. Every year but one since then the New England teams have gotten slaughtered, and you might think they would be ready to concede by now. But these Yankees are tenacious. "I think we still have a chance," George Hall says. We will soon find out.

The contestants are lined up in the arena and George Hall is holding out his hat to each man who draws for starting position. It looks like John Treadwell is going to pull first. Yes, it's John Treadwell from East Brookfield, Mass., the man wearing the wide-brimmed white hat and a white beard that's sticking out about three inches in front of his chin. It'll be a minute before Mr. Treadwell gets hitched up and in the meantime we can run down the rules.

Two strips of whitewashed two-by-fours are running parallel 12 feet apart down the length of the 150-foot arena. The oxen must stay between these rails. At one end of the arena is a "stone boat," which is a sledge with 3,600 pounds of concrete blocks on it. The oxen are hitched to the boat and have to drag it three feet along the dirt floor. If they do, the teamster can call for more weight. Then they tow it three more feet, the teamster calls for still more weight, and so on until the boat is too heavy to budge. The team that pulls the most weight three feet without stepping over the rail wins the contest. If a team can't pull the load in three tries, it's out.

The team is ready. Mr. Treadwell slips them some sugar, yells "Haag'h!" and the boat slides ahead easily. "Now he'll call for a load," George Edwards announces. "Whaddya going to have, John?"

"A thousand pounds," Mr. Treadwell says and a big rumbling tractor piles on three more blocks. "You're on your own, John," George Edwards says, but suddenly the cattle are pulling by themselves. "Whoa! Whoa! Whoa!" John Treadwell is shouting, but the cattle are over the rail once and heading over on the other side. "Wait! Wait! WAAIT!" he bellows, but the cattle are over the rail twice and they're out.

Mr. Treadwell heads for the barn. "We hope we have some teams from the U.S. that'll give us a little better show," George Edwards says.

"And now here's Oran Veinot from Nova Scotia."

Mr. Veinot, a man with a green-billed cap pushed to one side of his gray head, hitches up his cattle and they easily pull the boat three feet. They take on 800 pounds more and do the same. Mr. Veinot isn't making a peep. The load builds; 5,600 pounds, 6,400, 7,200, 8,000 pounds. The cattle just put their heads down and pull.

At 8,400 pounds Mr. Veinot begins to encourage them. He tugs down on their horns, whirls his whip over his head and screams: "Comeah! Heah! Heah! COMEAAAGH!" The load slips ahead. At 8,600 pounds they finally waver. Mr. Veinot shrieks, the head yoke creaks, but the stone boat creeps only 27 inches. The team is out.

"Nice job, Oran; that's the way to do it," George Edwards says over the loudspeaker.

The crowd is hushed in amazement at Mr. Veinot's display. People down here don't often see cattle trained the way they are in Nova Scotia. "In Nova Scotia you dassen't use the whip," Gordon Lohnes explains. "You got to get them to do what you want just by talking to 'em. They call 'em dumb animals, but they're smarter than we are."

The American way is to get the oxen to do what you want by whacking them on the haunches with the goad stick. And at most contests in the States, moreover, the rules are different. The oxen pull for distance with a set load within a time limit and the only place they aren't allowed to go is into the grandstand. This contest is being played with modified Nova Scotian rules, which are a bit more civilized. The Americans know they are at a disadvantage. (It's true, though, that at past matches American rules were used and the Canadians still won.)

Well anyhow, here comes Dwain Anderson from Webster, N.H., to give it another go. His black and white team takes loads with ease but at 7,800 pounds the pressure is too much. The oxen are blowing smoke from their nostrils and drooling heavily. A sweat stain is spreading across the back of Mr. Anderson's drab-green shirt as he roars "Heaagh!" and comes down with the goad. But the boat moves only seven inches, and the team is finished.

The next Nova Scotian is Darrel Watkins, with two fat, speckled oxen. He whoops and hollers a lot and takes the load up to 7,600 pounds. Then all at once he adds on 1,000 pounds and the team gives out. After Darrel Watkins comes John Mehuren, a strapping poultry farmer from Searsmont, Maine. He works the load up to 8,000 pounds, but with that much weight behind them his cattle bolt forward with all they've got and the boat doesn't move an inch.

And now, at last, we have Nelson Zinck, a Nova Scotian fish cutter and the reigning champion, with his two dark, mean-looking critters, Dynamite and Lightning. Mr. Zinck is smiling pleasantly, hitching his pants up around his rib cage, doffing his old blue sweater. He's walking over to the judge and it looks like he wants another 800 pounds on the boat even before he makes his first pull. "Ladies and gentlemen, this man knows what he's doing," George Edwards tells the crowd.

Mr. Zinck plants his feet firmly in front of his animals, opens his mouth and lets out a long "Eyaaaaaah!" as they draw the boat precisely three feet. Again and again, like clockwork, they take the loads up to 2,000 pounds. "He's calling for 800 more!" George Edwards shouts and the crowd is cheering. Mr. Zinck puts his hand on his chin and studies the situation. He motions to the judge. "Put on two more," he says. That's 9,000 pounds. The fans can't believe it.

Mr. Zinck is walking very slowly toward the front of his cattle. Suddenly he whirls, grabs their horns, pulls down hard and bellows as the team crouches and pulls as one, and the boat bolts ahead. It's done.

Even Nelson Zinck's team can't handle 9,200 pounds. They drag the load 34½ inches. But it doesn't look like anybody is going to beat 9,000 pounds and the fans are starting to filter out, heading over to the Exhibition Hall to check out the purple hoghorn potatoes and the rhubarb jam. Ernest Littlefield from Morrill, Maine, is in the arena now, looking helplessly at his oxen's splayed legs as they jerk at 6,600 pounds and can't move it. The last man is Gerald Woodworth from Nova Scotia, whose team stops cold at 8,000 pounds. "Oh shoot," says somebody in the crowd. Nelson Zinck is the winner.

Everybody is leaving now, trying to make it over to the midway in time to take in Zelda the Skeleton Girl. In the arena, Nelson

Zinck is being awarded a big silver cup and a first-prize ribbon as the flashbulbs pop.

"They putcha on a real show," George Edwards is saying over the speakers. "It looks like we got to do a little more practice if we're going to get ahead of them boys. But you got to give us credit; we're still working at it. We never give up here in the States. Now here's a list of licenses numbers that must be moved or they will be towed away . . ."

—BARRY NEWMAN, October 1974

32. *Another Thing to Grouse About*

NOCTON, England—Late on a dismal night, a man in jungle fatigues steps off 20 paces in his yard and fires into the mist. A lead ball zings through the dark and smacks the exact center of a can of car wax. "Haven't lost me touch," the poacher says, lowering his slingshot. "I hope ol' Alan heard that."

Alan Count is a gamekeeper who lives just two doors away. He, too, is plotting for the season ahead. "This time of year, you don't linger at the pub," he says, testing a high-powered lamp. "You don't want the poacher to know where you're lurking about."

In England each autumn, as pheasants grow fat and leaves fall from trees, gamekeepers and poachers begin a centuries-old rite. Prowling through the dark, deploying everything from horsehair to infrared beams, they duel over game that is reared for the sport of much richer men. At stake is their livelihood, and also their pride.

"The poacher knows most of my tricks and I know most of

his," says Mr. Count, a keeper for 35 of his 53 years. "We're heads and tails of the same coin."

Mr. Count's role isn't the romantic one of the gamekeeper who beds Lady Chatterley in D. H. Lawrence's novel. He began his career trapping rats and selling their tails for a ha'penny bounty. Later, he toted bullets and bagged game for a rich huntsman with a waxed mustache and manners to match. "The only thing he ever said to me was, 'Don't drag them hares through the mud!' " Mr. Count recalls.

Even so, game keeping offered some escape from class-ridden rural life. "The land belonged to rich people, and much of it still does," he says. "But if you're a keeper, the land is your beat. It belongs to you."

It also is his to defend. For the gamekeeper, poachers are but one of many pests with which he must wage nonstop guerrilla war. By day he sets traps for stoats and weasels, and uses ferrets to flush out hares. By night, he stalks foxes, feral cats, badgers and other "vermin" that prey on game birds, their eggs or their food. His only ally is a hip flask of sloe gin, "the keeper's drink."

Picking up the potent, garlicky scent of a fox, Mr. Count pans his lamp and spots a pair of flame-red eyes in a beet field. To lure the fox closer, he makes a squeaky sound with his mouth and hands, mimicking a wounded rabbit. "I reckon every predator's entitled to his share," he says, raising his gun. "But the fox is a wanton killer. He'll take every bird he can."

So too does Mr. Count's neighbor in Nocton, a poacher whose nom de guerre is Charley Peace, a 19th-century cat burglar famed for eluding the law. The modern-day Mr. Peace once dreamed of game keeping, but when he couldn't find a post turned to poaching instead. He tries, however, to target vast estates.

"I loathe aristocracy," says the 44-year-old laborer, a grizzled man with graying mutton chops. "Game was put on this earth for every man. I'm just part of the natural balance."

The workshop behind his home is decorated with huge antlers. "Them's from the Earl of Ancaster's estate," he chuckles. "Took that stag with a wire snare." His armory also includes a rifle fitted with a homemade silencer, a dragnet for sweeping up partridges, and raisins threaded with horsehair, which catch in a pheasant's throat and leave the bird flapping on the ground.

But Mr. Peace's preferred weapon is a simple, hazel-wood slingshot. "Silent, deadly and efficient," he explains. On bright nights, he picks out the pheasant's silhouette and downs the bird with lead musketballs he crafts himself. "Simplicity itself," he says. "And no need to spit shot out at dinner."

For cover, he relies on a face mask and foul weather. "The only night to go out is when it's fit for neither man nor beast," he says. In the wet and cold, birds roost low in the trees, sound doesn't carry, and keepers are less likely to venture out.

Mr. Peace clears about $400 a week in season illicitly selling poached game on the cheap to willing dealers. And in 25 years, he's been caught only once, when a jittery accomplice turned him in. Reveling in his roguish success, Mr. Peace wears his poaching camouflage to the pub and often leaves a bird or musketball at the scene of the crime, "as me calling card."

Even so, stealthy loners like Mr. Peace are a dying breed. To some degree, gamekeepers tolerate local poachers, particularly "one for the pot" men who catch birds for their own consumption. But city gangs have been moving in, taking 1,000 birds a night and disregarding the small timer's turf.

To defend against them, some keepers use night-sight binoculars, infrared beams to locate intruders and rubber pheasants that set off an alarm when hit. The gangs, many of them from depressed mining and mill towns, also have a certain flair. Alan Edwards, a

North Yorkshire gamekeeper, has found couples smooching in get-away cars—as decoys, while their partners poach game with lamps and dogs.

Mr. Edwards spends his Friday nights creeping with the fog across the desolate grouse moors. A light flashes in the gloom, shuts off, flashes again. Mr. Edwards checks his watch. "That'd be right," he says. "It's pub letting-out time."

Back in his jeep, he edges forward without lights. But the poachers hear him and break for a waiting car. Mr. Edwards hits on a spotlight and gives chase. "Jill, can you read me?" he yells into his radio phone. Jill is his wife, who relays messages from the Edwardses' cottage to the police. On this night, though, she is sound asleep.

Mr. Edwards bluffs instead. "Give it up, lads!" he shouts. "The police are on the way!" The driver, a scowling young skinhead, waves his fist and shouts a threatening obscenity. Then the two men begin a high-speed chase across a wheat field, with the poacher trying to bump Mr. Edwards's truck.

"Not worth getting killed for," Mr. Edwards says, as the car vanishes in the fog. Though poachers only face a fine of about $75, many have criminal records and would rather fight than face the police. Mr. Edwards once was badly beaten; other keepers have been wounded with crossbows, and occasionally shot dead.

For gamekeepers, such risks bring modest rewards. Those on traditional landed estates earn about $300 a week, plus tips from hunters and a range of rather feudal perks: a lonely cottage, coal for the fire, work clothes and a tweed suit to wear on shooting days. Mr. Count, the Nocton keeper, prefers to work for "shooting syndicates" that rent or buy land for use during the hunting season. But to "keep the wolf from the door," he says, he has often had to take second jobs.

This fall, Mr. Count began teaching game keeping at the Lincolnshire College of Agriculture. While passing on the age-old wiles of his craft, he also teaches his students how to deal with animal-rights activists, who often appear at hunts, shouting "Scum! Scum! Kill For Fun!" and tootling horns to mislead dogs. If the Labour party wins next year, it may well try to ban "blood sports," especially fox-hunting, which Oscar Wilde termed "the unspeakable in full pursuit of the uneatable."

"To most people now, we're cruel old bastards who murder and persecute every creature in sight," Mr. Count reflects, dropping a rabbit on the run at 75 yards. "I guess if there's justice in this world, I'll collapse out here one day, where the vermin can feast on me."

Game keeping also is under siege on other fronts. Many estates have broken up, thinning keepers' ranks to just 2,500, down from 23,000 in 1911. And as village life wanes, there are fewer men with the appetite or know-how for lonely patrol of woods, moors and fens.

But Mr. Count clings to one consolation: If gamekeepers go the way of the dodo, so too will his lifelong antagonist, Charley Peace. "He's not a villainous character, really," Mr. Count says, slipping out of the pub as his counterpart appears. "So in heaven, he'll still be poaching birds, and I'll still be there chasing after him."

—TONY HORWITZ, October 1991

33. At Least They're Not Elephants

PETALUMA, Calif.—Greg Gibson thinks people who appreciate something unique will want to get his goats.

"They're a novelty," says Mr. Gibson, an ostrich salesman

who recently diversified into selling "fainting goats," animals that have a genetic trait that causes them to stiffen up and fall when frightened.

The jittery critters were first noted in Tennessee in the 1800s, according to an article in *Exotic Farmer* magazine. But attacks by coyotes brought the goats near to extinction.

The American Tennessee Fainting Goat Association of Elkton, Md., with about 200 members, says its goal is to save fainters from extinction. The group ranks goats on a scale of one to six, with "six being the highest, meaning they lock up most of the time and fall over," according to founder Kathy Majewski.

"It's fun," says Ruth Prentice, registrar of the International Fainting Goat Association of Terril, Iowa, which is planning a show and sale next week. "People are getting excited about it." The organization, with about 100 members, advertises the animals as "The Fun Model of the Goat World," and prints a newsletter called "Fall in Love With Fainters." The group classifies goats as "premium" or "regular" fainters.

The best fainters command prices of as much as $1,000. Trouble is, once the goats get accustomed to their owners, it's harder to scare them. Says Mrs. Prentice, who was formerly involved with Red Wattle hogs: "One gal said she had to take a different route to the barn and come in a different door just to get them to drop."

But the Humane Society of the U.S. expresses "grave concerns" about the "whole fad of fainting goats" because of the "physical and psychological stress" involved. Lisa Landres, a society field investigator, says: "It's sad. It's people making money from the worst kind of exploitation; causing an animal physical stress."

"To raise animals with an abnormality for use as entertainment is sick," says Alexander deLahunta, a veterinary neurologist at Cornell University. "The whole phenomenon is mind-boggling . . . to breed for a disorder."

Still, Maureen Neidhardt, editor of *Rare Breeds Journal,* who owns about 50 fainters, expects their popularity to increase. But she doesn't think they're likely to become common pets: "I won't say they're a replacement for potbelly pigs."

—CARRIE DOLAN, April 1991

34. *The Polish Pickle Over Buffalo*

BIALOWIEZA, Poland—The Buffalo Movie House is down the street from the railroad station, which has a buffalo silhouette on its wall. Up the street from the hunting lodge, which has a buffalo head above its gate, is the Buffalo Restaurant.

And all around this village, a primeval forest teems with wild buffalo clear across the Soviet frontier into Byelorussia. Anyone can spot them. They're all over.

"I'm surprised you didn't see one," says a woman sitting in a rustic souvenir stand outside Bialowieza's zoo. "They stop right in the middle of the road." She sells buffalo post cards, buffalo-head plaques, carved buffalo.

"They walk around just like cows," says the man in the next stand. He has a carving for sale of an American Indian on horse-back, waving a rifle.

With buffalo everywhere, there is no need to go to the zoo. Far better to eat at the Bison Buffet, pass the night unpampered by heat or hot water at the Hotel Ewa, and forge into the wilderness in the morning sun with Polish buffalo scout Aleksy Bajko.

An under-forester in Poland's park service for 15 of his 45 years, dressed in green from peaked cap to rubber boots, Mr.

Bajko stalks buffalo most days on a yellow motorbike, keeping tabs on the herd. Today, his party has a silver Mercedes and a driver, but there's no need for a tougher car; one of Mr. Bajko's partners has sighted a herd over at the train tracks.

"It's not far," says the scout, climbing into the front seat. "I'll show you."

It was the crush of civilization that backed 1,500 wild buffalo into Bialowieza Forest. These are wood buffalo, a relative of the American plains buffalo. They are as humped and as shaggy, weigh 2,000 pounds and charge (sometimes in the direction of people) at 25 miles an hour. Here in their natural home they can feast on ash, alder and linden, hornbeam and spruce, unworried by wolves or bear. The forest is chock full of buffalo; the experts say it can't hold any more.

Mr. Bajko heads the Mercedes down a logging road to the tracks, and leads the way into the woods on foot. The air is still. Leaves float to the ground. "You need an instinct for this," says the scout. He can see that wild boar have roughened the earth, but those buffalo don't seem to have left a trace.

"We'll try the meadow," he says, walking back to the car.

This isn't the first time *bison bonasus* has swarmed in Bialowieza. The breed died out in Britain by the fifth century, but buffalo meat fed Poland's army not far from here at the Battle of Grunwald in 1410, and in the 1500s its kings decreed them protected game. One day in 1752, Queen Maria Jozefa bagged 21 while seated in the royal tent at Bialowieza. In 1990, buffalo are nearly as plentiful.

On the forest road, Mr. Bajko gets out twice, ducks into the woods, and traipses back shaking his head. "No tracks." The Mercedes soon comes to the grassy meadow. Bialowieza is renowned for its sweet-smelling buffalo grass. A blade of it is added to each bottle of Poland's Bison Vodka, and is said to impart a bison's hankering in matters of the heart. This meadow doesn't have any buffalo grass, though. It's just grass.

Mr. Bajko tromps around in it, finds some dry buffalo wallows, then powwows with a couple of woodcutters at the edge of the forest. "They were here long ago," he says, getting into the car and shutting the door with a bang. "We'll try another place."

It wasn't always so easy to stalk wild buffalo in Poland. Nineteenth-century Europe never had the mass hunts that almost obliterated the herds of North America, but in the 20th century it had wars. When World War I began, 700 buffalo lived in Bialowieza. When it ended, none did. Of 54 that survived in zoos, 12 were fertile. They were brought back to the woods they hailed from and were nurtured through World War II. In 1952, a few were set free into the wild. By 1970, they packed the woods once more.

"There's two!" Mr. Bajko yells from the front seat. "Black and white!" The milk cows watch as the Mercedes flies past them and turns down a muddy trail, which quickly narrows and snakes. Tires spin. "Normally, we don't have such cars," says Mr. Bajko as his party arrives at a cluster of park-service hayricks.

Buffalo congregate at the ricks to feed in winter. Nearby is a pen with a chute at one end, used to coax them into trucks. When the buffalo began to abound, Bialowieza began to export. Every European bison in the world has its roots here, including Brisket at the Bronx Zoo, and Phyllis, who belongs to Earl Tatum in Holiday Island, Ark. This is not winter, however, and there are no buffalo.

Mr. Bajko removes his cap and wipes his brow. "There's a place not far," he says. "Maybe there." Another meadow. Deserted. The scout opens his coat, stuffs his hands into his pockets and stomps to the meadow's distant edge. He enters the woods, and disappears.

The world's zoos now have all the buffalo they want. To keep the herd from overrunning the woods, Bialowieza's foresters must cull it—with rifles. No one else hunts buffalo here, but each year a few angry bulls are let loose in the Bieszczady Mountains, where they get angrier. Rich foreigners pay up to $3,000 to kill one. It is a real challenge. In the mountains, buffalo are hard to locate.

A half-hour later, Mr. Bajko steps out of the woods, raises his arms and lets them drop. "I have no idea where they can be," he says. "They must be underground." He guides the Mercedes along a swamp full of dark shapes that could be buffalo, but aren't. In a patch of sunlight, some woodcutters are taking a break.

"Didn't you see them in Siennicka?" one asks. "Maybe in Skladnica," says another. A third laughs: "You are the buffalo man and you don't know where the buffalo are?"

As the car moves on, Mr. Bajko goes quiet. "I'll make it up to you," he says finally. "I'll show you the Russian border. Then we'll go to the zoo, okay?"

The border has some curiosity value. Soviet and Polish buffalo used to mix. But in 1980, Moscow stopped that with a barbed-wire fence built to keep Polish people from mixing with Soviet people. The fence still stands. A grassed-over road to it ends at a closed gate. Beyond, a red and white post fixes democracy's eastern limit.

After photos are duly taken, Mr. Bajko retraces the trail to the zoo. He gets out, and the ticket-taker strolls over. "Did you see?" the man asks. "There's a herd up on the main road."

Mr. Bajko looks as if he's been gored. "Let's go!" he shouts, leaping back into his seat. The Mercedes races to the road, turns onto the asphalt, then slows to a stealthy creep. Mr. Bajko lifts a hand. The car halts. And there, a dozen yards into the forest and two minutes' drive from downtown Bialowieza, stand five huge beasts, slender of haunch and massive of shoulder.

His party to the rear, Mr. Bajko tiptoes toward them. A cow raises her great bearded head, swings her horns in his direction, and snorts. The buffalo scout turns, sticks both thumbs up in triumph and whispers: "Safari!"

—BARRY NEWMAN, November 1990

35. New Zealand's Woolly Problem

WELLINGTON, New Zealand—The sun eases up over a lush horizon, turning blades of grass into filaments of gold. Sheep, fluffy as cotton balls, gleam in the early morning light.

It's the kind of scene that makes you want to throw back your head and take a deep breath of fresh air. Don't. What you're likely to get is a mouthful of methane.

New Zealand may pride itself on its pristine landscapes and its rigorous environmental standards. It may eschew nuclear energy and build clean hydroelectric plants instead of dirty smokestacks. But that hasn't saved the country from the ravages of polluters.

The villains aren't cigar-chomping industrialists plotting in some multinational board room. They're sheep, millions of them, munching away on New Zealand's verdant hillsides.

Flatulent sheep, to be blunt about it. "Sheep are very efficient methane producers," says David Lowe, a geophysicist with the New Zealand Institute of Nuclear Sciences. Humans, he says, produce very little.

"If you could hook up a sheep to the carburetor of your car, you could run it for several kilometers a day," Mr. Lowe says. "To power the same vehicle by people, you'd need a whole football team and a couple of kegs of beer."

Trouble is, scientists haven't figured out how to hook sheep to cars, so instead of being a useful power source, the ruminants' copious methane output simply creates pollution. The problem is particularly acute in New Zealand because the country of three million people has more than 70 million sheep. Each produces about five gallons of methane a day.

That means the local sheep population is producing almost 2.5 billion gallons of foul-smelling gas every week, making New Zealand a big contributor to potentially serious environmental hazards.

Analysis of ancient air bubbles trapped in Antarctic ice shows that 30,000 years ago the concentration of methane in the Earth's atmosphere was only a third as much as it is today.

Along with carbon dioxide, whose atmospheric presence also is increasing alarmingly, scientists fear methane will contribute to the phenomenon known as the greenhouse effect, which could cause a dangerous rise in the Earth's temperatures and even a melting of the polar ice caps. While scientists know that higher levels of carbon dioxide are caused mainly by industry, the source of all the methane remains mysterious.

"One thing's for sure, it isn't just New Zealand's sheep," says Mr. Lowe. Other ruminants, such as cows, have in their digestive systems the same cellulose-eating bacteria, which produce methane. But the methane rogues' gallery also includes rice paddies, fossil fuels, volcanoes, Amazonian swamps and termites.

But why the drastic increase over the years in methane? Mr. Lowe and his colleague Rodger Sparks, a nuclear physicist, are trying to find out.

Through radio-carbon dating, the scientists can determine the age of various types of methane in the air, distinguishing recently produced gas from methane that is eons old. And by taking atomic "fingerprints" of methanes from various sources, the scientists hope to pinpoint which methanes come from sheep, swamps, people or industry.

But collecting methane samples isn't for the queasy. Sheep methane comes from a local agricultural university that is conducting research into the animals' digestion. The unfortunate sheep in these experiments have tubes protruding from their intestines, which makes methane collection simple, if unpleasant.

"It's horrible to look at and horrible to smell," says Mr. Sparks, who leaves most of the sample-collecting to Mr. Lowe.

When the scientists need human methane, Mr. Lowe calls at the local sewage-treatment works. The centerpiece of the plant is a 33-foot-high tank, filled to the brim with what the plant superintendent, Chris Butler, politely calls sludge.

The methane that rises from the mess is drawn away down a wide pipe and used to heat boilers that power the plant. Mr. Butler has his own hypothesis about the sudden increase in atmospheric methane. "It must parallel the rise of modern-day politicians," he says.

To get his specimen, Mr. Lowe, armed with a half-gallon vacuum flask and a dishcloth, gingerly approaches a valve in the pipe. "I've done some strange things in this job, but this is the strangest," says the scientist, wrapping the cloth around the valve to form a seal as he turns the tap.

A powerful burst of methane hisses forth. The smell is just about as bad as you would expect. Mr. Lowe's face crumples. "One of these days I'm going to have to talk Rodger into doing this," he gasps.

Mr. Lowe's next sample-gathering task isn't as malodorous,

but it can be just as onerous. It requires a trip to what he calls the clean-air factory—a bleak outcrop named Baring Head, where winds from the Antarctic first hit land after howling across thousands of miles of open sea.

Mr. Lowe gets his cleanest samples during southerly gales. That means he must do battle with blasts of icy wind as he sets up an array of flasks and pipes to trap air samples. "It's probably the cleanest air in the world," Mr. Lowe boasts. "In the Northern Hemisphere there isn't any clean air left."

To prove the point, the clean-air factory exports its product. It is hard to know what customs officers make of the apparently empty flasks regularly dispatched to destinations such as the Scripps Institution of Oceanography in San Diego, Calif., where the air is used in carbon dioxide research.

Back at the Institute of Nuclear Sciences, Messrs. Lowe and Sparks reduce the air samples to carbon particles that can be dated. So far, the scientists have found that about 75% of methane in the atmosphere is biological and of very recent origin.

Over coffee in the lab's cafeteria, the two researchers ponder a solution to the world's methane problem. "We can't just continue to use the atmosphere as a garbage dump for five billion people," Mr. Lowe says.

But a growing world population has to be fed, and that means more rice paddies, more livestock and more methane. "It's hard to figure how you cut down methane emissions," Mr. Lowe muses glumly. "About all we can do is stop eating."

Mr. Sparks stares into his coffee cup. "People will resist that," he says.

—GERALDINE BROOKS, June 1987

CHAPTER 5

FISH STORIES

---

36. *An Operative Theory of Caviar*

ASTRAKHAN, Russia—Be aware that patient comfort isn't necessarily a big part of sturgeon surgery. Be warned that knowledge of ichthyological gynecology doesn't necessarily enhance the pleasure of eating caviar.

Now, behold the caviar of the future.

Two competing Russian groups, called Ecoresoursy and VNIRO, say they have figured out how to make caviar without killing the fish. In both cases, the sturgeon gets a hormone injection to make it ovulate, and a sort of Caesarean section to remove the eggs. Both groups claim to have a secret method to give the eggs the consistency of normal caviar. The fish returns to the water and eventually spawns again.

It's about time Caspian Sea sturgeons got a break. The prehistoric giants—they have been known to live more than 80 years and reach 12 feet in length—have been fished onto endangered-species lists. The old Soviet Union strictly controlled production, but now the sturgeon is at the mercy of cash-hungry new countries and armed gangs.

"Within a few years, we're going to have to leave the old method and use the new one, without killing the fish," says Elena Chertova, director of Ecoresoursy, a firm that has a six-employee experimental caviar operation in Astrakhan, the Russian caviar capital on the Volga River. Mining caviar could be "just the same as milking a cow," she says.

By the conventional method, it's more mauling than milking. Nets haul in sturgeons before ovulation, when the eggs are still attached to ovaries. Workers kill the fish, pull out the insides, rub the eggs over a strainer to remove ovary tissue, and wash and salt the eggs to make caviar.

The caviar industry isn't exactly rushing toward slaughterless caviar. Suzanne Taylor, managing director of Hamburg, Germany–based Dieckmann & Hansen Caviar GmbH, says she imported 100 kilograms of Ecoresoursy's "special" caviar but was disappointed. "It just looks good," she says. For some reason, "the skin is so hard that you keep chewing on the skin." She ended up photographing much of it instead of selling it to shops and restaurants.

Russia's official caviar factories aren't gung-ho, either. Why should they spend to send sturgeons back to sea when outlaws are most likely to catch the fish next time around anyhow?

At Astrakhan's open-air fish market, a poacher named Samat describes what he does after catching a rare beluga sturgeon on the Volga at night: whack the beluga on the head, slice the still-living fish's belly from head to tail, scoop out about 10 kilograms (22 pounds) of caviar, and sell it locally for $40 a kilo. (In New York, it would cost 18 times that.)

"I'm sorry for the fish," says the laid-off ship mechanic, "but I have three children to feed." A 175-pound beluga, he adds, is worth an additional $250 dead because sturgeon meat is becoming popular.

So for now, the world's new sturgeon farms are the best hope, according to Igor A. Burtsev of the government-run VNIRO, the Russian abbreviation for the Russian Federal Research Institute of Fisheries & Oceanography. In May, Dr. Burtsev flew to Sarasota, Fla., with 100,000 eggs for the Mote Marine Laboratory's sturgeon farm. In about five years, when Mote strips the sturgeons' first spawn, Mr. Burtsev hopes the farm will keep the mothers alive, using VNIRO's method.

Maybe, maybe not. "We don't need that technique at all to be highly profitable," says Steven Serfling, director of the Mote laboratory's aquaculture program. True, he could get caviar out of the same fish 10 times over the course of 20 years, but the fish would get bigger and bigger and use up more and more tank space. Growing new fish might be cheaper.

Dr. Burtsev, a north Russia native with spiky hair, is a patient man. He has a black-and-white photograph of himself performing the world's first successful roe-extraction surgery on a sturgeon way back in 1967; in the photo, he sticks his hand through a slit in the belly of the three-foot-long patient as an assistant suspends it from its tail.

Twenty years later, another ichthyologist, Sergey Podushka of St. Petersburg, wondered why sturgeon eggs couldn't simply be pushed out the fish's genital orifice with head-to-tail massage. The eggs got backed up in the fish equivalent of fallopian tubes.

But if a small scalpel could sneak past the orifice and make a self-healing puncture in one of the tubes . . .

Thus was stitch-free sturgeon surgery born. A recent Podushka paper described the three-man job as follows: "The first man wipes the female's belly with a dry towel and holds a cup for the eggs in his hands. The second man holds the fish's tail, makes the oviduct incision and enlarges the genital opening with a small stick if necessary. The third man holds the fish's head and massages its belly." The surgery lasts 10 minutes.

Clumsy scalpel work can remove the fish's kidney. And wild sturgeons tend to swat their tails during surgery. Still, BIOS, a sturgeon hatchery affiliated with Ecoresoursy, says it has lost no sturgeons with the Burtsev method and only "one or two" with the faster Podushka method.

The trouble is, the Burtsev and Podushka methods work only with ovulated eggs. Eggs get a soft outer shell when they leave the ovaries, which makes them perfect for fertilizing with sperm and growing new fish. But try washing and salting them the traditional way, and you end up with mushy-sturgeon-roe porridge.

That problem has stymied efforts in Iran, France and the U.S. to develop death-free caviar. Regulatory concerns about hormones also hampered such research in the U.S., says Serge Doroshov of the University of California, Davis, fishery lab. When he operates on sturgeon, to breed them, he has to use anesthesia, stretchers, flowing water, iodine and surgical gloves.

Russia has no such restrictions, and its tradition of tinkering with roe includes developing long-lasting caviar for cosmonauts in the 1960s. Ecoresoursy and VNIRO both say they solved the mushy-egg problem, and will happily reveal how—for a price.

Ecoresoursy won't let outsiders into the room where it makes its experimental caviar. Ms. Chertova, the director, shows a copy of the patent for "way of processing eggs of sturgeon," but quickly pulls the patent away. Does the method use chemicals? "No." Special machinery? "No." Unusual temperatures? "No." Nuclear radiation? "That's too high-level for Russia," Ms. Chertova says, chortling. "Everything is very easy."

Well, not everything. Ecoresoursy doesn't yet have its own sturgeons; it uses eggs that the BIOS lab extracts for fish hatching but rejects as unhatchable. And Ecoresoursy would have to surmount tough new international rules limiting exports of caviar: The rules, though designed to save the sturgeons, have no exemption for caviar extracted without killing the fish.

Meanwhile, VNIRO is working on taste refinements; ovulated eggs seem to take on the characteristics of the grassy, soily river-bottom where they would end up if nature took its course. Asked to submit its work for taste-testing in Europe, the VNIRO team offers some caviar (a jar of eggs taken from live sevruga caviar) and some caveats ("It's not the best batch," "European experts don't know much about Russian caviar").

In London, John L. Stas, a caviar trader for 10 years, dons a white hat and lab coat and enters a tasting room. His company, W. G. White Ltd., imports eight tons of caviar a year from Russia and Iran, though he hasn't heard of caviar from live fish. "It's a lovely color," Mr. Stas says, dipping a mother-of-pearl spoon into VNIRO's jar. He puts a blob of light-gray sevruga eggs on his fist, and tastes. "It's very unusual. . . . It's not unpleasant. . . . It's very rubbery. . . ." An egg goes down the wrong pipe. The coughing lasts 10 minutes.

—DANIEL PEARL, June 1998

37. The Devil Ray as Angel Food?

Relaxing at a restaurant table, you sip your drink by candlelight and chat with your companion, appetite slowly building. The waiter brings the menu. With anticipation you begin to scan the seafood entrees: Broiled ratfish. Fried grunt. Poached mudblower with parsley sauce.

Ratfish? Mudblower? How disgusting. Maybe you don't want seafood after all. What else have they got?

This is the kind of reaction that frustrates the National Marine Fisheries Service. If only people knew. If only they realized how great ratfish tastes. If only they would try ratfish. If only ratfish had a different name.

Why yes, a different name. Butterfly fish, perhaps. Or sunshine fish. Honey fish.

The National Marine Fisheries Service is renaming fish. It has launched an ambitious program, involving more than 50 persons so far, to solve a problem acutely exasperating to those who manage our marine resources: While familiar kinds of food fish dwindle in population, dozens of delicious and nutritious species contentedly swim and jump, increase and multiply, protected by repugnant names. Living is easy when your name is toadfish.

The Fisheries Service has not, however, simply replaced the offending names. Rather, as a bureaucratic agency in good standing, it began some years ago to study the problem. Soon it discovered complexities. The red-ear fish, for instance, is called the stumpknocker and the roach. Moreover, new fish names might be unfair: How would a viperfish fisherman feel if lizardfish, which his competitor fishes for, got a prettier name?

In any case, is it certain that people want the names changed?

It is always possible that they have come to like names like croaker, hogsucker and hunchback scorpionfish.

So, late in 1973, the agency filed a public notice, asking the eating public for comment. Five hundred eaters responded. The Fisheries Service tallied the responses and reached a bureaucratic conclusion: "A need exists for the clarification and refinement of policies and procedures that govern the nomenclature of fish and fishery products for purposes of marketing and labeling of these products."

Now fish could get new names, right? Well, not yet. The Fisheries Service wasn't exactly sure how to go about solving the problem. Therefore, says one of its officials, James Brooker, "We decided to engage some expertise to make a proposal of how we could go about solving the problem."

A feasibility study was decided upon. Bids were sought. In 1974, the Fisheries Service awarded a $63,000 contract to a Chicago consulting company called Brand Group Inc. to study feasibility.

Brand Group found it feasible to rename fish. The company did not, however, actually rename any. First, it said, an "organizational framework" was needed. To obtain that, the Fisheries Service engaged Brand Group to do a second study. This study would develop a "prototype model identification system." Its goal: "to identify and prioritize a set of factors to be used in comparing and organizing the species."

Brand Group began to develop a prototype model identification system. In the sea, ratfish continued to multiply, uneaten. The prototype model identification system, it must be acknowledged, did not produce any new fish names either. What it did produce was a series of "edibility profiles." Fish were rated, on scales of one to five, for flavor, fattiness, odor, color, flakiness, firmness, coarseness and moistness.

Unfortunately, this did not simplify the renaming of fish. The fish did not fit neatly into edibility groups. In fact, a total of 390,000 different fish edibility profiles were possible.

Again the Fisheries Service asked the nation's fish eaters for advice. But they only complicated matters further. "I would like to know where a fish was caught, and by whom," wrote one citizen. A Florida man said the system should make clear "which of the eight edibility factors indicates whether ratfish tastes similar to tuna."

The agency vigorously rejected a third correspondent's advice: "About fish—leave it alone."

Frustrated, the Fisheries Service decided to call in the Army. It turned to the U.S. Army food research laboratory in Natick, Mass. The Army was not asked to suggest new fish names, however. Instead, it was told "to develop objective methods of measuring edibility and to determine the validity of the proposed eight edibility factors."

The Army, its mission assigned, referred the matter to a "flavor panel" and a "texture panel." It hasn't published any conclusions so far. When last checked, employees of the Army food research laboratory were eating fish.

To be on the safe side, the Fisheries Service asked Brand Group Inc. to do a third study. This one aims to produce a "uniform nomenclature" for fish forms, such as fillets, and fish modifiers, such as mustard sauce.

As for the Fisheries Service itself, it remains as concerned as ever about the sorry names some fish have. The service has so far spent seven years and $494,000 trying to find new names for them. It hasn't found any yet, but it is confident that it will.

Hogsuckers aside, many are pleased with this prospect. "The industry is enthusiastic," says Steven Pokress, head of the unit of General Host Corp. that markets frozen fish. "It will open up the market to a lot of species that have been ignored because their names are a turn-off."

However, there is one last bureaucratic hurdle the National Marine Fisheries Service must leap before it can bestow mouth-watering names on the lizardfish, the roach, the grunt and the croaker: The Food and Drug Administration says it alone is in charge of the names of fish.

—GAY SANDS MILLER, May 1980

38. A Wail of a Tale

Dan Jacobson's fish struck with fury and fought so gamely that it had to be nursed back to consciousness before being released into Canada's Lac Seul.

In retrospect, the fish had it easy.

For Mr. Jacobson, a Florida lawyer, last summer's catch of a lifetime has led to a cantankerous year-long fight with strangers determined to toss him out of fishing record books. Not that Mr. Jacobson asked to be put in the books in the first place; or that he tried to pass off a fish story. On the contrary, even his detractors admit Mr. Jacobson has done nothing but tell the truth and provide nine witnesses—and a videotape—attesting to his feat.

His problem? He caught a muskellunge—an astonishingly big muskellunge. Muskies, as they are called, are among the largest, fiercest and most prized of freshwater game fishes, and fishing for them isn't so much sport as religion. Among truly zealous muskie anglers, it isn't uncommon to spend a lifetime trying to catch a trophy fish.

The 38-year-old Mr. Jacobson, while a seasoned fisherman, is a muskie neophyte who caught his fish—63 inches long by his measurement—without a life of muskie toil. And in his version of events, veteran muskie zealots, largely out of jealousy, have since conspired through dubious investigations and technicalities to discredit his catch. Along the way, he says, they have impugned his integrity, not to mention his math skills. "I know that catching a muskie is a big deal," he says. "But these guys are fanatics."

The muskie folk are of a different school of thought. After first certifying Mr. Jacobson's fish as the world "catch and release" record for the National Fresh Water Fishing Hall of Fame, they simply did follow-up investigations, says John Dettloff, a muskie guide and historian. Based largely on interpretation of Mr. Jacobson's videotape, they have concluded that his fish probably wasn't more than 59 inches long. Furthermore—given that 59 inches would still better the world catch-and-release record by two inches—they have also decided that Mr. Jacobson mishandled the landing of his fish. Thus, on a technicality, his catch can't be any more than a footnote in muskie history.

This smells as foul as three-day-old carp to Mr. Jacobson and his supporters.

Says Mr. Dettloff, who has made something of a career of debunking muskie records he considers suspicious: "It may sound like you're splitting hairs or getting nit-picky, but a world record goes by accurate measurement."

None of this was on Mr. Jacobson's mind last August 17 when, on his yearly two-week fishing trip, he cast a chartreuse Swim Whizz lure into the shallow waters of Lac Seul in western Ontario. The day was fading; the lure plopped near a rock. Suddenly, the water exploded. "This muskie comes up and whacks this lure," recalls Marc Gordin, Mr. Jacobson's fishing partner. "Its gills flared; its mouth was tremendous." The pair carried a video camera; Mr. Gordin began taping the fight.

By the time Mr. Jacobson hoisted the monster out of the water, eight other companions who were fishing the lake had motored up to watch. The videotape later would show a giddy Mr. Jacobson raising his arms and saying, "Thank you. Thank you. You all may pay homage." It would also show Mr. Gordin holding the rod as Mr. Jacobson hastily measured the fish so he could release it. (As a conservation measure, Lac Seul is designated a strictly catch-and-release lake.)

Only after Mr. Jacobson got back to his fishing camp did he learn that his measurement of 63 inches was six inches greater than the muskie catch-and-release record. (The record for a kept fish, given by weight, is 69 pounds, 11 ounces; the fish measured 63½ inches long.) In no time, the informal muskie network—devoted fishermen, guides and historians—was electrified by news of a Florida novice catching a monster fish on flimsy 12-pound-test line.

Before long, the National Fresh Water Fishing Hall of Fame, in Hayward, Wis., got in touch with Mr. Jacobson and proclaimed him the owner of the world's record for catch-and-release muskie.

His euphoria evaporated quickly, however. He had freely provided his video to Mr. Dettloff, operator of a Wisconsin fishing camp, and copies began circulating among muskie purists. Mr. Dettloff did more than look at the video. He interviewed Mr. Jacobson by telephone. He studied the pictures of the muskie, comparing its length to Mr. Jacobson's height and to the length of the 7.875-inch lure used to catch it. His conclusion: Mr. Jacobson had mismeasured.

Mr. Dettloff is no stranger to this sort of investigation. He has done research, based on old photographs and anecdotal evidence, that persuaded the Hall of Fame to kick out of its books a trophy muskie caught by Art Lawton, a legendary New York fisherman in the 1950s and 1960s. Not everyone thinks Mr. Dettloff is doing the world a favor; Mr. Lawton's aging nephew is currently conducting a counter-investigation hoping to clear his late uncle's name.

Mr. Dettloff's friend Larry Ramsell, the Hall of Fame's fish historian and creator of its records program, reached a similar conclusion after his own study. Around Thanksgiving, Mr. Jacobson received a letter from Mr. Dettloff spelling out the two historians' verdict. They estimated his fish was only 56 to 59 inches long.

"I'm sure you couldn't have foreseen this predicament coming, but now you have one," Mr. Dettloff wrote. "Much of the muskie world now knows about your fish and most true muskie addicts know that your fish is much smaller than reported." He also warned: "Left uncorrected, your fish will remain tainted and uninformed gossips will spin accusations that your fish was somehow faked or exaggerated, painting you as less than honest." The recommendation: that Mr. Jacobson write the Hall of Fame and voluntarily relinquish his record.

When Mr. Jacobson declined—noting that he had nine witnesses to his catch—the Hall of Fame itself formally requested he withdraw the fish. "I'm sure it will enhance your credibility with the muskie anglers," wrote Ted Dzialo, the hall's executive director. "You come out looking like one of the 'good guys.' "

But Mr. Dzialo cited a different reason for disqualification: When the Hall of Fame viewed the videotape, it found that Mr. Gordin held the rod too long, breaking a rule that says a record fish must be landed without help.

"Mr. Dzialo, I already am one of the good guys," Mr. Jacobson fired back. And as for handing the rod to Mr. Gordin, he did this only after the fish had been brought to the side of the boat, he noted.

At this point, Mr. Jacobson's fishing buddies filed friend-of-the-fisherman briefs to the Hall of Fame. Joshua Feldman wrote from Lyndhurst, Ohio, that Mr. Jacobson wasn't one to tell fish tales. "The fish was about 63 inches when he caught it and it has not grown any since."

The Hall of Fame was unmoved, and in May wrote Mr. Jacobson that his record had been thrown out. "Wish you the best in your fishing," Mr. Dzialo added.

Mr. Jacobson's buddies want him to sue, but he thinks he would rather fish than fight. Still, he finds it ironic that, had he not provided the videotape, his record probably couldn't have been challenged—a fact that Mr. Dzialo readily admits. The whole affair "has been very irksome to me," says Mr. Jacobson. "I never really realized what I was getting into."

This very week, Mr. Jacobson is back fishing at Lac Seul. He says if he hooks a giant muskie, don't look for a videotape.

—ROBERT L. ROSE, August 1994

39. A Biting Reappraisal of Sharks

Memo to: Divers.

Subject: Surface People/Humongous Marine Predator Interface.

That sharks could be anything but unpredictable, marauding man-eaters was inconceivable to most Surface People 11 years ago when a story appeared on the front page of this newspaper defending them as much-maligned victims of media hype. Surface People (nondivers) saw it as a cruel joke. They deluged its author (me) with clipped reports of shark attacks (about 50 occur worldwide annually) and notes saying, "Guess the shark forgot to read your article."

While scuba divers had been peaceably interacting with sharks for decades, most Surface People still thought that the only good shark was a dead shark. And underwater filmmakers, as if to prove their point, offered up docu-babble of faux-macho divers fending off sharks with spearguns or blowing them up with bullet-tipped bang sticks.

These filmmakers knew the truth: that most of sharkdom's 350-odd species were harmless and that supposedly aggressive sharks generally eschewed divers and cameras unless they were lured in with food—speared fish, chum, a tuna carcass. But the truth didn't sell to Surface People. Evil sold, no matter that shark bites along American coastlines number only two or three a year. So NBC gave us sharks as "Death Machines" and Hollywood churned out *Jaws* sequels. Surface People loved it.

Evil sold everything except scuba-diving lessons. *Skin Diver* magazine kept sharks in the closet, virtually never mentioning or picturing them for fear of scaring off would-be scuba-diving readers. While experienced divers felt lucky to see a shark while diving, beginning divers white-knuckled their way along drop-offs, scanning the blue horizon for sharks. A sighting in the distance would send them swimming feverishly for coral holes.

How things have changed—except, of course, at this newspaper, where a headline-writing Surface Person in June came up with this canard: "Diving With Sharks Gets Even Scarier."

Gimme a break! Today, sharks are a major marketing tool for the booming recreational diving industry. Even novice divers pay extra to see them.

Skin Diver magazine prints loads of shark photos every month (the September issue has 18) in articles and ads. Last year, it had an unprecedented three cover sharks, beginning with a toothy six-foot gray reef shark in January over the headline: "SHARK DIVE! 30 Minutes of High-Voltage Action, The Ultimate Bahamas Adventure."

Advertisers, recovered from their jaws-ophobia, now use sharks to hawk scuba gear. Dive resorts and travel agencies not only tout them, they promise sharks, even guarantee them. *Skin Diver*'s June issue has 17 ads from dive resorts and charter boats using sharks as bait to lure divers.

"Sharks! Dozens of 'Em," says the Underwater Explorers Society, a dive operator on Grand Bahama Island. "World's Best Shark Dives," says an ad for Neal Watson's Undersea Adventures at Walker's Cay in the Bahamas. "Tiger, Bull, Gray Reef, Hammerhead and Lemon sharks swirl before you as they feed." Neco Marine and Sam's Dive Tours in Palau tout "guaranteed sharks" at a spot called the Blue Corner. "We can make your wildest diving dreams come true, face to face with schooling hammerheads, sea lions, whale sharks . . ." boasts the Aggressor Fleet, a firm operating live-aboard dive boats around the world.

In his spring newsletter, Chris Newbert, an underwater photographer who runs Rainbowed Sea Tours, Inc., touts Galapagos diving with descriptions like this: "Living up to my hopes, on the very first dive we were virtually deluged with hammerheads! They were making the closest imaginable passes. They came in three sizes, big, very big, and holy sh——!" Only $4,850 for two weeks, plus airfare.

On exotic dive trips arranged by See & Sea Travel Service, Inc., of San Francisco, sighting sharks in their natural settings has been an expected routine for 20 years. Owner Carl Roessler quietly started bringing sport divers to Rodney Fox's cages off South Australia to see and photograph great white sharks ("white fluffies," he calls them) in 1976, but kept it in the serious-diver family.

In the last five years, at least eight resorts in the Bahamas have begun offering "shark encounter" dives, in which dive guides (sometimes wearing steel-mesh suits, which do more to hype the danger than to protect the diver) take down squid or frozen fish to lure in sharks, then hand-feed them while diving customers ogle and photograph from nearby.

Critics say these popular dives have become underwater circuses that may eventually create the same kinds of problems caused by feeding the bears in Yellowstone Park. Proponents argue that these encounters and other shark dives have done wonders to rehabilitate the image of sharks and, thus, build a constituency for saving them from relentless slaughter by Surface People—commercial and sport fishermen and their customers.

Steve Blount, editor of Rodale's *Scuba Diving* magazine, pokes fun at these and other "guaranteed animal encounters," writing: "You got your stingrays in Cayman, you got your sharks in Nassau, you got dolphins and sharks in Freeport, you got mantas in Yap, you got morays in Key Largo, you got whale sharks in Perth, you got hammerheads in Cocos, and in the Turks & Caicos you got humpback whales plus JoJo the dolphin. Is it just me or is this starting to sound like the menu at a Japanese restaurant?"

That's just the point: These encounters may not be natural, but at least divers aren't killing these animals. Surface People are—by the millions every year. Asian poachers catch sharks live, slit off their valuable fins, and throw them back to die. Having practically wiped out billfish and tuna populations, fishermen turned in the 1980s to sharks for food and sport. Much commercial fishery today is undisguised ocean looting. So-called sport fishing in the oceans is a different story. Theirs is a fake contest. It takes a brain addled by testosterone deprivation to fall for the money-hungry charter-fishing industry's fantasy of a brave "Old Man and the Sea" struggle, a fair fight between man and fish. With today's techno-gear, the fish doesn't have a chance. If Hemingway were around today, he'd be a diver.

—JAMES P. STERBA, August 1994

40. *If Guppies Rise Up, You'll Know Why*

As pets, fish lead a dog's life—or wish they did.

They seldom inspire real affection and are frequently abandoned. At Iowa State University, for example, students who tire of their pet fish dump them into a fountain near the student union. A groundskeeper, in turn, removes them and, depending on their condition, flings them into a nearby lake or a dumpster.

Not all fish take this lying down. When the groundskeeper was cleaning out the fountain a few years ago, a fish chomped a chunk out of one of his fingers. It was a piranha, and it was hungry. The university flushed it down the toilet.

"Somewhere in the Ames water system," says a university spokesman, "there may be a giant piranha."

Numerically, at any rate, fish are the most popular pet, according to the Humane Society of the U.S. There are 340 million to 500 million tropical fish in the country, compared with about 100 million pet dogs and cats combined. Pet-store sales of fish totaled $219.7 million in 1985. Aquarium sales are up sharply from the early 1980s, thanks partly to a 1983 University of Pennsylvania study indicating that aquarium viewing reduces blood pressure.

But the way fish are treated—or not treated—makes them something more like organic ornaments than pets. Dogs and cats are members of the family; fish are luxuries or hobbies. If fish have feelings, they are probably hurt.

"I don't really consider fish pets," says Patricia Curtis, an animal-book author. "They're somewhere in between pets and plants. You can't hold them or walk them."

You can't read much about them, either. The Humane Society gets more than 800 animal periodicals, including *Dog Fancy, Cat Fancy, Bird Talk* and *Horse Illustrated*. Guy Hodge, the society's director of data and information, says he has never seen one for fish. Then, thumbing through a 300-page pet-industry directory, he finds three. "Until this moment," he says, "we didn't know any existed."

Few people seem to care much about fish health. Dr. Michael Fox, whose pet-advice column runs in 200 newspapers, says that less than 0.5% of the letters he gets are about fish.

Pet-fish doctors can swap tales with the Maytag repairman. Boston's Angell Memorial Animal Hospital sees 45,000 pets a year, everything from rabbits and dogs to birds, snakes and rats. It treated a hamster once for a stomach disorder. But Dr. Gus Thornton, the chief of staff, can't remember treating a single fish.

At the Animal Medical Center in New York, Susan Cohen, who counsels grieving pet owners, has helped people with sick horses, ducks, tortoises, canaries, ferrets, lizards, leopards and fire-bellied toads. "I went through a long thing with a guy who lost both his lovebirds in a matter of weeks," she says. "But no fish."

If fish owners cared enough to ask, they would find they can't get fish insurance. In Santa Ana, Calif., Veterinary Pet Insurance Co.—the company that once paid a claim on a dog's pacemaker—

has policies for 80,000 cats, dogs, horses, cattle, cows and birds. There is even llama insurance, but none for fish. Says Dr. Jack Stephens, the company's president: "It's always been easier and cheaper to throw fish out than to try to treat them."

Alternatives exist. The Sea Breeze Pet Cemetery in Huntington Beach, Calif., has buried a number of fish. The number is three. Dogs, cats, mice and birds fill the other 29,997 plots. Steven Stiles, the cemetery's assistant manager, doesn't want to discourage fish owners, though. "Whatever they want to bury, we'll take," he says.

Fish are more likely to die prematurely than other pets, veterinarians say, because they are fragile creatures living in a delicate environment. When fish cash in their chips, it is often because they are overcrowded or overfed.

Except for dying so easily, fish haven't done much to deserve such shabby status. But they also haven't done much to deserve attention. "When you walk in the house, they don't bark or lick your face," says Susie Rosenzveig, who has a couple of tanks of fish in her apartment in Farmington Hills, Mich. "I don't think they see my face and say: 'Oh, Susie's here!' " She and her husband would love to have a puppy, but apartment rules won't allow it.

It isn't at all clear that fish care how they are treated. A spokesman for the American Association of Ichthyologists and Herpetologists says no one knows for certain what fish can feel, if anything.

For people who don't want to spend much time caring for their fish, firms like Tank Goodness Inc. in Northbrook, Ill., are springing up to do everything but feed them. The company, which sets up, maintains and moves fish tanks, will clean aquariums for a monthly fee of $30 to $200.

If that is still too much hassle, there is Video Aquarium, a cassette that turns the television screen into an electronic fishbowl. "No fish to feed. No tank to clean," reads the box. One young man plays the tape to Beatles music at parties and puts a "Don't Feed the Fish" sign on his TV set, says Video Naturals Co., which makes the film.

Fish aren't cooperative actors. When a school of minnows bunched up out of the camera's view, Steven Siporin, the movie's producer, had to splash some water until they swam back into the picture. And, while filming, he couldn't find a big red fish—one of the movie's star fish—that had been cast for its bright color. Later he learned that it had hidden behind some coral to avoid the spotlights. Says Mr. Siporin, who owns Video Naturals, "I spent 25 bucks for that thing and it was light-sensitive."

—MICHAEL J. McCARTHY, October 1986

41. Getting With the Drill

WEST RUSH LAKE, Minn.—The ice was nearly two feet thick, but fisherman Dave Genz cut through it in about 15 seconds with his gasoline-powered drill.

He spent another 30 seconds setting up his canvas hut. Then he dropped his electronic depth finder down the seven-inch-wide hole, followed by a fishing line. After 15 minutes without a bite, he dragged his gear five feet away and drilled another hole.

"If you move, you'll stay warm," said Mr. Genz, dressed head-to-toe in Gore-Tex to fight the five-degree air temperature and 20-below wind chill. "And you'll catch more fish."

Most ice fishermen stay in the same place all day—or even all winter—sitting, drinking and playing cards. If they catch fish, so much the better. But Mr. Genz has no patience for that. Instead of waiting for fish to come to them, he thinks anglers should go after fish, no matter how many holes they leave drilled in the ice.

His approach has transformed the sport and turned Mr. Genz into a celebrity among buffs. It has also made him the object of scorn among traditionalists.

"They turn the ice into Swiss cheese," says 35-year-old Larry Johnson, an ice fisherman from Fridley, Minn., whose ice house has a wood floor and a space heater. He and his friends from high-school days have fished the same spot on Fish Lake for the past 18 years. "I know people who have sprained their ankles walking around all those ice holes. And the noise is really irritating."

Mr. Genz says every revolutionary has met with resistance. "Once they see I catch more fish," he says, "they start paying attention."

Mr. Genz, 55, was working as a maintenance engineer in Minneapolis when he launched his crusade 23 years ago. He had always loved the sport and was frustrated that men and women who fished through ice didn't realize how similar it could be to open-water fishing. Ice anglers, he believed, should move around a frozen lake just as readily as they would in the summer in boats, casting lines here and there. He found they were also reluctant to accept some of the technological innovations—including recent advances such as underwater cameras and location finders using global positioning satellites—that they were already using on boats.

In 1980, his wife, Patsy, helped him build a portable canvas ice house. While others were cozy in huts that have increasingly come to resemble double-wide trailers, Mr. Genz moved around like a heavily dressed nomad, his gear in tow. On his 40th birthday, he realized he wanted a career he would never want to retire from, so he quit his maintenance job to take up ice fishing full time. He began traveling almost constantly during the ice-fishing season, from North Dakota to New York, appearing at sports shows and fishing seminars, sharing his gospel on how the sport should evolve into something requiring more action.

Last winter, more than 1,000 people competed in five ice-fishing tournaments—referred to as "Trap Attacks"—organized by Mr. Genz and his partner, Dennis Clark. Nearly all the participants—and every one of the winners—used Mr. Genz's mobile and high-tech approach.

The contests served as qualifying rounds for the first North American Ice Fishing Championship in Alexandria, Minn., in December. Only anglers who placed in the top 10 of each Trap Attack were eligible to compete. The winning team won $10,000 and a Super Bowl–style ring.

"I wear that ring 24-7," says Jeffery Wright of Brooklyn, Mich., who won the championship with his brother Ben. They drilled holes nonstop for four days before the contest until they found the lake's hot spot, which paid off on the big day. Scoping out a lake in the days before a tournament, called prefishing, is a widely practiced though highly secretive strategy among fishing competitors. "It was definitely a dream come true. It would be for anyone who loves this sport," says Mr. Wright.

Mr. Genz's followers can be found now on frozen lakes all over the country. Brainerd, Minn., is home to the world's largest ice-fishing derby, held every year on Gull Lake. More than 12,000 anglers competed this year. Unlike Mr. Genz's Trap Attacks, where competitors drill their own holes, the Brainerd contest requires participants to fish in holes already drilled. It was never a problem—until followers of Mr. Genz's methods began insisting on moving around the ice. This year, the Jaycees of Brainerd, Minn., who organize the tournament, had to drill 20,000 holes.

Mr. Genz figured ice anglers would try his methods as long as they didn't have to sacrifice too much comfort. So he started promoting the canvas ice hut his wife had sewn. They began calling them "Fish Traps," and selling them for $169 each. The first year they sold five of them, the next year 80. To keep up with the growing demand, the Genzes outsourced the sewing to a local tent and awning maker, and enlisted their two daughters to help assemble the tents in a workshop they added on to their garage.

In 1991, he licensed the Fish Trap to a Minneapolis company, USL Outdoor Products Inc., which already had a similar portable fish house called the Clam that his partner, Mr. Clark, had invented. USL says it sold 20,000 fish houses last year, with $4.5 million in sales. The selling boom prompted Mr. Clark to buy the ice-house division last month for an undisclosed amount. Mr. Genz continues to get a percentage of sales but won't disclose figures.

Nationwide, sales of high-tech ice-fishing equipment are rising. Jeff Bergmann, vice president of marketing for Gander Mountain, a retail chain based in Bloomington, Minn., says sales of ice-fishing equipment rose 80% during the fiscal year that ended January 3.

Scott Peterson, president of Peterson Outdoors, an online ice-fishing-equipment retailer, says his sales have grown 30% each year for the past five years. "Almost every single aspect of the sport is changing and going high tech," he says.

For Mr. Genz, such momentum means a lot of product-endorsement opportunities. He won't disclose his income, but he has plenty of sponsors, including Vexilar electronic depth finders, StrikeMaster augers and Aqua-Vu underwater cameras. Mr. Genz has a series of Berkley ice-fishing rods named after him, and he helps design ice-fishing tackle for Lindy-Little Joe Inc., including a lure called the Genz Worm. Maggots are his preferred bait, bluegills are his favorite catch.

He has written two books and made a CD-ROM and an instructional video. Last August, Mr. Genz was inducted into the Minnesota Fishing Hall of Fame, the only person to win the honor based on achievements in ice fishing.

Still, some fishermen will never be converted.

A canvas ice house in the thick of winter holds little appeal for John Engerholm, 30, a technology consultant and weekend fisherman from Plymouth, Minn. As he fishes, his coat hangs from a hook on the wall of his $4,000, 6½-by-14-foot ice house on Minnesota's Lake Mille Lacs. Despite the howling wind outside, a thermostat-controlled propane heating system keeps the temperature in the ice house at about 72 degrees. Holding a Sierra Mist soda in one hand and his rod in the other, he waits over one of six fishing holes cut through the plush beige-carpeted floor. Bruce Springsteen plays softly from built-in stereo speakers. In the summer, the ice house sits on the lawn beside his lakeside cabin, where he goes to fish when the ice melts.

"I guess it comes down to the difference between leisure and work. I don't want to spend the whole day drilling," he says. "I can sit in here, never catch a fish and still have a great day."

—ELLEN BYRON, March 2003

42. Bugs, Bass and Loons in Moonlight

We're up in Maine and out on North Pond at midnight, Frank Spencer and I, casting for bass in a silent world by the glow of a bright full moon. Our lines whiz with each cast, the lures plop into the water, a loon calls a ghostly owhoooo in the distance, but that's it for big noise.

Izaak Walton, were he suddenly to be reincarnated beside us, would see only luminous water, a dark silhouette of shoreline woods, stars and a yellow moon. There would be nothing to tell him he was not still in the 17th century save our strangely colored lures and the odd craft in which he was floating—our bass boat, with one fishing chair perched in the bow and another in the stern. (Of course, when we cranked the 70-horse Evinrude into life to go ripping to another part of the lake, Mr. Walton might have the fantods.)

That's how it is up here, especially in this glacier-scooped chain known as the Belgrade Lakes, a region that includes Great Pond, the fictional "Golden Pond."

Maine takes you time-traveling, in aspect if not in reality. You can be out on North Pond or East Pond at any time of day and be transported: The wooden camps, one- or two-story lakeside cottages nestled along the shoreline among the tall pines, oaks, maples and birches, each with a little dock jutting into the water, were mostly built between the wars. Overhead, the occasional single-engine Cub or pontoon plane drones by, but you never see or hear jets. Unless some whooping lake cowboy on a jet ski roars past, there isn't a single thing to indicate that this is not, say, 1950.

Back in the boat with Mr. Walton's night shade: Frank (my father-in-law) and I have been waiting three summers for the ideal night-fishing conditions to recur—a full moon, clear sky and no wind. The big bass should be feeding on the surface and therefore attracted to certain lures. We remember the series of small adventures of our previous excursion—bats diving at our lures, bass rising in the moonlight—and anticipate a replay.

Sure enough, Frank's first cast is picked up on chiropteran

radar, and a bat swoops in. On the second cast, two more dive and flutter away. By the third, I observe that the bats, obviously confused, are also cross, for they begin diving at our heads. One flits two inches above Frank's head, but my companion never knows it, he is so busy reeling in his lure. I feel the swish of another past my left ear.

Hot, still nights provide high tea for hungry bats and fish, as swarms of gnats, mosquitoes and dragonflies dance above the lake's surface, beginning at dusk. At that time also, on shore, thousands of tiny spiders emerge to spin and capture their share of the insect feast. Their little webs are everywhere: in the trees and bushes; on the rocks, the dock, the dock lines, the boat, the motor and the instrument panel; on the rods and reels, on the porches, the chairs and the windows; even inside the camp on the lampshades, the bookshelves and the tables, and on any camper who sits still reading for an hour.

Every August seems to have a theme. One year it was exultations of chipmunks larking about the campground, as if we were part of some cute Disney nature flick. Another few Augusts featured rain, cold, fog, mosquitoes and Canada geese. Another year it was a hurricane and no running water for a week. This one, it's spiders.

Well, it figures. Flying insects are especially thick this summer, so there are more spiders to eat them, and, of immediate interest to Frank and me in the boat, more bass surface feeding on delectable bugs.

There's action on Frank's fourth cast. He's using the Jitterbug Lure, a classic of bass fishing going back at least 70 years. It's a small, wooden froglike thing with metal attachments that make it thrash about on the surface and emit little pup-pup sounds in imitation of an especially noisy frog.

I've reeled in and am watching his Jitterbug in action when the fish strikes. It hits with such strength and suddenness that we both jump at the turmoil in the water, so loud in the midnight calm. Frank jerks the rod back smartly, setting the hook, and lets him take off. The line whines through the reel as the fish goes deep, circles, heads west, doubles back and then, magnificently, rises and leaps high and straight up from the water right in the middle of the river of moonlight.

In those few seconds we can tell he's a bass. Then he plunges again and circles the boat. Bass are famous for wrapping lines around props, trolling motors or anchor lines, but Frank, an expert angler, keeps him clear. The fish leaps again, not so high as before, obviously tiring. Finally, Frank reels him in and out of the water, reaching down to grab his lower lip and lift him aboard.

He's a handsome, well fed small-mouth—about four pounds, we guess. Frank puts him in the live well and flips the aerator switch. When we return to the dock we'll weigh him with our other (expected) catches, take a photo, and then release them.

The next night we go out earlier, at 10 o'clock, and though we get fewer fish, and ones smaller than the four-pound beauties of the previous expedition, the night rewards us with uncommon beauty as we head back to camp under an even brighter, more wondrous full moon. Earlier, it was orange as it hung just above the trees; it turned yellow as it rose higher and now is white, sending a wide, glittering river of light across the still water to our boat.

We aim for the tiny point of light in the solid blackness of the eastern shoreline woods that we think is our camp. (I've left lamps burning in the main room.) It's easy to get lost on the lake at night, and we've done it before, despite having selected landmarks such as particular notches in the dark pattern of the tree line in the hills above North Pond.

Muted sounds from onshore camps drift across the water: laughter, music from a radio, a dog barking. It's cooler tonight, and we smell campfire, or possibly chimney smoke, and hear the faint clatter of tin plates and cups. I remember a romantic song from my parents' generation of the 1930s:

Smoke dreams, here by a campfire
Dreaming I see you near me.

We at last find our dock, hitch the lines, stow the rods and release the fish.

Out on the lake, the loons begin calling in that distinctive, maniacal giggling, unique in nature, that fostered the expression "crazy as a loon." What must they be saying to one another? Perhaps it's a love song.

Singing, here by a campfire,
Hoping that you may hear me.

Tackle boxes in hand, we walk up to the camp. As we go in, a breeze lifts from the lake, riffling the leaves of the pines and birches. All is well. Another smoke dream has come true.

—NED CRABB, August 2001

CHAPTER 6

WILD THINGS

―――

43. *Paddling With "Psycho Sam"*

MTONDO CAMP, Zambia—The Zambezi River slides quietly
by, a moving watercolor under a diminishing sun. From a
thatched-roof hut high on the riverbank, seven British and American travelers and their two Zimbabwean river guides sip drinks,
admiring this African postcard. Then a deep grumble comes from
midriver, scattering the silence.

It sounds like a bullfrog on steroids, amplified over a loudspeaker.

It is actually a hippo. Hippos are everywhere here. Hippos by
the dozens.

You know: those pudgy, cute, Porky Pig–like behemoths that lounge, snuggled together in the water, in big groups. Their likeness is a favorite for stuffed toys and cartoons. Scores of children's books feature friendly hippos as the main character. One of them is even called *The Happy Hippo.*

But in the distance now is a real hippo, a three-ton bull. He is not a happy hippo, however. A line of canoeists has swung in too close for his comfort and he has mounted a sand bar, mouth agape, tusks primed, bellowing in rage. The canoes slide by on a five-knot current, narrowly avoiding a confrontation.

From the safety of the hut, guide Murray Chalibamba shakes his head in awe. He has seen this behavior before. "Man, look at that guy! I just love it when they bite the water!" He tosses his head violently, in a jawing, slashing motion, mimicking this early warning sign of a hippo attack.

Mr. Chalibamba's clients have spent a day in canoes paddling down this very same river. With two more days to go, and perhaps hundreds more hippos to dodge, they have a hard time sharing his admiration. Later, Lloyd Shambira, the second of the guides, says somberly: "You do not crowd the hippo. This is an animal you must respect."

If you think the lion or cape buffalo is the most dangerous animal in Africa, think again. Cuddly reputation notwithstanding, it's the hippopotamus, a name that literally means river horse. Though no one tracks exact numbers, hippos by far account for more deaths on this wild continent than any other beast. Ask any guide, game ranger or river-dwelling villager to name Africa's most perilous place and they all name the same spot: "Between a hippo and its route to the water."

Next perhaps is between a hippo mother and her calf. Or in a canoe that foolishly, or inadvertently, floats atop a sleeping hippo.

"The hippo is very territorial and can be quite aggressive when challenged or surprised," says Riley Tolmay, Mtondo Camp's manager and a one-time river guide himself. Mr. Shambira, who has been taking canoe safaris down this stretch of the river for years, puts it more graphically: "A mad hippo can bite a crocodile in two. And a canoe to pieces."

For the skeptical, consider this: A New Zealand canoeist who floated into a submerged sleeping hippo on the river near here last year was rammed from his boat and mauled to death after the animal startled awake, according to river guides familiar with the incident. The year before, just 300 yards from where the Zambezi tumbles into Victoria Falls, an American river guide and his Zimbabwean partner were attacked by a male hippo as they tried to paddle around a female hippo and her calf. The American, in the widely reported incident, lost an arm but miraculously survived after the hippo literally swallowed him to the neck, then spit him out; the Zimbabwean was killed.

Even when a hippo encounter isn't fatal, it leaves an impression. Just ask Scott Wesley and Rob Callaway, two Australian college students who were recently fishing from an 18-foot pontoon boat on the Zambezi's Zambian side. Drifting quietly into a bay, they surprised a male hippo, which hammered their broad, three-quarter-ton craft with such force that it nearly knocked them over a rail. "The power of that thing. Amazing," says an incredulous Mr. Callaway.

Rural Africans, who take the brunt of attacks by the ubiquitous hippo, know that power well; at any remote settlement where hippos and humans coexist, stories of entanglements are common. One told to a visitor not long ago: In a village near South Africa's Kruger National Park, a woman returning home just after dark stumbled onto a hippo that had just moved into a nearby irrigation pond. The animal, caught off guard, made a mad dash for the pond—trampling her to death.

If all this is true, then why would anyone hop into a canoe and wittingly go paddling among them?

"Well, it's a beautiful way to see the river," says John Berry, director of Zambezi Safari & Travel Co. His is among a half-dozen or so Zimbabwe-based outfitters who book popular overnight canoe safaris along this 60-mile, hippo-thick stretch of the Lower Zambezi as it flows between Zimbabwe and Zambia eastward to the sea in Mozambique. Three vast game parks, including Zimbabwe's renowned Mana Pools, line this route; navigating their shores from the tranquility of a canoe often offers spectacularly close encounters with game—elephant and buffalo, particularly—that conventional driving safaris don't. Such animals usually pay little mind to canoes, and even if annoyed won't, without provocation, plunge into the river after them.

Mr. Berry and other outfitters also note that canoeing among hippos, assuming it's done under the watchful eye of an expert guide, is probably less dangerous than some of the other pursuits that tourists undertake in these parts: bungee-jumping 350 feet off the Victoria Falls bridge, for example, or hunting the unpredictable cape buffalo in brushy savanna.

In fact, among the hippo's virtues, and the one that makes these paddling expeditions possible, is that the hippo is usually quite predictable. "Hippos like the deep water. They stake out their territory there and they stay there during the day. That means we stay out of deep water and out of their way."

The speaker is the 20-something Mr. Shambira, a man with an easygoing manner and a sharp eye for river hazards. He's been down this river so many times that he's memorized all the hippo holes, and given names to the big territorial males living in them. The deep-voiced "Pavarotti" draws laughs when he bellows at a distance. Only later does Mr. Shambira reveal less-whimsically named others: "Mad Max" and "Psycho Sam."

And his admonition to avoid hippo contact by staying in shallow water turns out to be easier said than done when, on a cloudless morning, with the river a mirror of calm, he maneuvers his canoe into a slow-moving eddy and instructs the four other canoes in his charge to follow, in a single line, close to the bank.

By day, hippos tend to congregate, in pods of up to 20 animals, near deep midriver pools. They laze about, heads exposed, staying out of the sun that can blister their sensitive skin while keeping an eye out for predators—notably crocodiles and lions that want to eat their young, and humans who sometimes hunt them. It is there that, undisturbed, hippos do indeed often exhibit endearing behavior—grooming each other or snuggling, one hippo resting its head upon another.

They generally only leave the water at night to forage, sometimes roaming miles inland. But "generally" is the problematic word. Hippos do now and then invade the shallows by day, even climbing out on banks to feed; they also stake out territory in deep river pockets just off the river bank. So sticking close to shore isn't a panacea for avoiding contact with them.

This is driven home when, at one sharp bend, several hippos cascade off the bank about 30 yards ahead of Mr. Shambira's canoe. They disappear; then heads pop up—squarely in his path. He barks an order to the other canoes to hug the bank and observe the single-file rule—no use giving hippos a wide target. He then stands, to make himself more visible, rapping the side of his canoe with his paddle.

This is his warning to the hippos: We're here and we're coming through.

A tense minute later, the canoeists float past the point where the hippos submerged. They breathe a collective sigh of relief when the hippos pop up, one at a time, well out in the river. Before the trip is over, there will be at least a half dozen of these adrenaline-filled encounters.

And what if a hippo had attacked? Mr. Shambira shrugs. Guides here are unarmed and the defense is three-prong: shouting, slapping the water with a paddle, then paddling away as fast as possible.

Later, sipping tea on high ground, two of the canoeists, David and Cynthia Onions, a middle-aged British couple who live on a farm, are happy to have made the trip and seem happy, too, to be off the river and out of the hippos' way. "I have to say, well, there were apprehensive moments," says Mrs. Onions. Agrees Mr. Onions: "There was certainly an element of risk. If you didn't have someone with you who knew what they were doing, you could find yourself in trouble quickly."

Mr. Shambira admits that all he thinks about is staying out of trouble. In fact, he confides that he pulled the group off the river about two miles above a stopping point he sometimes uses. Below that is a place he calls "Hippo City," a treacherously narrow meander with one of the highest concentrations of hippos in the world—and little room to avoid them.

"I only take two kinds of people there," he says, only half-jokingly. "The young, and the foolish."

—KEN WELLS, August 1998

44. We'd Guess Punxsutawney Phil Is Next

ROSEBUD, S.D.—From a windswept hilltop, two men study a cluster of prairie-dog holes across the valley. One animal is spotted perching on the cusp of its mound—a twitching sentinel for the rest of the colony. John Parker, an English professor from Nashville, fires a shot and misses. The animal doesn't flinch.

"Give him a quarter-dog of windage," says his friend, James Lappin. What he means is that Mr. Parker should aim slightly into the wind by a distance equal to a quarter of a prairie dog's height. Mr. Parker adjusts his aim almost imperceptibly, and shoots. This time, he hits. "That's sweet," says Mr. Lappin, breaking into a smile.

These men are on a prairie-dog safari. Dozens of people—from Texas to Montana—now lead such expeditions. The hobby has exploded in recent years, fueled by ranchers who detest the burrowing rodents and gun enthusiasts who view this as the ultimate target practice.

"Some guys do this for the macho thing," says Mr. Parker. "But I'm more into the science, the precision of it."

Consider the challenge. Since prairie dogs, which stand about a foot tall, scamper into their holes at the first sight of a human, it isn't unusual to fire on them from distances the length of four football fields or more. When you factor in crosswinds, hitting the critters—which often flit around the edges of their holes—can be a daunting task.

"Anybody can hit a deer at 100 yards when it's standing still," says Scott Elrod, a dentist and avid hunter of many types of game. "But it takes a certain skill to hit something the size of a can of tennis balls."

Not to mention a certain amount of heavy equipment. Rifles that are used to kill prairie dogs often weigh up to 14 pounds and can easily cost $5,000. "Dogtown Varmint Supplies," of Newport Beach, Calif., offers everything from hunting clothes and high-powered rifle scopes to the services of gun technicians who will answer questions by telephone. Another company sells "Roto-Benches," which look like ironing boards on steroids; they are portable shooting-tables that pivot 360 degrees and have a built-in stool and resting place for a rifle.

Fans of the sport call themselves "shooters" rather than hunters, since there is really no need to search for animals. Prairie-dog colonies—or "towns"—are all over the Great Plains, some as big as 1,000 acres. Indian tribes and landowners produce maps to help people find dog towns. Some spots are overrun by shooters, especially in summer.

So in recent years, guides have become popular because they can lead tourists to secluded prairie-dog towns. Safaris tend to last about three days, with shooters staying at motels or local ranches and going to a new dog town each day.

Jerry Geidd, proprietor of South Dakota's "Western Safari," drives people to dog towns in his mud-splattered Chevy Suburban, then sets up a table and lets clients sit there for hours, blasting away. Miles Hutton, who operates a guide service in Turner, Mont., called "Dogbusters," has played host to shooters from as far away as Israel and Sweden. But most of his business, he says, is American, including a couple of police SWAT team members who were "plumb deadly, once they got the hang of it." He charges shooters $160 a day, which is about average.

Raymond and Lisa Velez went out with Mr. Hutton on their honeymoon in May 1993. "We got married on a Saturday, and on Tuesday we were out shooting," recalls Mr. Velez. The couple, from Oxford, Conn., got funny looks from some people when they announced their plans. "We just had to explain to them that the prairie dogs may look like cuddly little animals, but they also compete with sheep and cattle for grass and carry the plague," he says. "Shooting them is really doing something good for the environment."

That is hotly disputed. While the animals can carry disease, many biologists believe they are also crucial to the natural order of life on the prairie. Black-footed ferrets, for instance, can live only in conjunction with prairie dogs, which are their staple diet.

Shooting them as sport is "pretty macabre," says David Crawford, codirector of Rocky Mountain Animal Defense, of Boulder, Colo., which often tries to disrupt organized prairie-dog hunts. "Whenever you're killing simply to kill—with no utility whatsoever—it's wrong."

Such arguments carry little weight with the prairie-dog crowd, which is part of a niche in the gun scene called "varminters." A varmint is any animal viewed as a pest and, therefore, fair game. Ranchers complain that prairie dogs devour grass their livestock could be eating, that cows and horses sometimes trip in prairie-dog holes, and that farm equipment can get damaged going over the mounds. Shooters note that far more prairie dogs are killed every year by ranchers' poisoning programs than by bullets.

Other frequently hunted varmints include ground squirrels, coyotes and crows, but the prairie dog seems to be the most-prized prey. The logo of the Varmint Hunters Association—a Pierre, S.D., group that claims more than 30,000 members—features a prairie dog. The most recent issue of the group's glossy magazine carries an article titled "A North Carolina Hunter Goes Prairie Dog Hunting," as well as an ad for Nosler Inc.'s bullets, showing a pair of prairie dogs under the slogan: "Betcha Can't Shoot Just One."

There is a subtle split within the ranks of prairie-dog shooters—between those who emphasize the precision side of the sport and those who focus on firing as many bullets as possible. "The rule, rather than the exception, is that guys want to see the dogs blown to smithereens," says Mr. Hutton, the Montana guide. The terminology among shooters reflects that. A "chamois shot" is when the shooter sees a hide flying through the air, while "red mist" is self-explanatory.

"I'm not into the killing part of it at all," counters 26-year-old Ruth Elrod, an enthusiastic shooter who was introduced to the sport three years ago by her husband, the dentist. "Once I tried it, he couldn't get the gun out of my hand," she says. Yet she refuses to even look at the animals after she has killed them. "That's gross," she says.

Ned Kalbfleish, executive editor of the magazine *Varmint Hunter,* concedes that part of the appeal of prairie-dog shooting is the sheer number of animals that can be killed in a day. But, he says, the "social aspects" of the sport are another big draw. "People can talk to each other and sit in lawn chairs under an umbrella," he says. "And for a lot of guys, this is the only type of shooting they do with their wives and girlfriends."

Today, Mr. Kalbfleish scans the horizon with binoculars for potential targets, while his wife, Christi Heller, reels off what she likes about the sport: She loves to shoot, she says, the more the better. And on nice days, she can work on her tan. "Plus," she adds, "I get to be with a man—doing what he likes to do and I like to do, which is pretty rare these days."

—TIMOTHY AEPPEL, August 1995

45. Not Only That: Rudolph
Sells Crack!

BELLE FOURCHE, S.D.—A long career in law enforcement failed to prepare Capt. Larry Roberdeau for what he encountered outside a mobile home here one morning in September.

"I never saw anything like this," he says. "I came on the scene and there was a reindeer trying to kill Santa."

The man known here as Santa survived unscathed. His reindeer didn't, though. And neither did the popular Christmas image of reindeer cheerfully carrying Santa Claus in his sleigh. Here in Belle Fourche, the reigning image is that of a reindeer furiously stomping around with Santa caught up in its antlers.

The Santa in question is James Emery, 40 years old. He owns a backhoe business that digs ditches for septic tanks and such. But he is better known in Belle Fourche (pronounced foosh) for his hobby. Ever since he graduated from high school here in 1975, he has played Santa, and not just at Christmas. This year, he won "Best Float" in the Belle Fourche Fourth of July parade for an entry called "Santa on Vacation."

Mr. Emery takes the role of Santa so seriously that much of the year he bleaches white his long red hair and beard. Just last week, he spent $160 getting his hair done at the Mane Attraction beauty parlor in nearby Spearfish. That was to prepare for today, his first official appearance of the season. He stands six feet tall, weighs 370 pounds and has the gregarious nature of St. Nick. "He's Santa to everybody in town," resident Terry Arpan says.

Two years ago, Mr. Emery took his act a step further and, for $6,500, bought three reindeer. Last Christmas, he parked them in a corral outside the empty storefront on Main Street he used as

Santa's headquarters, attracting lots of shoppers downtown. This was a blessing for local shops, many of which are struggling. Mr. Emery didn't charge anyone a cent. "Jim touches on one of the true meanings of Christmas, which is about giving your time to people," says Bill Davis, a town councilor.

"There were kids he restored the belief in Santa in," adds Verlyn Hespe, whose wife's jewelry store benefited from the crowds.

Nobody foresaw any reindeer hostilities. His largest beast, a 550-pound bull, was so shy that Mr. Emery's ex-wife named him Casper, after the Friendly Ghost. During last summer's Fourth of July parade, Casper rode calmly atop Mr. Emery's float. "Tame as a kitten," Mr. Emery says.

But in early September, Mr. Emery introduced two year-old females to the reindeer herd he keeps in the pasture beside his mobile home. It was mating season, and it didn't occur to him that love would drive Casper mad. As Mr. Emery entered the pasture to put grain in the trough at 6:30 one morning, the big bull snorted and attacked. Casper, Mr. Emery now theorizes, feared "I was going to take his two women."

To avoid impalement, Mr. Emery grabbed hold of Casper's four-foot-high, 31-point rack of antlers. The animal lifted his head and for 45 minutes marched around with the big man in his antlers. Then Casper lowered his head and pinned Mr. Emery to the ground.

Eventually, Debbie Johnson stepped out of the mobile home next door to get her son's shoes. "I heard Jim yell: 'Help! Can anybody hear me?' " she recalls. She ran down for a closer look, saw what was happening and went into Mr. Emery's place to call 911.

Capt. Roberdeau was first to arrive. Thinking Mr. Emery was being gored, he got ready to shoot Casper. Mr. Emery said, "No. That would be a $10,000 bullet."

Capt. Roberdeau grabbed Casper's antlers, but the animal didn't budge. Next to arrive was Rocky Millis, Butte County deputy sheriff, who grabbed hold too. "I never realized reindeer were that strong," he says.

Even after two more men arrived, Casper could not be pulled off Mr. Emery. The beast began dragging him and his four would-be rescuers toward a water hole. Mr. Emery told Capt. Roberdeau to go ahead and shoot if Casper pulled them into the water.

Just then, local rancher Merlin Porterfield showed up and could hardly believe that Mr. Emery was unhurt. The antlers pinning him to the ground gave him the appearance of "one of those guys they stick in a box and put swords through," Mr. Porterfield recalls.

Mr. Porterfield lassoed Casper's hind legs and pulled him down, allowing Mr. Emery to escape essentially uninjured.

Casper, however, had had enough. He gasped and fell dead on the spot. "He had a heart attack," Capt. Roberdeau says.

The battle with the bull made news as far away as Rapid City, about 70 miles southeast of Belle Fourche. "Bell Fourche man rescued from love-struck reindeer," ran the headline in the *Rapid City Journal*.

But the publicity hasn't diminished demand for Santa and his reindeer. Mr. Emery will make as many local appearances as ever this holiday season with his remaining reindeer, which now include two young ones fathered by Casper. Mr. Emery aspires to the big time; he wants someday to be in the Rose Parade in Pasadena, Calif.

Here in Belle Fourche, however, the Casper story has assumed mythic proportions, and townsfolk rib Mr. Emery wherever he goes.

"Hey Santa, like the way you ride those reindeer," says Cleve Schmidt as he saunters into the Circle Lounge. Mr. Schmidt is a rodeo star who ranks ninth nationally for riding broncos bareback.

"At least I can last more than eight seconds," Mr. Emery shoots back as he drinks a rum and Diet Coke.

Jokes aren't all that have been made of Casper. Last Saturday, a gathering at the home of Mr. Emery's parents found his father, Chuck, at the stove.

"It's not bad, Chuck," said Mr. Emery's mother, Leota, as she bit into a piece of fried Casper. "But I would rather have beef."

—ROBERT BERNER, November 1997

46. Feral TV

On a recent prime-time TV program, the camera caught four young females chasing an older victim in their neighborhood in broad daylight. One jumped on his back while the others grabbed his legs and slashed him to death.

Members of Congress who decry TV violence may be complaining about the wrong species. Forget cops and robbers: The real mayhem, as in the scene above, is all about lions and water buffalo. Also hyenas and wildebeests, killer whales and sea lion pups, and a bestiary of other feral stars of unabashedly blood-soaked nature documentaries. Viewers are zeroing in on the shows like cheetahs to a gazelle carcass.

The Discovery Channel's top-rated series is *Fangs,* a new hour-long bloodbath featuring carnivores stalking, killing and devouring. Recent episodes: "Wolf—The Spanish Outlaw," a shark-fest called "Teeth of Death" and "Hyenas—Nature's Gangsters." In the world of home video, Time-Life is setting a sales record with its *Trials of Life* series, which the Time Warner Inc. unit promotes in TV ads featuring a shark munching on a large brown gull. "See why we call them animals!" thunders the voiceover, as "UNCENSORED" flashes on the screen. "Violent footage shows you the life-and-death struggle to survive in a tough and brutal world!"

Even grand old *National Geographic,* known for its distinguished public-TV nature shows, is wading in gore with such high-body-count fare as *Shark Attack,* featuring assaults on humans and vicious mating scenes among nurse sharks.

All this is a long way from Mutual of Omaha's *Wild Kingdom,* the 1960s nature series hosted by affable, white-haired Marlin Perkins, with such episodes as "Bear Cubs in Painted Canyon." Today, notes Clark Bunting, an executive of Discovery Networks-USA, "There's a saying in this business: The bigger the teeth, the better the ratings." *Fangs* is such a hit that Discovery is ordering up a gusher of bloody shows about carnivorous Komodo dragons, Australian saltwater crocodiles and "Animal Cannibals." "Large, dangerous megavertebrates have been good to us," Mr. Bunting says. Some viewers, he adds, "have seen more cheetah kills than most cheetahs."

Only recently have nature shows begun looking like Quentin Tarantino movies. The filmmakers had always captured stark footage of beasts devouring one another, but slow film and old-fashioned equipment made shots of long chases and nighttime scenes almost unusable. "I've spent my entire life watching animals doing rather mean things to each other," says David Hughes, an award-winning producer of *National Geographic* films. "I was resentful about not being able to show it all."

Then filmmaking technology and techniques improved—and, more to the point, audiences developed a bigger appetite for slaughter. Time-Life began rolling out its *Trials of Life* series, beginning with "Hunting and Escaping," in which a giant killer whale bursts out of the water and snatches an unsuspecting sea lion pup from the shore. "Very often, the successful hunter takes its victim out to sea without even killing it, and there it plays with its catch as if it were exulting in triumph," a grim-voiced narrator says. On screen, the whale tosses the maimed pup high into the air.

The series was such a hit that Time-Life quickly followed up with *Predators of the Wild,* backed by TV ads with roaring grizzlies and tigers shaking bloody corpses. "You are in a nightmare filled with monsters that bite and crawl and kill," the narrator intones. "A nightmare more terrifying because it's real. Welcome to nature's dark side. . . ." The new genre really took off last year when Discovery, which is 49% owned by Tele-Communications Inc., entered the fray. During a new-show brainstorming session, Chairman John Hendricks mentioned that he had always wanted to do a show called "Teeth." Programming Vice President Michael Quattrone, who keeps a saber-toothed-tiger skull in his office, shot back: "What about *Fangs?*"

Soon, Discovery was airing some of the most graphic scenes on TV. In one show, two wild dogs, after chasing and killing a baby gazelle, literally rip it in half. Later, a pack of hyenas chases and nips at a young wildebeest until it falls, and they immediately begin feeding on its soft, bloody belly. As the animal, still alive, looks out with what seems a serene stare, a narrator explains: "By this time, it is so numbed by shock that it hardly reacts. . . ." Soon, the hyenas are chased away by vultures, which claw and peck one another to get at the meat.

Audiences devour this stuff. "There's a primal feeling to it," says Andrew Coale, a 23-year-old *Fangs* fan who cools down by doing graduate work in English literature at the University of Maryland. "It's like 'boom!'—this is what they do! We go out and pick up a pound of ground round and never see a cow."

Fangs and its ilk draw howls from some animal lovers, however. "It's ironic the way they portray predators and prey when we're the biggest predators of all," says Ingrid Newkirk, chairwoman of People for the Ethical Treatment of Animals. The new nature shows, she says, are "voyeuristic and not respectful."

Too many are aimed only at the ratings, complains Jim Fowler, who was Mr. Perkins's sidekick on *Wild Kingdom* and now runs Mutual of Omaha's Wildlife Heritage Center. "Unfortunately, sometimes it gives the wrong impression," Mr. Fowler says. "On *Wild Kingdom,* we were selling real-life adventure."

Today's nature programmers and filmmakers come back with a fierce defense. They say the shows offer valuable education in animal behavior and aren't the nonstop orgies of violence that the ads for them sometimes suggest. Besides, killing is "a fundamental part of earning a living as an animal," says Keenan Smart, head of the *National Geographic* TV division's natural-history unit.

At the start of one especially vicious show, "The Super Predator," Discovery's narrator warned viewers: "We must be careful not to judge the predators by human standards. They pursue their prey not in anger or with hatred, but because nature has equipped them so superbly."

Yet predator programmers do have their limits. Discovery says it won't air human footage in a planned cannibal show. And Mr. Hughes, the National Geographic producer, drew the line in a pending film about crocodiles. In one section, he says, "a crocodile takes a baby fawn, a real-life Bambi, and another croc tries to take it away. . . . There's no way we'd run it."

—MARK ROBICHAUX, August 1995

47. Where's Dumbo?

KAKUM NATIONAL PARK, Ghana—How does an elephant hide?

"Very, very well," said Yaw Boafo, who should know. For three years, he has been trying to count the elephants of Kakum.

"I've seen them maybe eight or nine times. Well, not seen with my eyes. Maybe I've seen them four times with my eyes," he said while peering through a thick cluster of trees. No elephants here.

"Other times," he said, "I've seen them by hearing. We can see they are around by hearing them."

"Once we came so close to a group of elephants, 20 yards, and we couldn't see them," added Mildred Manford, a fellow elephant counter. She was walking on a suspension bridge hanging high in the Kakum canopy, looking for movement below. No elephants in sight here, either. "They were around us, but we never saw them," she continued. "We just heard them leaving."

So it goes at Ghana's Abrafo Academy, informally called Elephant University, where the main subject—*Loxodonta africana cyclotis,* or the West African forest elephant—is an elusive critter. *Loxodonta invisibilis,* the students joke, would be more like it.

Thus, the students—four from Ghana and one each from neighboring Ivory Coast and Burkina Faso—have learned the fine arts of counting what you can't see: analyzing dung piles, measuring footprints and listening to low-frequency elephant chatter captured by recording devices hung in trees.

As West Africa's first homegrown elephant experts, they will soon leave the small white house on the edge of Kakum forest that serves as Elephant U and take up a challenge of elephantine proportion: conducting a census using all the senses. "First, we have to establish how many elephants there are in West Africa," said

Umaru Farouk Dubiure, one of the six students in Elephant U's first class graduating this week. "You can't preserve and manage something if you don't know how many of it there are."

The forest elephants of West Africa are the most endangered—and least studied—of Africa's giants. The savanna elephants of East and Southern Africa tower above the bush and can be tracked by aerial survey or foot patrol. But the forest elephant lives in dense rain forests.

The students could barely conceive their subject's elusiveness when they entered Elephant U, which was founded by Ghana's government and the U.S.-based Conservation International in 1999. Sure, the forest elephant is a bit smaller than its savanna cousin, maybe two-thirds the size. But it is still a massive creature, reaching 18 feet in length and nearly eight feet in height, and weighing as much as 7,700 pounds.

"Ah, but the forest elephant is very secretive," said Cletus Nateg, the senior wildlife officer at Kakum Conservation Area and an instructor at Elephant U. Kakum, a 144-square-mile rain forest, may hold the largest group of forest elephants in West Africa. Various models from dung surveys put the number at between 183 and 241. Still, in three years, the students have managed only one grainy photo of a single elephant, and that was from an automatic infrared camera mounted on a tree.

"The elephants themselves have a good sense of smell and hearing, but poor sight," said Mr. Nateg. "You rely on sight, but the forest is dark. So an elephant detects you before you detect the elephant. That's why they're so elusive."

The forest that once stretched for thousands of kilometers along the Atlantic coast of tropical West Africa has been whittled back by human beings. Expanding fields of cash crops such as cocoa and food staples including corn and cassava have shrunk the elephants' habitat, cut off their instinctive migratory routes and isolated them in islands of forest surrounded by farming villages. That has greatly increased the contact zone between humans and elephants, and conflict has escalated as the elephants emerge from the forest for a snack.

Over the years, the elephants have developed quite a taste for cocoa. Cocoa is the main pampered species in Ghana, for it provides a vital source of foreign currency to buy imports and pay off debt. Thus, the more that elephants eat cocoa and disturb the crop, the more agitated the nation's bean counters and farmers become. In recent years, reports of elephant shootings have increased.

"There's a lot of pointing going on, some with fingers, some with trunks," said Brent Bailey, a forest-resource specialist at Conservation International and one of the coordinators of Elephant U. "Elephants have good memories. They may see the land as theirs, and the villagers think it belongs to them."

The students have become adroit analyzers of elephant dung. Working with U.S. researchers, the students have participated in dung DNA testing as a way of counting elephants. But mainly they stick to counting piles of poop.

Their tools of tracking invisible elephants are always at the ready: a compass to keep trackers hewing to a straight line, a rolling measuring wheel to record the dung details, some machetes to hack back low-hanging branches and a global positioning box taped to a stick to pinpoint the location.

"When we're very, very lucky," whispered Emmanuel Danquah, one of the Ghanaian students, "we see fresh dung and a dispersal of urine that will tell us whether a female or male left this gold nugget behind."

No dung nuggets were found this day—and no elephants—but the memory of a counting expedition in Tai National Park in Ivory Coast kept them going. "We first searched the east side, we searched and searched and didn't find any dung," remembered

Mr. Danquah. "Then we moved camp and went to the western side. We walked and walked and finally we found some dung.

"We started pumping our fists and yelling 'Yeah!' " he said. "Then we found a lot more dung. That day, we were so dung hungry, we skipped lunch, we just kept counting."

—ROGER THUROW, November 2002

48. The Monkey Bomb

DACCA—The government of Bangladesh has thrown a wrench into the machinery of America's National Primate Plan.

A diplomatic controversy has ensued, involving an international corporate struggle between MOL Enterprises Inc. of Portland, Ore., and Scotty's Pet Farm of Oregon City, Ore., which also operates Scotty's Roadside Zoo.

At issue are the neutron bomb, the health and well-being of all mankind, and a lot of monkeys.

"The monkey file is one of the more highly classified we have," an American diplomat says. A. Hamid, Dacca's inspector general of forests, agrees that "this is a sensitive matter." And a Bangladeshi monkey dealer whispers, "America will remember this."

Some background is in order: For several years, the U.S. has been in the grip of a "severe and long-term shortage of nonhuman primates," according to the U.S. government Interagency Primate Steering Committee in Washington. The crisis intensified in April 1978, when the world's largest primate-exporting country, India, imposed a monkey embargo. America responded with a conservation and breeding campaign aimed at achieving monkey self-sufficiency by 1982. This is the National Primate Plan.

The monkey of moment to America is the rhesus. Each year, the country must enlist 14,000 rhesus monkeys to test vaccines, gauge the dangers of drugs and chemicals and serve the general cause of medical research. To bring America's breeding colonies into full flower, the Primate Steering Committee needs 12,000 more of these monkeys. But it can't get them.

This is because the only source of rhesus monkeys outside India is Bangladesh, and Bangladesh has also banned their export. India's ban was straightforward. The Bangladeshi ban was not—and there's a story in that.

It begins in 1977, when Bert Vieceli, then a vice president of MOL, dug in at the Intercontinental Hotel here in quest of some nonhuman-primate business. He left a variety of impressions.

"Mr. Vieceli has a great faith," says Mother Agnes, a frail nun at Bottomley Home orphanage, "He came often and gave sweet-meats to the children."

"Bert Vieceli had a lot of money," a banker says. "He insisted on paying for everything in dollars. He used to come around banging on desks."

Whatever his technique, Mr. Vieceli met initially with success. In March 1977, Bangladesh awarded MOL an exclusive 10-year contract to trap rhesus monkeys and send them to America. MOL would pay $81.50 per monkey, a high price compared with the rate then prevailing in India. No other exporter even bothered to bid. Mr. Vieceli proceeded to Washington, and by June 1978, MOL had a delivery contract at $185.00 a monkey with the National Institutes of Health.

In the meantime, India banned monkey exports. Entirely by accident, Mr. Vieceli found himself with a monopoly on America's monkey supply. Under the circumstances, however, it wouldn't have been unreasonable for anyone to conclude that the monkeys of Bangladesh were suddenly underpriced.

Enter Scotty's Pet Farm. Paying little mind to MOL's exclusive contract, Scott Campbell came to Bangladesh in mid-1978 and began beating the bushes for a contract of his own. Reached by telephone at Scotty's Roadside Zoo, Mr. Campbell says he was acting on the request of U.S.-based monkey exporters India had recently put out of business. "I knew some of the elite in Bangladesh," he says. "I had done some real favors for some of the families there."

Mr. Campbell didn't get much help from the American embassy in his raid on MOL's turf. He did persuade Oregon's Sen. Mark Hatfield to complain that an Oregon company was getting short shrift, but the senator had to reverse himself when he found out MOL was from Oregon, too. In December 1978, Mr. Campbell sent a furious Mailgram to President Carter, broadly suggesting that some palms at the embassy had been greased by Bert Vieceli.

"He is throwing money around in great quantities," Mr. Campbell wrote, "and states he could buy the countries of Bangladesh and India any time he desired."

From his home on Palomino Way in West Linn, Ore., Mr. Vieceli parries: "I wouldn't pay anybody off, all right. That's putting it to you straight out. I give from the heart, and I don't care if no monkey ever comes out of it. But the competition!"

Less than a month after Mr. Campbell sent his Mailgram to the White House, Bangladesh abruptly canceled MOL's contract. At least two loads of monkeys were then sent to America by other companies, a U.S. official says. Mr. Vieceli raised a rumpus, and in August 1979 the government announced its decision to ban monkey exports altogether.

Officially, the ban was touched off by the neutron bomb. It seems that another American interest—the International Primate

Protection League of Sununerville, S.C.—also engaged the attention of Dacca's policy makers. It informed them that the U.S. military was using monkeys exported by MOL for "inconceivably ghastly experiments" with the warhead, whose enhanced radiation is designed to kill living things but leave buildings standing.

While Muslim Bangladesh may not share Hindu India's concern with the fate of animals, its leaders seem to have developed a profound desire for good relations with the monkey lobby in the U.S. "We don't want to hurt the feelings of our American friends," says inspector general of forests Hamid, a man of polish who wears starched white shirts and smokes Dunhill cigarettes. "I must tell you there is a strong reaction in America against Bangladesh for using these monkeys. You might know the Primate Protection League. They are bitterly accusing us. Believe me, the feeling in America is very much against this trade."

The feeling isn't shared by the American government, an interest that curiously seems to have less influence in Dacca than the Primate Protection League. Ever since MOL lost its contract, the U.S. embassy here has tried mightily to get the monkeys flowing again. Every American monkey-using agency has disclaimed in writing any link to the neutron bomb. From the highest levels of the State Department came this telegram:

"No Bangladesh monkeys have been used in neutron bomb or atomic weapons development. Moreover, if exports from Bangladesh are reinstituted none will be so used."

A formal diplomatic note was delivered. "The embassy of the United States appeals to the Government of Bangladesh to reconsider its position," it said. "The United States is approaching a critical situation in its supply of rhesus monkeys for medical research and testing. These programs are not only important to the United States, but are vital to the health and well-being of all mankind."

The government of Bangladesh apparently was not moved. It has made no reply. "This is a case of expropriation," says an exasperated U.S. official. "Aid could be cut off. We don't want to threaten, but there's a stage when this has to come into play."

There is talk in Dacca that the government is merely biding its time until MOL decides its monkey monopoly is no longer worth fighting for. The ban could then be lifted and a new contract awarded to another company. One who leans toward this view is Mohammad Neyamat Ullah, a stout man in sky-blue trousers who goes by the name Sabu.

When it comes to the business of nonhuman primates, Mr. Sabu is an old war horse. At the moment, however, he is proprietor of the New Elegant Tailor Shop in an arcade of shops that sell brass pots to tourists. "I have been deprived of my business," he says, seating a visitor beneath a rack of limp suits.

Mr. Sabu used to be a trapping agent. He says he has connections in America. He doesn't offer the name of his contact, but it certainly isn't Bert Vieceli. "He asked me to work for him and I said no," Mr. Sabu says indignantly. "Monkeys are to serve the human. But he was exporting these monkeys for the destruction of the human. There is the difference."

Selling monkeys is more profitable than selling suits, though, and Mr. Sabu is sure there is still a future for the monkey traffic in Bangladesh. "I understand the government is thinking of breeding for export," he says, watching one of his tailors cut a pattern. "They may hire a company to do it for them. I have already applied. Someday, I will get the permission. I will not give up the hope. It will come—today or tomorrow."

—BARRY NEWMAN, March 1981

49. *This Zoo's a Killer*

HARBIN, China—An unfortunate Black Angus calf skitters from the bed of a dump truck near here and stumbles onto a muddy track. Moments later, the truck gone, two thick-necked Siberian tigers chase the confused animal in a tight circle, bringing it down by the throat.

"Wahhh!" gasp a half-dozen Chinese tourists crowded at the windows of a waiting minibus. As the tigers gorge, a young girl snaps pictures and two middle-aged men discuss the merits of drinking blood.

Feeding carnivores live quarry is a growing attraction in China, where sightseers can watch alligators chomp chicks, lions mangle goats or big snakes swallow rats. But none of the entertainment is as popular—or as misguided, some animal experts say—as the killing at China's Siberian Tiger Park here in far northern Heilongjiang province.

The park is supposed to be a scientific endeavor to teach tigers bred in captivity how to hunt for themselves in the wild. But money is tight, so the park sells prey to tourists who watch the cats kill to order. Want to see a Siberian tiger make a pig squeal? It costs $120. Visiting company groups and some individuals gladly pay, and everybody who happens to be present gets to see the kill. Someone on a tighter budget can sacrifice rabbits to a saber-toothed maw for just $12 apiece.

Started 12 years ago by zoologist Liu Xinchen, the project has been remarkably successful in propagating Siberian tigers, the world's biggest cats: An original population of just eight tigers, rescued from poor conditions in Chinese zoos, has increased to 110. Worldwide, there are only about 2,000 of the animals in captivity and just 400 or so left in the wild.

Strolling along a dark, foul-smelling passageway in the park's main building, Mr. Liu, a boyish man with a mop of salt-and-pepper hair, points out litters of orange cubs nuzzling their 500-pound mothers in cages on either side. "They watch their mothers kill chickens and start eating meat when they're one month old," he boasts, adding that he has 30 young tigers that can already chase down deer.

The cats may be killers, but few tiger specialists think the feeding frenzy will truly help them adapt to the wild. Some experts worry that Mr. Liu would be doing the endangered species a disservice if he were to set his tigers free, which he has no immediate plans to do. Howard Quigley, codirector of the Siberian Tiger Project at the University of Idaho's Hornocker Wildlife Institute, says, "The worst thing you can do for local impressions is take a tiger from a farm, release it in the mountains and have it show up in someone's backyard to kill a dog or, worse, a child."

The concept of introducing captivity-bred carnivores into the wild was first popularized by the 1960s book and movie, *Born Free*, which chronicled the rearing of a lioness by a pair of British game wardens and her happily-ever-after departure when she heard the mating call. But the real story wasn't so idyllic—Elsa died a year after giving birth, and another lion released from captivity was later shot when it killed a man. Zoologists say there are no clearly documented cases of predators bred in captivity being sent successfully back into the wild. Mr. Quigley argues that there are enough Siberian tigers left in China's forests to repopulate the species if provided enough protection.

Animal-rights activists, meanwhile, are outraged at the killing shows. The World Society for the Protection of Animals says it is creating a Web site to alert tourists about what to avoid in China if they can't stomach the sight of suffering.

Mr. Liu has faced international scorn: In 1993, the U.S. threatened China with sanctions, in part for allowing the state-owned park to sell tiger bones as medicine. Chinese traditionally ascribe curative powers to various tiger parts, including the relief of impotence by eating tiger penises. State-run media reported at the time that the park was financed by the trade. China has since banned the sale of tiger bones, and Mr. Liu says he has a freezer filled with about 60 frozen carcasses that he can't sell (he denies that he has ever sold any, in fact, but is holding on to the remains in case the laws change).

Tiger-feeding, meanwhile, has proved so lucrative that Mr. Liu says introducing tigers to the wild won't happen for at least 10 years—the current generation of cats are spoiled by the steady supply of captive quarry.

A butcher in blood-soaked camouflage fatigues attaches wire cable to the remains of a big animal, with plans to drag it through a gate in the park's 12-foot chainlink fence. "He's going to get the cow," says a woman in a red polo shirt and white pedal pushers. "The tigers won't eat a whole one, so we bring it back and cut it up to feed to them later," she explains.

Tourists occasionally complain that the sated tigers ignore the frightened animals released for them to kill. A Toyota Land Cruiser, its windows covered with heavy steel mesh, scares up lounging tigers and herds them toward two white rabbits dropped in a sandy clearing. "They've already had 40 or 50 chickens today—and a cow," snorts the driver of one of three buses waiting nearby as the tigers lie down again. They ignore a thin man in the closest bus as he bangs on the window and roars.

Finally, a man hops from the Land Cruiser, plucks up the rabbits and drops one under a tiger's nose. The tiger slowly settles the rabbit between its massive paws and tilts its head to bite as a child might a candy bar.

Mr. Liu remains confident that he can nurture the wild nature of later tiger generations. Walking along a raised walkway in a walled-off section of the park, he describes how visitors will soon be able to watch young tigers kill deer. It will be good for business, he believes, because they will be more elusive. Rabbits and cows don't understand danger and too often freeze when faced with imminent death.

—CRAIG S. SMITH, September 1998

50. Gentle Ben's Big Bad Brother

KODIAK, Alaska—Gregory Furin won't soon forget the time he met a brown bear up close and personal.

Hunting deer, he had shot and field-dressed a buck when he noticed the bear about 150 yards away. "I'd always been told bears want no part of you and I thought it was a good idea to scare him off," the local dentist says. He took a deep breath and, in his most threatening tone, shouted "Hey." The bear stood up, stared and charged.

Shaken, Dr. Furin fumbled through his pack for more rifle shells. But when the bear galloped out of the nearby bushes, the hunter revised his survival plan, and "came off that hill in three great leaps." From a distance, he watched the intruder eat most of his deer and bury the remains for a later snack.

Such scrapes are a normal part of the adjustment process on an island that 14,000 people share with 2,500 of the world's largest carnivores. Brown bears, variations of grizzlies, may weigh 1,500 pounds and stand eight feet tall when they rear up.

Considering what could happen, the accommodation between

bear and man is remarkably harmonious. Kodiak, in fact, is something of a modern-day wildlife success story, where local industries have been inconvenienced but not destroyed and where wildlife has thrived despite a growing population and surging tourism.

This mountainous island is a bear's Eden: 100 miles of steep slopes luxuriant with vegetation, roots and berries, and sliced by streams where salmon spawn. Almost two-thirds of the island is dedicated to the Kodiak National Wildlife Refuge, where hunting is permitted but the bears' welfare comes first.

There are only 87 miles of roads, none into the interior. Island development is strictly regulated, as is hunting of the brown bears. As a result, their population is believed to be at its highest in 30 or 40 years.

The industry most cramped by the bears is cattle ranching, which dates back to Russian ownership of Alaska. Touches of bitterness aren't hard to find among ranchers. DeWitt Fields has raised cattle here for 38 years and says he once lost 16 head to bears in a single night. "Bear refuge is a misnomer," he says. "It's a bear hatchery producing bears for the wealthy to hunt."

In the 1960s, the state fought the bears with an arsenal that included a plane outfitted with a semiautomatic rifle and flown by an ex-fighter pilot. But sympathy for the cattle industry has ebbed, partly because bears provide quite an industry themselves. A single tourist will pay $7,500 for a 10-day guided hunt, while spending more money during his stay. Now, official bear control is minimal.

So ranchers adapt to the bears. William Burton, who has access to some 21,000 acres of Kodiak range, is gradually switching from cattle to buffaloes. He says bears annually kill 20 to 30 head of his cattle but have yet to take so much as a newborn calf from his herd of the quick and aggressive bison. (As livestock, the buffaloes do have their drawbacks; so far they have gored to death four of Mr. Burton's ranch horses at roundup time.)

One thing that worries bear overseers is an increasing number of confrontations involving deer hunters. Beyond regulated hunting, state law permits killing bears if they threaten a person's life or certain property (not including deer carcasses); in recent years the number killed under the law has jumped from an average of four annually to 11 a year, most of them shot by deer hunters.

The problem isn't so much the numbers; after all, licensed hunters bag about 190 bears a year. But about two-thirds of those are males, thanks to the timing of hunting seasons. The ones killed by deer hunters tend to be females protecting cubs. Their loss affects the bear population without returning any economic benefit. One reason deer hunters are having more bear trouble is that there are more hunters now. They have multiplied sixfold in the past 15 years as Kodiak has become a playground for Anchorage, less than an airline hour away. But bears also are getting wiser to the ways of the hunter.

It doesn't take a bear long to sense that the easy way to get hold of a deer is to muscle in on one a city slicker has just shot. The smell of a deer carcass being field-dressed can draw a Kodiak bear from far away. And now, some hunters claim, the bears have another cue.

"Like Pavlov's dogs, which began salivating when he rang a bell, those bears are conditioned to know that a rifle shot means a free meal," contends Donald Brenteson, a 41-year-old vocational counselor. "There's absolutely no doubt in my mind they come to a rifle shot."

Though state game biologists are skeptical, Mr. Brenteson tells of a hunt in which he and two friends shot two deer and began dressing them, one hunter standing watch. A bear soon approached. While the hunters dragged one deer away and hid it,

Mr. Brenteson fired two shots over the visitor's head. It ignored them and kept coming, first devouring the dressed deer and then following the scent trail to claim the one hidden away.

"To a bear," notes a veteran guide named Joe Want, "possession is ten-tenths of the law."

Despite such encounters, no one has been killed by a bear on Kodiak Island in more than 30 years. In the past 15 years, seven people have been chewed to varying degrees.

Few people anywhere live as intimately with giant predators as the 200 residents of Larsen Bay, a string of little houses along Kodiak's western coast reachable only by air or water. A stream runs through the village, and in late summer the bears gobble up spawning salmon as residents go about their business as close as 50 feet away.

When the bears aren't fishing, says safety officer August Aga, "they wander around the village like cats and dogs." Yet in residents' memory, the only villager even slightly hurt was a drunk who one night fell over a bear sleeping in the street. It slapped him and left.

Bears, though, sometimes get hurt themselves. Alberta Aga, August's mother, recalls the night she heard something beating on her house, shined a flashlight out the window and looked directly into the face of a brown bear. While she was out the next evening, it broke through a window, thoroughly trashed the house and left through the front door carrying a box of groceries. Her son, passing by, came upon the looter and shot it.

Normally, "Bears walk past my house like cattle," Mrs. Aga says. "That bear was crazy."

As there are survival rules for the bush, there are specific elements of bear etiquette for Larsen Bay, Mr. Aga says. Among them: "If you leave the house and there's a bear directly in your path, you wait till it leaves."

"If you're walking up the road and a female is on one side and her cubs are on the other, you don't walk between them."

And if a bear decides to chase you, as they sometimes do?

"You run like hell."

— KEN SLOCUM, May 1987

51. Barking Up the Right Tree

Robert Butler of Wadesville, Ind., is planning a little raccoon hunting next week. He'll take along Big Creek Jack, his favorite coonhound, and if Big Creek Jack does big stuff and trees a half-dozen or so coons, it could be worth several thousand dollars.

Not that coonskins have suddenly become a hot commodity. They're worth only 50 cents or so apiece. But Big Creek Jack will be competing in the world championship hunt of the American Coon Hunters Association.

A win in the annual event, which begins Monday and lasts five days at Van Wert, Ohio, could mean that Big Creek Jack would be in instant demand as a sire. About all Mr. Butler would have to do would be to sit back and rake in the loot. Currently stud fees run up to $125.

Mr. Butler says that he paid $400 for Big Creek Jack five years ago and that now "you just couldn't buy him regardless of how much you were willing to pay." That's because the coon-dog business is booming.

"Coon hunting is the fastest-growing" of sporting-dog events, says Bill Boatman, an authority on coon hunting who operates a large hunting-equipment company in Bainbridge, Ohio. In the past four or five years, he adds, coon hunting has increased by at least a third. He estimates there are 150,000 coon hunters across the country.

"A boy can either go to town and be a hippie or go to the woods and be a coon hunter," Mr. Boatman says.

All kinds of people, ranging from lean tanned farmhands to paunchy professional people, are taking up the sport. "A businessman needs exercise to keep in shape," says Walter Mayors, a De-Soto, Mo., car dealer, who didn't let a heart attack nine years ago stop his hunting. He says his dogs tree an average of five coons a week.

"There are more young boys in it than I can ever remember," says Dr. E. G. Fuhrman, president of the United Kennel Club, which registers six breeds of coonhounds—black and tan, redbone, treeing walker, bluetick, Plott and English.

What type of dog is best—an object of hot dispute among enthusiasts—depends on the kind of event the dog's owner is interested in, for coon hunting has become a specialized sport. No longer does a hunter just take up a gun, hit the trail and see how many coons can be treed and shot. These days many hunters are more interested in how their dogs perform, and in organized events nowadays the hunters almost never shoot their prey.

Consider the nation's largest field trial—technically, not a hunt at all—which was held over Labor Day weekend at Kenton, Ohio. More than 1,000 dogs, and only two coons, participated in that event. To test the entrants, officials laid out a mile-long trail by dragging a heavily scented coonskin through a wooded area. The trail ended at the base of an ancient white oak tree, atop which sat a lone caged coon.

Such field trials reward two distinct skills—speed of the line dog, the first to cross a line several yards in front of the tree, and the nose of the tree dog, the first to jump at the tree and bark. Top line dogs often have more than a trace of greyhound in them, so they're fast but reluctant barkers. On the other hand, tree dogs may finish late, but they're eager to yelp at the coon.

At night the Kenton field trials included water races. These involved releasing six dogs at once at the end of a 160-foot-long four-foot-deep water-filled trough. A caged coon was pulled overhead along a wire in front of the dogs, which swam the trough to a tree at the opposite end. Prizes for winners totaled more than $6,000.

Some lovers of true coon hunting, however, decry field trials and water races. Clyde Routh, a farmer and dog dealer at Losantville, Ind., says that "a dog has to be a lot smarter for coon hunting—he has to have a lot more nose" than is required for field trials.

At the Autumn Oak Hunt near Greencastle, Ind., which drew more than 500 dogs and their handlers over the Labor Day weekend, not a coon was hurt, although several were treed. Competing for three-foot trophies topped by a silver hound treeing a silver coon, the entries were divided into "casts" of four dogs and sent out to hunt with their handlers and a judge. Since each hunt lasted three hours and required separate hunting grounds, some teams had to drive as far as 40 miles before finding a suitable spot.

In organized coon hunts, dogs earn points, depending on how they perform. The first one to "strike," or sound the deep howl indicating a coon scent, earns 100 points. The first dog to "chop" or start a rapid, excited bark at the base of a tree, runs up more points, provided a coon is in the tree.

Dogs lose points for such grievous faults as fighting or running "trash"—fox, rabbit, deer or possum. One well-known coon hunter lost a great deal of prestige recently when his highly rated but overanxious hound treed the same alley cat twice during a crucial hunt. Coon dogs have also been known to kill lambs; farmers, therefore, aren't always friendly toward coon hunters.

Coon hunting takes place at night because coons are generally nocturnal animals. Hunters roam around the woods looking like coal miners, wearing heavy overalls and hard hats with lights attached. Hunting coons is one of the nation's oldest sports. Coons were hunted first because they damaged crops and later because their pelts sold for as much as $20 during the Roaring Twenties, when they were widely used for raccoon coats. Today individuals often shoot coons for the sport of hunting and sometimes give one to their dogs to keep their appetites whetted. Some hunters consider coons a kind of delicacy as food, but others say they can't stand the thought of eating one.

Raccoons weigh up to 20 pounds or more and are distinctive because of their black-and-white facial markings, which resemble a mask. Today the coon population seems to be rising, partly because mechanical harvesters, increasingly used on farms, leave more foodstuffs on the ground.

If coon hunting is exciting for men, it's sometimes perilous for dogs. More than one dog has tumbled down a mine shaft, and many have been injured fighting coons. Others just disappear. Mr. Butler hopes Big Creek Jack will fare better at the world hunt next week than he did in 1968. That year, says Mr. Butler, "the dog got lost the first night" and wasn't found until the next day.

Hunters want their dogs to avoid such dangers because they cost so much. Estelle Walker, editor of *Full Cry,* one of several magazines for coon hunters, says some dogs have sold for nearly $10,000.

"When you put that much into a dog, you tie him to the bedpost."

—JIM HYATT, October 1970

CHAPTER 7

BUZZ

━━━━━

52. After the Oscars, Please Call Orkin

Steven Kutcher, a Hollywood agent with a creepy specialty, gets a phone call. The makers of a documentary film want to use one of Mr. Kutcher's clients, but there is a catch: The actor is to be killed—squashed, actually.

No problem. The film makers merely want to swat a fly, and Mr. Kutcher has an endless supply of those, also an array of other insects he finds jobs for in movies and TV. Stardom, unfortunately, sometimes requires the ultimate sacrifice.

As one of a handful of insect agents in the industry, Mr. Kutcher, a short, slender man of 45 with a bushy beard, is more

217

interested professionally in attracting flies than he is in, say, Michelle Pfeiffer. "I work strictly with invertebrates," he says. "It's got to have more than four legs to get me excited."

In some ways, of course, Mr. Kutcher's work isn't all that different from that of regular Hollywood agents. He has to deal not only with death but with early retirement, temperamental outbursts on the set and tensions with costars.

And he does have casting problems. For this documentary, called "The Secret Life of 118 Green Street," an ABC television special to air next fall about the little creatures people share their houses with, the film makers need silverfish, spiders, ants, cockroaches and a fly.

Mr. Kutcher, who himself lives in a small house in Pasadena, scouts talent at home, or grows his own. In his kitchen, for instance, a rotting orange is left out to attract fruit flies. Bread and dead butterflies are kept side by side in the refrigerator; scorpions, also deceased, are stashed in the freezer next to the turkey potpie. In the living room is a tank of newly hatched caterpillars munching on broccoli. Termites in a box are nibbling wood, and cockroaches are eating Purina dog chow. Hundreds of dead insects rest in dresser drawers and in cabinets in the bedroom. The chirping of crickets fills the night, from inside the house.

Mr. Kutcher gets quite attached to some of his crawly house guests. "I've learned so much from her," he says, tenderly stroking a tarantula named Dolores. "She feels just like velvet."

Dolores, now 15 years old, performs primarily for school groups. Joy, a tarantula with orange knees, has film credits that include crawling on a scantily clad actress in a threadbare film called *Barbarian Queen II*.

Some bugs require going on safaris of a sort. And bug-hunting methods vary. While one insect agent tells of picking fleas off the backs of dogs at the local pound, two men were dispatched to

Costa Rica to find harlequin beetles for *Indiana Jones and the Temple of Doom.*

Andy Miller, a special-effects man, provided 50,000 crickets for a scene in that film, and when an actress got a little squeamish about letting a centipede crawl in her hair, he put on blond wig and blue bathrobe so movie makers could get their shot. "My arm was in a soap opera," says another bugman, David Brody, who climbed into bed with a scorpion on his arm when an actor balked.

Bugs don't make anybody a lot of money, but the overhead is low. A common roach raised in a lab sells for $2.50, while a fancy Madagascar Hissing roach can command $7.00. Sometimes stand-ins are cheaper: Worms can be used instead of caterpillars and coffee beans can sub for beetles. The cockroaches that actress Mink Stole ate in a John Waters cult film actually were raisins.

Rubber look-alikes are sometimes used in background shots, or substituted for living creatures that are about to be filmicly exterminated, so the real bugs live to work another day. Humane concerns seldom enter the picture, except in odd moments of sentimentality. Mr. Kutcher says most film makers feel that "killing flies or cockroaches is OK, but why kill a beautiful monarch butterfly?"

Complaints about insect-abuse are as rare as a June bug in January. "The SPCA doesn't care about flies," says Mr. Brody. Which is not precisely correct. John Kullberg, the president of the American Society for Prevention of Cruelty to Animals, says, "We're not indifferent to insects."

When Mr. Kutcher did a commercial for Glad-Lock food-storage bags that showed angry bees tightly sealed in the company's product, the ad agency had him sign an affidavit swearing that none of these industrious creatures were harmed in the filming. "We wanted [the public] to know the person who handled the bees actually cared for and loved bees," says a spokesman for Leo Burnett Co., the Chicago agency that made the spot. "We didn't want to offend anyone."

People in Mr. Kutcher's line of work often base their fees on how much time it takes to rustle up performers. While he is working on the set, Mr. Kutcher takes in $250 a day, "More than a union-rate dog trainer," he says. And he gets on-screen credit, too, as an "insect consultant" or "bug wrangler."

As a child, Mr. Kutcher says, he was a loner who played with bugs. And his fondness for insects got him treated as "a social outcast." But he was able to get his revenge: "When relatives pinch your cheek, you have a tarantula ready."

Growing older, he became less shy. As a guest on *Late Night With David Letterman*, he let them dump a hundred thousand mealworms on him. "I've worked with Steven Spielberg and leeches," he says proudly.

He got his big break as a biology graduate student, employed in a Los Angeles county mosquito-abatement program. Warner Bros. called looking for someone knowledgeable about grasshoppers. Before long, he was sticking the orthopterous ornaments on Richard Burton's face.

Doing that, for *The Exorcist II,* turned out to be relatively easy because the late Mr. Burton had bad skin; the smooth complexion of costar Linda Blair proved to be the greater challenge. "They kept falling off. I had to stick them in her hair and her ears," he recalls.

Cosmetic surgery (on insect, not actor) is sometimes necessary for safety's sake. Mr. Kutcher snipped off the stinger of a wasp before it walked across Farrah Fawcett's thigh, and he performed "ant dentistry" on insects that worked with Lynda Carter.

Bugs can be counted on to be repulsive, so horror films are their obvious métier. Mr. Kutcher concocted a cup of maggots that an actor pretended to drink in *Prince of Darkness*.

For one moving moment in the film *Creepshow,* Mr. Brody (who works in the entomology department at the American Museum of Natural History in New York) loaded 15,000 sedated roaches (they'd been given the gas) into a thin latex body, made up to look like E. G. Marshall. "When they woke up, they just broke through," says Mr. Brody.

Some bugs have box-office staying power. Scorpions, for instance, can live six to eight years; tarantulas can top 20. But for others, fame is fleeting, careers brief, life short. Mr. Brody once spent two days clipping the wings of 3,000 flies so they wouldn't buzz off a set in Central Park. But the shoot was rained out, and the flies, which live only a week to 10 days at best, died before their debut. (He had to put out some fish entrails to attract new talent.)

Since insects don't take direction well, it takes an expert to coax a good performance from some of these reluctant Oliviers. But for most bug people, that's hardly a career. Mr. Kutcher, who teaches at two community colleges, says he couldn't live off bugs, although he occasionally does eat bee pupae, which he says are nutritious and interesting. And he has eaten ants and crickets, which he notes are "closely related to lobster and shrimp."

To supplement his movie income he has stooped to doing commercials. Once he shined snails with furniture polish to make them look sharp for a Subaru television spot. There are consulting possibilities, too: He once was hired by a cereal company, he won't say which one, to determine how moths were getting into its muesli.

On the set of the documentary, a cameraman, who has worked with dogs, cats, elephants and whales, says "bugs are almost always a problem. People freak out. Last time I did roaches, we lost about 50%. They head for any crack they can find." Seasoned bugmen rein in their talent by surrounding the set with Vaseline, flypaper, tape sticky on both sides, and the like.

. Between takes, Mr. Kutcher crawls around on his hands and knees, trying to recapture escapees. "I want him to land on this dot, upside down, wiggle around, and then get a good mash," the producer says of the fly in question. Mr. Kutcher selects one fly from a group he has raised from little maggots.

The flies have been chilled in an ice chest, so they will move slowly as they warm up. The producer blows on one, hoping to rouse it, fretting that viewers will think it's made of rubber.

At last, a fly awakens, and the cameras roll. A star is born. And dies.

—CARRIE DOLAN, December 1989

53. A Grubby Little Secret

Harold Taylor's right leg had turned gangrenous; that was the bad news.

It was also crawling with maggots.

That was the good news.

The lowly, loathsome maggot, it turns out, is a swell, all-natural surgeon; sicked on Mr. Taylor's necrotic flesh by doctors, scores of the tiny grubs went to work, dining on infected tissue while bathing healthy tissue in an ammonia-like excretion that is a kind of natural disinfectant.

As a result of months of intensive maggot treatments, Mr. Taylor, a diabetic hospitalized at the Veterans Affairs Medical Center in Long Beach, Calif., beat his gangrene. He has since regained partial use of his leg—a leg that surgeons were on the verge of amputating.

Many people find maggots disgusting, but the 59-year-old carpet salesman sings maggot praises. "I tell you, my thoughts were, I don't want to lose my leg, let's take every shot," he says.

Maggot therapy, a medical mainstay as far back as the Napoleonic Wars, had all but been abandoned in the U.S. by the 1940s as modern medicine rushed to sulfa drugs and antibiotics to treat wounds and infections. But a small but growing number of doctors, casting off notions that maggot therapy is some medieval relic, have begun to embrace maggots anew.

At the Long Beach veterans hospital, Ronald Sherman, who oversaw Mr. Taylor's case, has treated more than 100 patients in the past four years. In Louisiana, Grady Dugas, a general practitioner, has used maggots to battle severely infected bedsores. And a group of British doctors affiliated with Oxford University hopes to begin treating patients there with maggot therapy using techniques taught by Dr. Sherman. He is maggot therapy's undisputed guru, having published numerous maggot-treatment treatises in respected medical journals, including the *Journal of Plastic and Reconstructive Surgery.* He also serves as a kind of one-man clearinghouse for queries from other doctors interested in his specialty.

Dr. Sherman turns positively missionary when he ticks off maggot-therapy virtues: It is low-cost and requires no anesthesia; wounds heal with minimal scarring; and there are seemingly no side effects. And producing maggots, the larvae of blowflies or even common houseflies, involves simple kitchen-sink science— a few chunks of decaying meat and a swarm of randy flies.

"People don't think about maggots until other methods have continued to fail," says Dr. Sherman, a bearded and bespectacled 37-year-old, as he sits in an office piled high with cardboard filing cabinets stuffed with maggot data and maggot lore. "If maggot therapy is so effective . . . if everybody could sing its praises when everything else had failed, then why, I asked myself, why are we waiting?"

Probably because people—even those who see the virtue of maggot therapy—tend to find maggots disgusting. "Biologically it makes sense," says Laurence Beck, chief of internal medicine at Georgetown University Medical Center in Washington. But Dr. Beck has never seen maggot therapy practiced, and that is fine with him. "It seems rather gross superficially," he adds.

Edward Pechter, a plastic surgeon and former medical-school colleague of Dr. Sherman's at UCLA, recalls the incident that was pivotal in Dr. Sherman's interest in maggot treatment. While on rounds at UCLA, Dr. Pechter unwrapped the bandages of a patient who had just been brought in for a lower-leg wound—and maggots came crawling out.

"Everyone kind of gasps and takes a step back. It's not something you expect to see," Dr. Pechter recalls. Still, when he noticed that the wound seemed surprisingly healthy, his curiosity was piqued. He consulted with Dr. Sherman, and the two decided to collaborate on an article on the history of maggot therapy. Among the nuggets they dug up: Baron D. J. Larrey, Napoleon's famed battlefield surgeon, was one of the pioneering physicians noting the healing properties of maggots among soldiers suffering untreated wounds.

For Dr. Pechter, who practices in Valencia, Calif., "Maggots were more of a passing fancy," he says. Dr. Sherman became maggot-obsessed.

An avid bug collector as a child, Dr. Sherman holds a degree in entomology, the science of bugs, as well as in medicine. "I had always been interested in the therapeutic uses for insects," he says. Since 1991, he has used MDT—shorthand for maggot debridement therapy—both as what he terms "salvage therapy" and to curb infections that seem resistant to more conventional treatments.

On a recent day, he unlocks double doors and takes a visitor into his "insectary," essentially a maggot farm housed in a tiny converted kitchenette in the hospital's recesses. Thousands of blowflies buzz and swarm in three small cages holding putrid liver. The stench is overpowering—but maggots would rather starve than eat fresh food.

The flies lay their eggs in the liver; left alone, the maggot eggs would hatch, engorge themselves and turn into flies. Dr. Sherman intervenes by removing the eggs from the liver and bathing them in a chemical solution that sterilizes them without killing them. After hatching, they are sewn into a patient's wound, which is sealed with a mixture of glue and gauze. This creates a little window allowing the maggots to breathe, and Dr. Sherman to observe them at work.

Barely a millimeter long when they go into the wound, they come out two to three days later five to 10 times bigger. Removing them is no problem: Feasting maggots become drowsy, reaching a state of near-hibernation.

Sometimes a few days of maggot therapy does the trick; but Mr. Taylor underwent a five-month maggot regimen. For many patients, the biggest obstacle is the idea. Edward Wicks, a 73-year-old former bombardier captain and car salesman, resisted treatment for a diabetic foot infection until his wife talked him into it. Revolted at first, he has now become a maggot convert. "They are creepy-crawly little rascals," Mr. Wicks says, "but they sure do a job on infection. When the things were done with me, I was well."

The maggots generally do their work silently—though patients occasionally feel them. "Once in a while you could feel gnawing or scratching, but it didn't bother me," Mr. Taylor recalls.

The interest by British doctors in maggot therapy—which they euphemistically call "biosurgery"—was, like Dr. Sherman's interest, initially fanned by accident. Some years ago, John Church, an orthopedic surgeon, came across a patient who had been in a car accident. The impact had thrown the man through his windshield; covered with cuts and bleeding, he rolled into a ditch and wasn't found—by humans, at least—for three days.

"His wounds were full of common housefly larvae, but they had done an excellent job on him," says Dr. Church, who, with a group of Oxford physicians, plans to set up an insectary there based on Dr. Sherman's model. Not only did the maggots stanch his infection; extensive lacerations that normally would have required costly surgery "had been done by Mother Nature for zero charge."

—DAWN BLALOCK, January 1995

54. The Dean of Doodlebugs

GAINESVILLE, Fla.—Although this article is about doodlebugs, which aren't bugs at all, we preface it with a riddle about Mr. Horsefly's grandfather.

Lionel Stange, the nation's foremost authority on doodlebugs, is leading a visitor through his place of work—a big Florida Department of Agriculture museum in this university town—when he spots a white-haired man in khakis and a wrinkled shirt, working at the end of a row of tall wood cabinets.

"There's Mr. Horsefly," he announces.

He introduces the man as Dr. Fairchild, an entomologist who has one of the world's biggest horsefly collections, with about 125,000 specimens. G. B. Fairchild, whose friends call him Sandy, has just celebrated his 87th birthday.

"Can you guess who his grandfather was?" Dr. Stange asks.

Well, here are some more clues. Dr. Fairchild's maternal grandfather was one of the best-known inventors in American history. Dr. Fairchild's father, David, was one of the most celebrated exotic-plant hunters of the early 20th century; Miami's Fairchild Tropical Garden is named for him.

So, we'll drop Mr. Horsefly until later.

Now, doodlebugs.

Doodlebugs are tiny insects that live in loose soil or sand. They also are known as ant lions, which aren't bugs any more than they are lions. True bugs belong to the order *Hemiptera,* and doodlebugs belong to the order *Neuroptera*—but that's nitpicking. Nits aren't bugs, either.

Doodlebugs are so named for the doodlelike lines the larvae describe in the sand as they scurry about—often in reverse, because some species have lost the ability to move forward. Ant lions are named for the ferocious way they prey on ants. A larval ant lion will dig a hole in the sand in the shape of an inverted funnel and then wait at the bottom. When a wandering ant falls in, the lion pounces.

Technically, the term doodlebug applies only to the larval stage, because adults have four wings and fly. The term ant lion applies to both young and old, though it is mainly the young lions that eat ants. Older ones prefer aphids and caterpillars.

A classic of doodlebug literature—*Demons of the Dust,* a 1930 tome by a Harvard entomology professor named William Morton Wheeler—calls the larvae "ugly, if not repulsive," and says adults lead "rather futile lives."

Such comments may help explain why doodlebugs have never been particularly trendy. The latest catalog of ant lions was published in 1866. It included 17 genera and 317 species. By now, 180 genera and some 1,300 species have been described in scientific papers. But nobody has pulled them together in one volume.

Which brings us back to Lionel Stange.

Dr. Stange (pronounced STANG-ee) is a taxonomic entomologist. In other words, he classifies insects—by species, genus, tribe and the like. He has published about 20 scientific papers on ant lions—plus another 50 or 60 on wasps, bees and snails—and he has named a score of new ant lion species.

And now, from a battered beige desk in a cluttered corner office, he is putting the finishing touches on the first whole-earth ant-lion catalog in more than a century.

"I've got it done, essentially," says the 58-year-old Dr. Stange, a gray-haired man with a pleasant manner. He adds that it has been delayed by the rigors of establishing some new classifications—two new tribes and six new genera—with which to define ant lions.

Dr. Stange has been working on the catalog for about 15 years, while performing his regular job identifying insects for the state agriculture department. He hopes to publish the catalog next year. It will include descriptions and drawings, plus a system he devised for quick identification of any given ant lion.

His subject is rather a moving target. "There's always a new species coming up," he says. "You can't wait on that, or you'll never get done."

The catalog should confirm Dr. Stange's already redoubtable reputation as the dean of doodlebug studies in the U.S. He can list the world's other doodlebug experts on the fingers of one hand. The only other American is a man with whom he often works—Bruce Miller, a research associate with the museum here, who makes his living as a snake breeder. ("My formal training is as an entomologist," Mr. Miller explains, "but at the time there were not a lot of jobs available.")

Oliver Flint, a curator in the Smithsonian Institution's entomology department, credits Dr. Stange with making the ant lion "fairly well known" in U.S. insect circles. If that sounds like faint praise, consider that there are millions of species of insects in the world. Many aren't known at all. What's more, Dr. Flint says ant lions aren't particularly easy to identify, "unless you're Lionel." He explains: "Some of them are very cryptic."

Speaking of cryptic: The term doodlebug is a relatively new one, dating to between 1865 and 1870. The term ant lion is an old one found, in the original Latin, in manuscripts from the sixth and seventh centuries. The family's scientific name, *Myrmeleontidae,* is Greek for "ant lion."

Doodlebug also is the name of various vehicles. Divining rods are called doodlebugs. And Doodlebug is the name taken by a member of the popular rap group Digable Planets; the others are Butterfly and Ladybug.

Dr. Stange's interest in ant lions began in his teenage years in California, when he encountered them on insect-collecting trips. He wrote his Ph.D. dissertation on ant lions, at the University of California at Davis in the mid-1960s. He has worked on them ever since, for 12 of those years at a university in Argentina.

He concedes that his specialty is rather arcane. However, he says, "I'm sure there are numerous cases of that in entomology."

Which brings us back to Dr. Fairchild, otherwise known as Mr. Horsefly. He attributes his longevity—87 years and counting—to his being an entomologist. "The thing is, you always have an interest—you don't give up and say the hell with it," he says. "There is always one new species to be described, one new bug to be moved to a different box."

As for the riddle of his grandfather, the answer is in Mr. Horsefly's full name: Alexander Graham Bell Fairchild.

"The whole damn business," he says.

—ERIC MORGENTHALER, September 1993

55. With Crickets, I'd Try a Nice Pinot Grigio

They want you to eat your grub.

And crickets. And wax moths.

A small but energetic group of entomologists, farmers and chefs are promoting edible insects, a foodstuff better known in academic circles as "microlivestock."

But moving bugs off the science-fair banquet circuit and onto the American dinner table is a hard sell. Though insects are a dietary staple in much of the world, squeamish Western palates resist. This perplexes people like David Fluker.

The Baton Rouge, La., cricket farmer, a supplier to zoos and pet stores, recently began marketing the insects as a human snack: freeze-dried, oven-roasted and dipped in melted chocolate. Mr. Fluker, who says he shipped 200 cases of chocolate crickets in the first two weeks, introduced them at a trade show last year, along with Cajun-spiced sautéed cricket. "We ran out of all 400 or so crickets we served," he recalls.

William Schultz, who sells Mr. Fluker's crickets at his roadside fruit stand in Port Allen, La., says, "It's just a real exciting thing here. We are selling them, not by the thousands a day, but 20 to 25 a day, at $1.89 apiece." Observing that most customers buy one to taste and more for friends, he concedes: "I haven't had anyone buy two for themselves."

McDonald's isn't about to offer mealworm burgers or deep-fried crickets. "But the idea of eating insects is beginning to get some serious attention," asserts Gene R. DeFoliart, an entomologist and professor emeritus at the University of Wisconsin in Madison. He edits the Food Insects Newsletter, a 2,000-circulation quarterly that runs recipes for fried bee larvae, sautéed giant ants and the like.

At the International Symposium on Biodiversity in Agriculture in Beijing last September, a third of the scientific papers dealt with microlivestock. Topics ranged from insect farming and harvesting to identification of edible species and their nutritional value. "I think it shows insects' new status," says Dr. DeFoliart.

Ronald Taylor, an entomologist and coauthor of *Entertaining With Insects,* a cookbook about to go into its third printing, has a hard time fathoming resistance to bug cuisine. Noting that insects are closely related to popular crustaceans, he says: "It's interesting that we prefer lobster and crab, which eat dead and decaying flesh. Insects are far cleaner."

Next summer Dr. Taylor will demonstrate his beetle, moth-larva and cricket recipes at a food fair in Orange County, Calif. His pièce de résistance uses the larvae of wax moth, a pest that invades beehives. "When you drop them in oil, they expand and explode like popcorn," he says. "It's particularly tasty." How tasty? "If you can tell me how bacon tastes, I will describe how wax moth tastes," he says.

He is especially partial to the wax moth's soft skin, and explains: "With mealworm and cricket you end up with cuticles between your teeth."

Last June, edible insects got a public-relations boost of sorts, when Air Force pilot Scott O'Grady ate them to survive after being shot down over Bosnia. Amid the media frenzy, "We received quite a few calls from people inquiring about eating insects," says Dale Cochran, president of Grubco Inc. in Hamilton, Ohio, which grows moth and beetle larvae for zoos and aviaries.

Though Mr. Cochran says, "We've donated a lot of insects to entomological societies for their dinner events," he doubts that demand is strong enough to justify going into commercial production of insects for human consumption.

That sort of attitude poses problems for the Insect Club in Washington, D.C. The supper club opened in 1992 with a menu featuring such dishes as mealworms Rockefeller and grilled cricket polenta. But the bug items have been discontinued, partly because of raw-material shortages. "People were interested, but getting the insects was a real hassle," says Robert Newkirk, one of the owners.

Entomologists, nutritionists and other insect fanciers scoff at Westerners' bias against bugs. Insects are a prized source of protein and vitamins in many countries of Africa, Asia and South America. As much as 60% of an insect's dry body weight is crude protein. Termites and caterpillars are among the fattiest.

Dr. DeFoliart cites research showing that over half of the 94 insect species eaten in Mexico—including caterpillars, beetle grubs and ants—had more calories than soybeans. He says 100 grams of cooked insect can provide more than the daily requirement of iron, copper, zinc, thiamine and riboflavin.

Advocates also promote bug eating as a boon to the environment. If the food market expands, they reason, it could reduce the need to spray crops with harmful pesticides.

During locust attacks in Thailand and the Philippines, for example, the government pays people to collect them for food; during Mexican plagues, local agricultural authorities hand out locust recipes.

Insect harvesting isn't for amateurs, however. There are more than a million species, and Dr. Taylor says that as rule of thumb, the most colorful shouldn't be eaten. "Bright colors are often an indication of foul taste or toxins," he says. Ladybugs, for example, evolved their red coloration to deter birds and other prey. But some edible insects mimic the bright coloration to throw off their enemies. The orange-and-black monarch butterfly, for instance, is foul-tasting, but the viceroy, which resembles the monarch, is edible.

Dr. DeFoliart estimates that there are more than 1,000 species of insects suitable for human food. Silkmoth pupae, a by-product of commercial silk production in many Asian countries, are already produced by the ton for human consumption there, and canned pupae are imported into the U.S. Fried in oil with onion and spices, they make a delectable meal, according to Dr. DeFoliart. He says that in the past few years, Asian groceries in Madison have begun carrying them, as well as giant waterbugs.

Then there are the various domesticated bees, whose larvae and pupae are eaten in many parts of the world—56 species in Brazil alone.

"A taste panel in Canada described honeybees fried in butter or vegetable oil as like walnuts, pork cracklings, sunflower seeds and Rice Krispies," Dr. DeFoliart says. "We have a whole new class of food out there."

—AMAL KUMAR NAJ, January 1996

56. The Roach Has No Friends . . .

PALO ALTO, Calif.—It has no head, no legs, but in the name of all that entomologists find holy, its heart beats.

It is the abdomen of a cockroach; specifically, an American cockroach, *Periplaneta americana,* aka palmetto bug, water bug and the Bombay Canary. Fluid pulses through its scaly membranes, magnified on a TV monitor. It lies in a petri dish beside half a dozen other torsos. A wire runs from one to an electrocardiograph that scratches out its life pace. A scientist in a white coat drops a tiny amount of a clear liquid onto the roach's belly.

Suddenly, the needle of the electrocardiograph jumps to twice the normal level. This is step one of a new, sophisticated assault on the cockroach and its insect brethren.

The scene takes place in an upstairs laboratory at Zoecon Corp. of Palo Alto, an insect-control unit of Sandoz Ltd., based in Basel, Switzerland. Researchers here probe the deepest workings of the roach, hoping to use its own hormones against it. The company's chairman, Carl Djerassi, used the same strategy when he helped invent the human birth-control pill. "It's different chemicals," he says. "But intellectually it's the exact same approach."

Zoecon (zoe from the Greek word for life, con from control) hopes to sidestep roach defenses that have let the bug accompany man from cave to condominium largely unimpeded by more conventional roach fogs, powders, sprays and traps. This latest effort may offer a way to get back at roaches by giving them what they have given man all these years: heart attacks. There's just one problem.

"We have these compounds, we've been able to put them on the heart, we've been able to show an increase, but we haven't been able to kill a roach," says Steven Kramer, an entomologist leading part of the project. Moreover, he says, no one knows how long you would have to stop a roach heart to kill the thing.

This should come as no surprise. The hearts in these headless roaches—the bugs were decapitated and otherwise trimmed for easy handling during the experiments—will beat for as long as 30 hours. A headless female roach can still find a place to lay her eggs before dying. Roaches can taste poison with tiny taste hairs without ever ingesting it, then avoid the poison the rest of their lives. Their folding wings let them hide easily; their tight cuticle, or shell, keeps in moisture so well that they can survive a long time without water. Their sensors send warning signals directly to their legs, bypassing the brain, allowing them to start sprinting in 0.054 seconds (someone clocked this).

Urban entomologists love to tell how the roach has been around 350 million years, far longer than man. Emperor Nero's physician had a use for roaches—he mixed their guts with oil and plugged the concoction into ears as a cure for earaches. Early seamen reported that when they slept roaches munched on their fingernails and eyelashes; when really hungry, roaches will still do so. In the 1920s, *New York Sun* columnist Don Marquis wrote of Archy, a free-verse poet reincarnated as a cockroach. Archy composed poems at night on Mr. Marquis's typewriter, typing only in lower case because he couldn't hit the letter and shift keys at the same time. More than once, Archy called on bugs to revolt:

rise
strike for freedom
curses on the species
that invented roach poison

Scientists certainly treat roaches shabbily, blasting them with radiation, running them on treadmills, hacking off their limbs and heads, grinding up their brains, even dangling them before the dreaded *Bufo marinus,* a tropical toad that eats roaches. Still, they thrive. Four species torment man: the German cockroach, the most common and found around the world, and the American, Oriental and brown-banded cockroaches.

Fugitive roaches have escaped the insectaries at Zoecon, going over the wall, and, for that matter, up the wall, across the desks, into the desks. Gerardus B. Staal, director of insect research, pulls a sheet of postage stamps out of a drawer and holds it to the light. The glue on back is scored and mottled, signs of a past roach feast. (Roaches will also eat soap, paper, bookbindings.) "I don't mind roaches," he says. "But I don't like them to lick my stamps. I can tell you I won't lick those stamps."

Roaches can resist the most toxic of pesticides. In 1967, entomologist Stanley Rachesky tested propoxur, then a new roach killer, in the cage of Sinbad the Gorilla in Chicago's Lincoln Park Zoo and bagged 132.5 pounds of dead American roaches. Now, in some areas, roaches shrug the stuff off. This is evolution, natural selection under the kitchen sink.

Zoecon figures this is one key area where its products can top the conventional killers. "There is no way in theory for an insect to get resistant to its own hormones," says Mr. Djerassi. "That would be like us becoming resistant to insulin."

To develop its biological weapons, the company needs a supply of roaches. This is not difficult to acquire. In the insectaries, a kingdom ruled by David L. Grant, manager in charge of insect culture and special projects, Zoecon raises German, Oriental and American roaches, tobacco hornworms, cotton budworms, grasshoppers, houseflies, dermestid beetles (relatives of the kind museums use to strip flesh from dead animals being prepared for exhibit) and Aedes aegypti mosquitoes, notorious for spreading yellow fever.

In the grasshopper room, which smells like a freshly mowed lawn, a chubby grasshopper fixes itself to Mr. Grant's back and hitchhikes to a neighboring roach room. Here, about 20 five-gallon pails teem with roaches fed on Gaines-burgers dog food. "We can raise probably 5,000 roaches in one bucket," says Mr. Grant. He reaches into one of these pails of scampering, clacking, rustling, flailing, antenna-waving, almond-sized roaches and turns over one of the cardboard egg containers stacked there as bug shelters. The shiny horde flits for cover. (Occasionally a roach will seize this opportunity and dart up Mr. Grant's sleeve.) "Gross, isn't it," he says mildly.

He remembers the hopper on his back. "I'll take him to lunch," he quips. He takes him gently between finger and thumb, turns toward the door, then changes his mind and squeezes. Freedom is a transitory thing at Zoecon. He drops the grasshopper into the trash.

Zoecon hopes to market its first antiroach product to consumers next year. Called hydroprene, it mimics the hormone in roaches that controls when they advance to the adult stage. The compound in effect locks the roaches in their youth. They will still grow, but hydroprene crumples their wings, leaves them unable to bear young and, incidentally, can cause homosexuality in adult male roaches.

The results of tests of the product now grace a wall of Mr. Grant's office. He has hung two Roach Motels there (Zoecon is the world's largest producer of roach traps, including Roach Motels, marketed by Boyle-Midway Inc. of New York). But these traps are open, glue side out, each with hundreds of roaches stuck to it. On one, there are dead adults and babies tragically born in the glue and stuck there. The other trap, from a treated apartment, shows adults with crumpled wings and no babies. Roach birth control at work.

There's a hitch. Since the product doesn't kill adults and works by halting reproduction, a consumer won't see a decline in roaches for several months. That poses a marketing problem, says Roger Gold, professor of entomology and a roach specialist at the University of Nebraska. "Most people we deal with want to see dead roaches on the floor," he says. Zoecon therefore expects to sell hydroprene to consumers along with an "adulticide," something to yield a satisfying number of roach bodies right away.

The "heart-attack" research takes Zoecon even deeper into

roach physiology. Zoecon now knows what the hormone is that controls the cockroach heart, and knows how to synthesize it. In the labs, however, there is doubt about ever really giving roaches heart attacks, although company executives still seem optimistic about it. "Heart rate, it turns out, just isn't that important to the roach," says Robert Scarborough, senior research chemist. What the researchers would really like to discover is a hormone that controls the roach's urinary system. "If you can possibly mess that up, you can get rid of them," says Mr. Kramer.

Will Zoecon's weapons help overcome resistance for once and for all? There is pessimism among entomologists who have seen roaches wade through once-lethal pesticides. "It's beyond belief unless you've seen it," says William Bell, professor of entomology at the University of Kansas in Lawrence. "In the big battle, they're going to win."

—ERIK LARSON, May 1984

57. . . . Save One

PLANO, Tex.—Once a man has talked Johnny Carson into walking a cockroach on a leash, and ridden the talk-show circuit with three-inch hissing Madagascar roaches crawling on his chest, it's hard to go back to workaday life in Plano.

For Michael Bohdan, the tan and telegenic Dallas exterminator who adopted the moniker "Cockroach Dundee," it has been particularly difficult. He used to jet around America judging big-bug contests sponsored by deep-pockets corporations. He hobnobbed with stars on TV talk shows. He was mentioned in *People* magazine. Then, last summer, his corporate backer pulled the plug on the competitions, and Mr. Bohdan was brought back to earth.

Now, home in his suburban Dallas strip-mall Pest Shop, amid the souvenirs and the detritus of celebrity (a signed photo of TV host Gary Collins, an aquarium full of roaches feeding on dog food, a small display case of his favorite bug dioramas) Mr. Bohdan plots his return to the big time—a book, a radio show, movie work.

"I'm going through a metamorphosis as an exterminator," he says, "I need . . . something more."

It's not that after 18 years, the thrill of stalking the wily arthropod is gone. Mr. Bohdan, 46 years old, says he has enjoyed "a close personal relationship with cockroaches" since his first significant contact with them—as a restaurant inspector in Chicago 19 years ago. "Roaches have been very good to me," he says. Resting a reverent hand on his aquarium, he adds, "I like to just sit here at the end of the day and watch them, see how they try to communicate."

But he longs to return to the limelight.

Seven years ago, with Barnumlike perspicacity, Mr. Bohdan parlayed his idea of offering a prize for the biggest cockroach in Texas into a short feature story on CNN's *Headline News*—which led to an appearance on the *Tonight Show Starring Johnny Carson*, and an offer from American Cyanamid Co., at that time the maker of Combat roach killer, to take the contest national, with him as head judge.

By last year, his Texas roach roundup, which got off the ground with a $1,000 first prize, had become a national event with a $50,000 purse and categories such as Most Creative Presentation of Roach Art—tiny dioramas with roaches dressed up as, say, Elvis Presley or Marilyn "Monroach."

"It was a really positive experience," says Abby Ross, a Miami psychologist whose eight-year-old son, Blake, won a prize last year for his "Roach Perot" display, which featured a jumbo Florida roach with a photo of Ross Perot's head, ears akimbo, attached to the body.

For six years, Mr. Bohdan rode his big-roach contests to dizzying media heights: appearances on *The Joan Rivers Show, To Tell the Truth* and *Live with Regis and Kathie Lee.* On *Hour Magazine,* he brought fly swatters so hosts Gary Collins and David Leisure could prod their roaches along a table top to the strains of "The William Tell Overture." From comedian Chevy Chase, Mr. Bohdan picked up the trick of carrying a box of rubber roaches he could "accidentally" spill. His roaches were featured in a display at the Smithsonian Institution's insect zoo. And American Cyanamid asked him to field-test the newest bug killers in such places as Seoul, South Korea, and Madrid.

The publicity didn't make him rich—he was paid $200 for his appearance on the *Tonight Show*—but he had broken into show business. There were company-sponsored trips to lecture sales crews and eager invitations from Dallas schools and homeowners' associations. Just about every public appearance brought in more customers back home in Plano, he says.

Then, last summer, Combat's new owner—Clorox Co.—put an end to the contest after sponsoring it one last time. It had served its purpose, the company felt, in publicizing its product. Just like that, Mr. Bohdan became passé. The attention—and the offers—dried up. "They just moved on," he says. Famous no more, he fears his extermination business may shrivel like a bug in a Raid ad. "I have to keep my face and my name in the turnpike," he says.

The need he feels to skitter back into the spotlight hasn't endeared him to some of his peers. At a recent pesticide trade show, grouses a competitor, Mr. Bohdan elbowed his way to the front of a crowd for a ribbon-cutting. He says he didn't do that. "I'm a new breed of exterminator," he says. "Some of my peers get jealous."

Even Ron Shapp, who made Mr. Bohdan a partner in his Bizzy Bees Pest Control Co. in 1977, says the bright lights "just went to his head" after the first big-roach contest took off. Mr. Shapp says the partnership ended after he asked Mr. Bohdan to set aside the contests and the talk shows and help run the business. "It wasn't fair" to Mr. Shapp, Mr. Bohdan agrees, to remain a partner when he was on the road so much. The two men remain friendly.

Neither criticism nor sagging fortunes seem to faze Mr. Bohdan. Friends say he is like a kid's punching bag that bounces back up every time it is knocked down. Observes his wife, Sharon: "Saying it's a stupid idea will never stop him."

So, the would-be Marlin Perkins of the bug world contemplates his prospects. He still makes occasional appearances on a local children's TV show, *Peppermint Place,* and teaches the odd class for the Plano Parks and Recreation Department on safe pest control. He has left his name with a Dallas movie studio for possible work bug-wrangling. But for movie work, he says, "You have to keep a pretty big inventory of bugs on hand."

Meanwhile, he has launched a new diorama contest. The first prize is just $300, and his efforts at publicity, to date, have yielded just a brief spot on a local TV show and an article in the *Plano Star-Courier.* Three weeks into the contest, he still awaits the first entry—not that he is worried about it. "It takes time to catch them and for people to create their displays," he says.

His wife concedes that she won't be sorry if the contest flops. "I was glad," she says, when her husband's star faded. "He's home more."

That may not last long if Mr. Bohdan pulls off his latest scheme: to appear on the *Late Show With David Letterman.*

"I could do stupid roach tricks," he says. He scoops up a handful of live hissing Madagascar roaches to demonstrate that, when a ringing phone interrupts. He explains to his caller that there are better ways to kill slugs than to crawl around your garden with a saltshaker. Meanwhile, a roach heads across his chest, while another clambers up his collar. He redirects it with a finger before it disappears under his shirt.

When he hangs up the phone, he bounds excitedly to a display case, labeled Cockroach Museum Hall of Fame, to show a visitor his "secret weapon" in the Letterman campaign. Reaching delicately past an Imelda Marcos roach, which sports tiny gold shoes on four of her six feet, he gently picks up a particularly Brobdingnagian deceased Madagascar roach with a photo of Mr. Letterman's grinning face glued on, long roach antennae protruding jauntily from the temples.

This is sure to get him on the show, he believes. And if it doesn't? Well, there's always the possibility of an infomercial for this stuff that kills bugs by drying them out: "Diatomaceous earth," he says, caressing each syllable with his voice.

—BOB ORTEGA, November 1993

EPILOGUE
ONLY IN AMERICA

═══════

NEW YORK—American Home Products Corp., the maker of the "Roach Motel," asked a federal court here to squash the sale of another insect trap, the "Roach Condo."

American Home and its Boyle-Midway Inc. unit, in a lawsuit, accused Hampton Chemical Inc. of trademark infringement and unfair competition over the distribution of the Roach Condo.

The lawsuit alleges that Hampton Chemical's product "closely and colorably copies, imitates and simulates" that of the Roach Motel and that the company seeks to "capitalize upon the good-will" associated with it. As a result, American Home contends, it has been "irreparably injured."

The lawsuit seeks an injunction against Hampton Chemical to prevent it from selling the Roach Condo. American Home also is asking that Hampton be forced to give up its profits from the insect trap.

The Roach Motel, part of American Home's Black Flag line of insect-control products, has been on the market since 1976.

Hampton Chemical couldn't be reached for comment.

—DOW JONES NEWS SERVICE,
February 1985

ACKNOWLEDGMENTS

Thanks to Steve Adler of Wall Street Journal Books and Fred Hills of Free Press for their support of this project and to Fred for his additional patience and sage input during the editing process. Thanks, too, to Roe D'Angelo and Daniel Nasaw at WSJ Books for their indispensable input and research and editing help as the book came together. A further thanks goes to Lottie Lindberg in the *Journal* library for her speedy assistance in finding stories that resided outside the *Journal*'s electronic database, thus saving the editor long sessions sleuthing through microfilm. Thanks also to my numerous *Wall Street Journal* colleagues who greatly aided this effort by their helpful story recommendations. And last, thanks to Jim Sterba, a gifted *Journal* writer, and Glynn Mapes, a gifted (and now retired) *Journal* writer and editor, for sharing their institutional knowledge of the *Journal*'s fascination with animal stories.

INDEX TO AUTHORS

———

ABOUT THE AUTHOR

———

KEN WELLS is a 21-year veteran of *The Wall Street Journal,* having served stints as a reporter in the paper's San Francisco and London bureaus, and as an editor on the Page One staff in New York. This book is his second anthology for Wall Street Journal Books; in 2002, he edited a collection of the Journal's fabled "Middle Column" features titled *Floating Off the Page.* A native of Cajun, Louisiana, Wells is also the author of three novels set there: *Meely LaBauve, Junior's Leg* and *Logan's Storm.* (You can visit Wells and bayou country at www.bayoubro.com.) In his spare time, he dabbles in blues and jazz guitar and often wishes he were fishing. He lives with his family in the Greater Manhattan area.